The National
Charity Company

I do really take it for an indisputable truth, and a truth that is one of the corner stones of political science—the more strictly we are watched, the better we behave.

Jeremy Bentham

The National Charity Company

Jeremy Bentham's
Silent Revolution

Charles F. Bahmueller

University of California Press
BERKELEY · LOS ANGELES · LONDON

University of California Press
Berkeley and Los Angeles, California
University of California Press, Ltd.
London, England
© 1981 by
The Regents of the University of California
Printed in the United States of America

1 2 3 4 5 6 7 8 9

Library of Congress Cataloging in Publication Data

Bahmueller, Charles F
    The National Charity Company. Jeremy
Bentham's silent revolution

    A revision of the author's thesis, Harvard
University, 1975 published under title: The end of
contingency.
    Includes index.
    1. National Charity Company. 2. Bentham,
Jeremy, 1748–1832. 3. Poor—Great Britain.
4. Poor laws—Great Britain. I. Title.
HV245.B29 1981   362.5'0941   80-20632
ISBN 0-520-03796-0

To my Father
and
To the memory of my Mother
Grace Estelle Skilton Bahmueller

Contents

Preface

I have tried in this book to give Jeremy Bentham his due. Whether I have succeeded is not for me to say. I believe that more criticism than praise, so far as his writings on the reform of the English Poor Law are concerned, is his just desert, and I have not attempted to conceal my judgment. However, my strictures on Bentham and the Poor Law, to state the obvious, are not an essay on or an evaluation of his work as a whole. Such an evaluation, of course, is a much larger and complex task, and it cannot be undertaken until more of the parts of his work are better known and studied. It is a great pity that certain scholars are in the habit of passing sweeping judgment on Bentham by way of historical hearsay and a passing acquaintance with his published writings or even with a deeper knowledge of his published writings and little or none at all of his unpublished manuscripts, which are voluminous. When these scarcely known works and accurate versions of better known ones are available, Bentham will be seen, I believe, as a far more complex figure than he is usually considered to have been, and more discriminating judgments than sweeping ones will have to be made.

This book began as a doctoral dissertation submitted to Harvard University in 1975. I would like first of all to thank my teachers at Harvard—Professor Michael Walzer and Professor Judith N. Shklar, to whom I owe more than I can express here. I especially appreciate the freedom I was given to approach my subject in my own way and the positive encouragement and criticism I received. I would also like to thank the Department of Government at Harvard for having granted me a Traveling Fellowship, without which the basic research for what has become this book could not have been undertaken. The department also generously granted me summer aid for the purpose of consulting the Dumont papers in Geneva.

During four years at University College London I accumulated more debts both of friendship and of intellectual aid and stimulation than I can state briefly. Janet Percival, Archivist of University College Library, patiently aided my first halting efforts to read Bentham's hand and greatly assisted in making my stay profitable, as did Dr. N. D. F. Browne, Mr. Robin Hankey, Mr. John Rae Harby, and Mr. Dermot Morrah, F.R.C.S. I would also like to thank the Bentham Committee for employing me for three years and therefore allowing me to increase my acquaintance with manuscript sources. My colleague on the Bentham staff Judith Legoff opened her fund of knowledge of Bentham, especially her knowledge of his writings on the Poor Law, to me and later agreed to read my manuscript. I appreciate all of her help. I also appreciated the unfailing intellectual stimulation and hospitality of Dr. Frederick Rosen, Professor William Twining, Dr. Michael James, and Dr. Michael Woodcock.

Professor Amnon Goldworth and Professor H. L. A. Hart kindly consented to read the manuscript, for which I am most grateful. Each contributed many comments and criticisms which helped me very much, though I am sure I have fallen short of their high standards. Professor Peter Euben, whose colleague at the University of California at Santa Cruz I was privileged to have been, read parts of the manuscript and made invaluable comments on substance and style. Yvonne Quinlan lent her fine ear for the English language to correct my writing at a number of points. I am grateful to her as well for meticulously typing and correcting the notes at short notice. I would also like to thank Mr. Gregory Karns and Mr. Klaas R. van der Weg for generously giving of their time for last-minute research assistance. I was fortunate to have the editorial advice and criticism of an old and trusted friend, Richard A. Anderson, who was good enough to read and correct the conclusion.

This book owes a special debt to Professor Douglas Long of the University of Western Ontario. He undertook to make painstaking, detailed corrections on every page of the manuscript and in addition made dozens of suggestions for improvements on every aspect of my work. This would be a better book had I been able to follow all of his advice. As it is I hardly know how to thank him.

Above all, though he bears no responsibility for the inevitable shortcomings of these pages, I must acknowledge my debt to Professor J. H. Burns, whose depth of humanity is matched only by his depth of learning.

Introduction

At the end of 1795, Jeremy Bentham, temporarily forsaking all other major projects of intellectual creation, began work on a proposal for the reform of the English Poor Law. By the time he had stopped writing—characteristically, the Plan was never completed and was only partially published—he had amassed more than twenty-four hundred manuscript pages, the fruit of nearly two years' work. An analysis of their content (which forms between three and four percent of Bentham's gargantuan life production) and of the historical circumstances surrounding them is the principal subject of these pages.

The years during which Bentham thought out his reforms of that confused jumble of local practice that had hitherto cared for the poor were crisis years both economically and politically. Bread, the most important staple in the diet of the southern English laborer, was in short supply, its price rising at an alarming rate; but revolutionary ideas were abundant and cheap. Bentham, having flirted with democratic ideas soon after the outbreak of the Revolution in France, dropped them altogether[1] and adopted an attitude notable for its fear of political eruption from below—an attitude which in one way or another figured prominently in his thoughts on the affairs of the poor. The poor, suffering as they were in the grip of economic misery, had to be both mollified and controlled; but on the other hand complaints were loud that the poor rates were increasing catastrophically

1

and would soon become unbearable. (The incompatibility of the needs of the poor and the cries of the taxpayer is not exactly unknown in our own time.) Thus Bentham was confronted with a seemingly insoluble problem: what could be done with the poor that would alleviate their distress and dampen the fires of revolutionary fervor without simultaneously courting revolt among ratepayers by driving taxes still higher?

The solution Bentham adopted—the involuntary imprisonment (under a semipublic joint-stock company to be called the National Charity Company) of all those seeking relief (and many who were not) in his own peculiar version of the workhouse—has been seen both as historically progressive and as retrograde: progressive because it entailed a single national administrative policy for poor relief; retrograde because it meant the end of "outdoor" relief.[2] ("Outdoor" relief meant relief at home—outside the doors of a work or poorhouse.) In what follows we will try to show that even though the first view has some merit, the second carries the day: Bentham's Poor Law reform was replete with a repressiveness so pervasive, so soul-destroying, and with so little regard for either the civil liberties or the emotional sensitivities of those whose health (moral as well as physical) and happiness it set out to promote and protect, that its administrative progressiveness pales in the comparison. Left in Bentham's hands, the Poor would, in respects essential to those who refuse to travel "beyond freedom and dignity," be worse off by far than they in fact were.

But this is not to say that Bentham's efforts were without value, for many of his arguments are worthy of our attention. He argued, as we will see, that public relief is overwhelmingly to be preferred to exclusive reliance on private charity; that is, he gave justification for the Welfare State. This 'Welfare State'* of Bentham's, however, was not the modern Welfare State as we know it: it provided no cash benefits (leaving aside small loans) for the unemployed, the old, or the otherwise helpless. But it did try to promote voluntary social security insurance (for those who could afford the premiums); and it sought in a variety of ways to keep the independent poor from falling into the abyss of abject indigence.

In proposing his reforms, Bentham brought to bear a perspective whose components, though when taken individually were not always original, when added together were unique and went far in forming an answer to the question: What shall be done with the poor? Before setting out on the body of our work, we should know something of its most salient ideas.

*In this book ordinary double quotation marks appear only to indicate a direct quotation; single quotation marks do not denote a quotation.

One element of Bentham's perspective concerned population. At last the question of overpopulation had reared its menacing face amid the torpor of the common eighteenth-century opinion that an increasing population is desirable as a blessed sign of national prosperity and happiness. But first for Joseph Townsend and later for T. R. Malthus, growing population was an omen of crisis: how would the poor be fed? The historical placement of Bentham's Poor Law reform is that it was in part an attempt to deal with the foreseen population crisis without succumbing to demands that public poor relief be abolished on the ground that it exacerbated the very problem it sought to assuage—that taxation for the relief of the indigent demoralized the independent laborer and finally forced him into pauperdom. One possible solution was forced emigration—not necessarily in such utter wretchedness as occurred in Ireland half a century later, but forced emigration nevertheless. Another was contraception; but whatever its merits, it could hardly touch the immediate crisis of the late 1790's. By the 1820's, however, this course was being openly advocated by such disciples of Bentham's as John Mill and Francis Place, with his private blessing and in the face of Malthus' explicit condemnation.

Bentham chose emigration of the poor as the short-term solution to hunger—but the form of the emigration he chose was novel; it was *internal* emigration. It was emigration to a separate economy and a separate society, the "pauper kingdom" of the enterprise proposed to deal with those seeking relief, the National Charity Company. There food itself would be separately grown on otherwise uncultivated land (or separately harvested from the sea), none being subtracted—as was the practice of the common eighteenth-century poorhouse—from the market supply. Such internal emigration served the dual purpose of increasing production during hard times and of decreasing the financial burden on ratepayers—perhaps in time eliminating the poor rates entirely, as the "colonies" became wholly self-sufficient. And that was not all, not nearly all.

Gathered in strictly regulated establishments modeled and managed on Bentham's famous Panopticon principle, the poor would be weaned from what he believed to be a malignant habit of the first magnitude: idleness.[3] His depth of passion on the subject, his frenetic, even fanatical search to abolish idleness in all its forms, can hardly be exaggerated. For Bentham idleness led only to evil: idleness, the state of having no purposeful activity, whether productive or not, created an inner emptiness whose inherent instability led inevitably to antisocial behavior—nature tolerated no vacuums. The worst fault of the laborer left idle, so far as Bentham was concerned, was his habit of excessive drinking—no collateral vices could be far removed from the drunkard. Over and over he condemned the misuse of alcohol by the lower orders; and although it need hardly be said that there was more than a little historical justification for his concern, it should be borne in mind that the worst days of dram drinking were long since past—the climax of gin consumption, when the poor were dying like flies from its effects, had come in the 1740's. The need for solace, for relief from a life of dreary toil that held little prospect of amelioration, seems never to have occurred to him. Still, drinking was (and is) a problem of no inconsiderable dimensions in working-class England.

The cure for idleness with all its attendant emptiness and *ennui* was busyness: any "innocent" activity sufficed, but some activities were more valuable than others. In the case of the poor, labor was the obvious remedy. Work—Bentham did not distinguish between work and labor[4]—was not only the source of present and future subsistence, but also fostered a further good: it promoted moral health. Bentham carried this emphasis on work to its furthermost extremes—under the direction of the National Charity Company, every moment of the pauper's life would be filled with productive activity; even the one day demanded by religion would be converted from uselessness to utilitarian purposes; and if Bentham had his way, the church itself would be subtly subverted from within for the sake of promoting Utilitarian ends.[5] The result was that, so far from wallowing in 'pleasure' in the ordinary sense, life for the poor under the regime advocated by this philosopher of the pleasure principle was positively *ascetic*. The poor would be remade as models of the secularized Protestantism of the work ethic.

Another constituent of Bentham's perspective on the reform of the Poor Law was his definition of poverty itself. Poverty was not merely the state of possessing little or no money or property. Rather, it was the state of being compelled to work in order to live: thus for Bentham nearly all of us are and always have been in a state of poverty; only the very few whose property was sufficient to sustain them without recourse to labor could be called rich. Those who stood in need of public relief were not only poor, they were *indigent*. Indigence was the condition of those who, although obliged to work for subsistence, were nevertheless either unable to work or unable even if they did work to earn enough for subsistence.

This definition of poverty fitted neatly into the main tenets of Bentham's thinking on Poor Law reform: it underlined the nearly universal necessity to labor, implying that instilling the habit of labor ought to be among the first preoccupations of any program for the relief of indigence. Poverty itself was beyond cure, and there was no excuse for providing relief without requiring productive exertion. Thus the pauper newly arrived at Panopticon poorhouse was to be subjected to what Bentham called the "earn-first principle": first he would perform an assigned task, then and *only* then would he be allowed to eat.[6] Those who were sustained through the fruits of others' labor were considered little (if at all) better than parasites; natural justice demanded that every laborer have a right to the fruits of his own labor, and only by the most compelling need could dispossession for the sake of others be justified. Still, such dispossession *could* be justified.

This view of the distinction between poverty and indigence had subtly conservative implications, for there is no sense in attacking wealth if one's status as poor can be altered only temporarily. Redistribution of the property of the wealthy would add no more than a token of abundance when stretched among so many, and escape from a life of toil would not for long endure. Moreover, class distinctions among the "poor" were conveniently blurred—the prosperous manufacturer or shopkeeper was as much a poor man as the day laborer, and so the condition of every class but the highest shared the same unchangeable essential attribute.

A study of Bentham's Poor Law reform reveals characteristics of his mental baggage which have as yet been inadequately understood. One is the passion with which he pursued the administrative unity of an entire society. Again and again he railed against the parochialism of eighteenth-century English government. Aghast when he looked out upon the mélange of diverse, even contradictory, local practices in the treatment of indigents, he felt that knowledge of the social order was as impossible as knowledge of the common law. "In a cluster of small pauper establishments," he wrote, "straggling over England, dispersed and unconnected . . . all is opacity and obscurity. . . ."[7] Or again, "Here, every thing is insulated—every thing is *particular*: every thing is out of reach, every thing is out of knowledge: and while every thing is growing worse and worse, every thing is out of the reach of cure."[8] What was particular and unknown could not be *controlled*: the search for the means of control was characteristically Benthamite.[9] Knowledge, real knowledge, would only be possible with a single administrative entity pursuing common policies. This meant creating a *system*, a network of pauper establishments, binding together what had been scattered: "in the proposed system of Industry Houses all connected together by one authority, the management might be . . . as transparent in the figurative sense, as each House, if constructed in the Inspection Architecture principle, would be in the literal sense."[10]

This almost religious quest (our word religion, after all, derives from the Latin *re-ligare*—to bind again that which is broken) for connecting what was separate is mirrored in language that recurs in much of Bentham's work. In particular, he repeatedly used the imagery of a *chain* to express what he had in mind. In his *Essay on Indirect Legislation* (1782), for example, he compared the legislator to a commander looking over a battlefield to plan future strategy:

> Thus instructed, at every considerable turning of the road, he . . . opens a new battery and from a chain of diversified but connected works, brings the artillery of the law to bear upon the path in every direction, and throws fresh danger and difficulty in the way of every step.[11]

He spoke of a "chain of policy" and a "chain of causes,"[12]—even expectation was a chain: "Expectation is a chain which unites our present and our future existence, and passes beyond ourselves to the generation which follows us. The sensibility of the individual is prolonged through all the links of this chain."[13] The system of Panopticon workhouses which formed the heart of his reform was itself a chain of a sort; it was, as he put it, "a chain or rather a net-work"[14]—networks are like series of interconnected chains. With all that was particular chained together within a rationalized administrative unity, the cause of mental anguish over uncertain policy and contradictory practice would be removed: again, practice could be *controlled*. Thus one advantage of national administrative unity was that sheer size attracted attention and invited public scrutiny. The "transparency" of the new Poor Law administration would be meaningless without "the existence of an observing eye," Bentham wrote. "To the eye of the public, an object might as well not be transparent if it be not of a certain magnitude." The literal observation of Panopticon expanded to metaphorical public observation, but the purpose remained identical:

> Management which can hope to elude observation may be, and often is, extremely bad. Management which is sure to be looked at—and generally looked at—and constantly looked at can scarcely fail of being as good as the managing hands know how to make it.[15]

This system also did something else, something profoundly Benthamite, which the idea of control obviously entailed: it eliminated—or sought to eliminate—contingency in the treatment of poverty, controlling the free play of whim and accident, of chance itself. Hostility to the role of chance in social life is already visible in some of the earliest of Bentham's writings that have come down to us. In his *Preparatory Principles* of the 1770's, he spoke of what most characterized the "infancy" of English history—"force and chance were every thing."[16] In *An Introduction to the Principles of Morals and Legislation* (printed in 1780), "caprice," an alternative term for the principle of "sympathy and antipathy," was on the list of proscribed grounds of moral judgment, the "principles adverse to utility."[17] In *The Influence of Place and Time in Matters of Legislation* (1782), he spoke derisively of the "lottery of the law,"[18] and he complained that in the transfer of English law to Bengal, although much of what was bad was left behind, "this omission is not owing to judgment but to chance."[19] In *Indirect Legislation*, he spoke of the "caprice of terrible punishments" and also of the policy of placing convicts in the ordinary poorhouses of the day: "True it is that there is a chance that the punishment may have operated with effect in the way of reformation: still, however, it is but a chance." As for the pillory, it was a "game of chance in which the life of the patient is staked upon the caprice of the multitude and the accidents of the day," such as bribery—the weight of whipping depended on the impression made on the executioner's palm; and burning in the hand, in a like manner, was "performed as he and the patient can agree, either by a cold iron or a hot, by which nothing suffers but a slice of bacon."[20] In the same work he again suggested a connection between the role of chance and the absence of civilization: "Look into the history of the barbarous ages and you find perjuries so abundant that chance was trusted to as a safer guide than testimony. . . ."[21] In the writings on Evidence composed after the turn of the nineteenth century, he again complained of the sway of contingency: the legislator who allowed courts to "remake" law was like "the ostrich, who drops her eggs and leaves it to chance to see if they come to life."[22] And in his great propaganda pamphlet *Truth versus Ashurst*, he condemned the rule of mere contingency with overflowing emotion:

Ashurst.—No man is so low as not to be within the law's protection.

TRUTH.—Ninety-nine men out of a hundred are this low. Every man is, who has not from five-and-twenty pounds, to five-and-twenty times five-and-twenty pounds; to sport with, in order to take his chance for justice. I say *chance*: remembering how great a chance it is, that, although his right be as clear as the sun at noon day, he loses it by a *quibble*.[23]

As we will often have occasion to notice, Bentham's writings on Poor Law reform are replete with this same concern—the very purpose, in the first instance, of public provision for the relief of indigence was to eliminate the contingency that was the scourge of man: hunger. A Poor Law could create security of expectation that one would not, come what may, be left to starve. This security was the hallmark of civilization: barbarians were "ill provided for against casual and particular exigencies" and haunted by "the constant sense of general insecurity." Barbarism "leaves the indigent to take their chance, leaves the chance of indigence to be provided for by the chance of bounty": "In a state of society more or less advanced, the first step and the widest is to make a regular and secure provision for this branch of exigency."[24] Nevertheless, the hand of the uncivilized "Dark Ages," as the Enlightenment called medieval Europe, was still seen on the practice of poor relief in England. Once more there was the theme of eradicating contingency by joining fragments into a single whole. "Looking at the Parochial divisions," he wrote, "at this and that and t'other Parish, begotten by chance in the night of the darkest antiquity, I see in them an aggregate of heterogeneous fragments essentially incapable of entering as consistent elements into the composition of any tolerably regular or convenient system."[25]

Within the walls of Panopticon poorhouse, contingency in all it endless varieties would find its match at last—"In the world at large, fashion and caprice bear sovereign sway: here their authority is utterly disclaimed."[26] It was the "dominion of Chance" which allowed such unwarranted extravagancies as meat on the menu of some poorhouses seven days out of seven.[27] In the same way, through complete control, through rigorous foresight, no such changeable and unknown a force as weather would determine the continuation or cessation of labor: outdoor and indoor employments would both be available so that "not a particle of time shall remain necessarily unemployed: and relaxation shall be measured out by reason and humanity, not commanded by necessity and blind chance."[28] Nor would the quality of management (a subject that will be examined at some length) be left to the whims of local desire: "the chance in favour of good management . . . is encreased by an encrease in the strength of the junction between interest and duty."[29] This theme, the struggle against contingency, will recur throughout the pages that follow.

In the first chapter, we will look at Bentham's thoughts on the poor and the relief of poverty prior to 1796. Some of his remarks were directed to the Law of Settlement, especially to its form before 1795, and a section is devoted to the subject of Bentham and the Law of Settlement. This is followed (in Chapter Two), after a brief look at the practice of eighteenth-century English poor relief, by an account of the crisis of 1795 and reactions to it: in particular, we will examine the responses of Samuel Whitbread and William Pitt. Bentham criticized both men and devoted great attention to an attack on Pitt's Poor Law reform bill, an attack which will be analyzed in some detail. Whitbread's bill, which proposed a minimum wage, fared little better in Bentham's estimation, and the chapter closes with a discussion of his view of wages. After this, in Chapter Three, there is a description of the circumstances surrounding Bentham's own reform proposal. At the very moment he was writing voluminously on the poor, he was vigorously negotiating for land for Panopticon prison and intriguing on French affairs. He nevertheless found the energy (and time) to carry on extensive researches on the poor and to ally himself with leading men in English society to further both Panopticon prison and the National Charity Company.

At this point, we begin analyzing the substance of Bentham's arguments for the *public* (as opposed to purely private) relief of poverty. He had a stock of arguments ready-made for a variety of the Poor Law's enemies. Some critics took the position that public relief made the practice of Christian charity impossible; others argued the virtues of private charity as furnishing a kind of social glue—gratitude. Joseph Townsend made the further argument that inevitable overpopulation made public relief socially disastrous: the poor would have to be left to fend for themselves—perhaps, he implied, even left to starve. Bentham's answers to such arguments and his position vis-à-vis the entire population question are set forth in Chapter Four.

The final three chapters critically dissect Bentham's reform proposal. In the first, the structure of the National Charity Company is described, as well as the history of prior proposals for ventures of its kind. We also take up Bentham's defense of the common eighteenth-century practice of "farming" the poor—the National Charity Company was a variation of such "farming." We will question whether the poor themselves were intended to be the primary beneficiaries of Bentham's plan, and an attempt will be made to show that he saw his plan as a method of preventing revolution—a widely shared preoccupation at the time—through a policy of 'divide and rule.'

Next (in Chapter Six), the system of Panopticon poorhouses is considered as an alternative economy—an economy which, far from being modeled on the principles of Adam Smith, was planned and controlled from beginning to end. Planning, it will be argued, was necessary for the economic stability of the Company: the uncertainty inherent in a market economy would be banished altogether.

The remainder of the chapter is devoted to three topics. The first concerns Bentham's mania for utilizing every particle of available labor and for saving money and money's worth. Not only would the "save-all principle" be applied with maximum force in the Company's operations, but the independent poor would be encouraged to adopt the habits of thrift. The second topic concerns the general roundup of beggars, prostitutes, and a variety of other 'marginal' social elements. Since this was all quite involuntary, and since no trials for vagrancy would be held, Bentham had somehow to justify what would undoubtedly have been among the most controversial aspects of his plan had it ever been enacted. Finally, we will look at his propensity to seek total control within Panopticon poorhouse.

In Chapter Seven, the account of Bentham's reform proposal is completed through an analysis of his ideas on idleness and work, on education, on the system of management within the Company, and on religion. Throughout we will see a common thread—the urge to recreate the poor as the models of Utilitarian men and women; and we will see that a certain price is paid, namely, the institution of an overwhelming repressiveness (there was one single exception—an enthusiasm for maximizing, in a 'proper' manner, the sexual pleasures of the young). The poor would be taught to work and save, to be happy in their unchangeable station in life and therefore politically quiet. Made secure through savings, through insurance and through the very existence of the Company, they would find happiness in the knowledge that their sustenance was forever safe. Even that 'unutilitarian' institution, the Church of England, would be co-opted into service. But this 'happiness,' it will be argued, was at the lowest, the crudest levels of human—even animal—existence. Finally, we will conclude with a statement of the burden of these pages, that the indigent as a class, their literal freedom either in jeopardy or, as Panopticon inmates, terminated altogether, their dignity as human personalities hopelessly compromised by Bentham's workhouse regime, would have been placed in an immeasurably worse position had Bentham's plan not met the fate that in fact awaited it—burial in the graveyard of discarded ideas.

Having said this, two further points ought to be borne in mind. First, since much of what follows is critical in tone, the positive side of Bentham's thinking on the Poor Law should not be overlooked. We have already noticed that Bentham provided a spirited defense to indigents' right to relief as a matter of public law: that this was of no small importance is a point to which the conclusion of this book will draw special attention. And we have also seen that Bentham's reforms would have entailed an end to the often arbitrary and chaotic nature of England's parochial Poor Law administration; centralized administration would at last give the poor security of expectation. There were, furthermore, other benefits both to paupers and to the independent poor. At long last pauper children would receive at least a modicum of systematic education; and the independent poor could look forward to a variety of assistance. Several forms of medical treatment would be available at home; travel would be facilitated through cheap lodging; small loans would be available in times of stress, including pawnbrokers' facilities at less than commercial rates; and banks would be established that accepted the hitherto spurned pittance that the better-off of the independent poor could afford to rescue from the oblivion of present consumption. Thus made possible and encouraged, habitual saving would provide a prop to continued independence.

The second point is that in considering Bentham's proposed reforms, it should not be assumed that his position on the relief of poverty is *the* position of Utilitarian philosophy. In the first place several versions of Utilitarianism have emerged since his death in 1832. Often more subtle and complex than Bentham usually was (though that is not to say that he was neither), those who have revised and deepened Utilitarianism cannot necessarily be expected to apply their philosophy to the poverty problem as Bentham did. It must surely be obvious that the involuntary imprisonment of the poor, even assuming that afterwards they were happier, would be rejected by many if not all Utilitarians as a sacrifice impossible of remedy by future benefits. Apprehension of the occurrence or recurrence of imprisonment added to the pain of incarceration itself and the "pain of sympathy" (to use Bentham's own phrase) of those left otherwise untouched by this apprehension and pain must all weigh heavily in any calculation of the merits of Bentham's plan. Practitioners of Utilitarianism should not be expected to accede to his reckoning, for it lacks the character of necessity. Of this I hope to make readers very sure.

1

Poverty and Society:
Preliminary Reflections

The 1790's were prolific years for Bentham, even by his own standards. Besides the great bulk of Panopticon materials, he produced tracts on French affairs such as his *Emancipate Your Colonies!*, his treatise on the French judiciary, and his denunciation of the French Declaration of Rights of 1791 and 1795 in *Anarchical Fallacies*.[1] In tracts such as *Truth versus Ashurst* and *A Protest Against Law Taxes*, more salvos were shot off in the never-ending war against English legal practice;[2] and there were a host of economic writings of both a theoretical and a practical nature—the *Manual of Political Economy* was written between 1793 and 1795, *Supply without Burthen* in 1795, and a proposal for a new species of paper currency in 1795–96.[3]

But in addition, probably toward the end of 1795 and certainly by the beginning of 1796, Bentham turned his attention to a new subject which was just then agitating the English reading public as it had never done before: the Poor Laws. By the autumn of 1797, he had ransacked the extensive literature on the subject, compiled hundreds of pages of statistical and other information on the poor and on the operation of the Poor Laws, and produced a plan for a systematic reform, or rather, as he so aptly put it, *"revolution"* in the treatment of the poor.[4]

This was not Bentham's first excursion into the subject of poor relief. His concern dated from at least as long before as 1776. In a passage from what Bowring called his "Commonplace Book," Bentham suggested a public works program—"digging of canals, deepening of harbours, making of roads, building of fortifications"—to employ manufacturing workers (and only manufacturing workers) who were temporarily out of work. This employment would be available only near manufacturing towns, and then only upon production of a certificate showing that the holder was a *bona fide* manufacturer "having been so for such a time." Payment would be lower than their usual rate ("else they would quit their manufacture"), but greater than that of the ordinarily lower-paid common laborer. It is not clear precisely who would pay for such projects, but, since it would in Bentham's estimation be a "great relief" to the poor rates, the parishes affected would be one source and a county or national fund another.[5]

This brief passage is of interest in several respects. The twenty-eight-year-old Bentham had singled out a problem seldom treated by eighteenth-century writers on the Poor Law, a problem which would assume a greater importance in his writings of 1796–98: the social discontinuities created by the business cycle. "The greatest evil manufacturers are liable to," he wrote, "is that of a temporary stagnation of trade, which leaves vast numbers at a time without employment and without subsistence."[6] Moreover, it is clear that he wanted relief, for this particular class of poor at least, to be accompanied by the "extraction of labour": in his writings of the 1790's, the "extraction of a maximum of labour" from every conceivable category of the poor became an obsession, as we shall see. Finally, it seems implicit in his proposal that Bentham envisaged public works as part of a *national* rather than purely local policy—hence the reference to a "national fund"; in any case, the problem of manufacturing unemployment would not be dealt with on a purely parish basis. One great deficiency of eighteenth-century methods of relief had been the lack of any coherent national policy for dealing with poverty: local government reigned supreme, with units as small as the parish itself the usual dispensers of poor relief.[7] Bentham's Poor Law reform of the '90's sought to reverse this situation, replacing local autonomy with a single national authority.

Interest of a more extensive nature in the problem of poverty and poor relief is evident in Bentham's correspondence for 1781. Early in July of that year, Earl Shelburne succeeded in meeting the hitherto elusive Bentham[8] through the device of descending upon him at his chambers in Lincoln's Inn. Subsequently, the two men met at Shelburne House (in London) where Shelburne mentioned that he was planning to improve the Poor Laws. This was undoubtedly some spur to Bentham's thinking on the subject, but he had been thinking seriously about the Poor Law prior to his meeting with the soon-to-be Prime Minister. He had discussed the matter with his Scottish friend James Anderson[9] some time before March of the same year,[10] and Anderson subsequently replied with a fascinating letter describing the Scottish method of caring for the poor.[11] Bentham, however, was not very impressed with what he read, at least so far as it had any bearing on English practice.

Anderson began by claiming the superiority of the Scottish to the English method of treating the poor: the English Poor Law he considered as "the most destructive system of laws that were ever invented, which must at last prove the ruin of that nation. . . ." He went on to describe the Scottish "system" (it was hardly very systematic) of relief, which consisted almost entirely of "gratuitous Donations"[12] distributed by the parish parson and a group of Elders ("grave well behaved Persons") chosen by him, with some additional power of oversight over the distribution lodged in the property owners in the district.[13] Anderson made it clear that relief always was very scanty indeed, and that receiving it was universally regarded as a matter of disgrace: it was strictly a matter of Christian charity and not one of legal right as in England. Moreover, the small sums available were depleted by paying the salary of the local "Session Clerk" (who usually was the school master) out of the poor funds. The same source provided the salary of the parish sexton. Things were even worse in parishes which were not Church of Scotland, for then there were no legal funds even for paying the parson, and the money had to be raised by extra taxes of an evidently regressive nature: ". . . as the lower Classes among these Sectarists feel these Taxes very heavy, there is always a greater proportion of the Poor among them than in the Established Church." Anderson admitted that this was a "radical defect" in Scottish practice, but nevertheless hoped never to see the day that involuntary contributions to the poor might come to Scotland.[14]

For Bentham, Scottish practice thus described could be of little use in reforming English law. The letter was, he told Shelburne, "a matter of curiosity." The system in Scotland was predicated on three factors—humanity, frugality, and "honest pride," that is, the shame of receiving "alms." Bentham did not doubt England's humanity—"it is to this that we owe, such as they are, the present system of the Poor Laws"—but in the other factors, England was, "and perhaps ever shall be, far behind." Consequently, ". . . the view it presents to us, is rather that of a state of things to be envied and of a system of manners to be admired than that of a plan of policy to be pursued."[15]

It may seem curious that to Bentham the Scottish "state of things" was enviable when it was obviously so defective on Anderson's own showing, but one need not be very shrewd to guess just what it was that Bentham envied in Scotland: there was no poor rate. Property owners had long been groaning at the increase of the poor rates, and in the years following 1781 they were to groan even more.[16] It was their interest rather than those of the poor that Bentham had in mind when he rued the state of English manners. After he devised his plan for Poor Law reform in the nineties, he said that he had "heeded the cries of the poor"; but it might well be asked whether the cries he was heeding were not those of the ratepayer, and we shall have occasion later on to inquire whether or not it was the interests of the poor that Bentham had primarily in view. Be that as it may, what Bentham's letter does show is that even in his early thinking on the Poor Laws, he never contemplated what not a few Englishmen were to demand: their complete abolition.[17]

The year following his discussion with Shelburne saw Bentham's first extended writing on the question of the poor. He was composing his *Essay on Indirect Legislation* (1782) and thought it proper to include a section called "Expedients for Satisfying Indigence."[18] Since this was an essay on indirect rather than on direct legislation, many important considerations were deliberately excluded, principally the question of how to relieve those whom Bentham termed the "honest poor." Here he was concerned primarily with two questions, how to deal with various categories of unemployed persons who would work if given the opportunity, and how to deal with those who were unwilling or who were suspected of being unwilling to work.

With respect to the first question, Bentham repeated his early suggestion of public works for the able-bodied, but omitted the specification that they be "manufacturers." More interesting are his thoughts on the treatment of the handicapped. As we shall see, the 1790's saw Bentham develop a mania for saving every conceivable form of labor which might otherwise be "lost." In 1782 this concern was already evident: the deaf, the dumb, the blind, and the mutilated all should be put to work in "houses of industry" rather than kept in hospitals. "Those with no eyes can knit: those who have no feet can work at any sedentary employment. Those who have but one hand can write. Those who have none can carry a message." Ominously, he added a further point. "In the pin and other manufactories employment is found for children of four years old."[19] The great vice of idleness was as detrimental to the idle as to the community: "Time must be filled up as well as existence kept alive. The good things of this life do not produce half the enjoyment when they are the wages of idleness, as when they are the price of industry. The wages of idleness are never half the enjoyment as reward of industry."[20]

Bentham was also concerned with the poverty caused by unemployment among women. Women were at a marked disadvantage compared with men, due to the "superior activity, liberty, and perhaps dexterity of the men." Here indirect legislation could alleviate poverty by reserving certain suitable occupations exclusively for women. Bentham argued that employments "which seem particularly suited to the female sex and which can scarcely be practised without indecorum by the male are either shared in by the latter or engrossed." It would not be unjust if custom were overturned by law in such cases.[21] One effect of such a policy might also be the reduction of prostitution, since lack of employment among uneducated women could "fairly be reckoned among the causes of prostitution."[22]

But the greater part of Bentham's discussion of indigence in *Indirect Legislation* was directed toward the second of his categories, the "dishonest" poor. His arguments here had a direct bearing on his proposals of the 1790's, and it is important to understand his terminology. He spoke of "the honest or unsuspicious" poor and the "dishonest or suspicious." In this logic whoever was "suspicious" was considered dishonest—an obvious *non sequitur*. This class included "sturdy beggars, persons suspected of crimes of indigence but not triable [and] persons suspected of crimes of indigence after acquittal."[23] The question was, could it be right to force any of these "suspicious" poor into a House of Industry—that is, to imprison them? Bentham's answer was affirmative. After all, if your object is to minimize social contingency—contingency such as crimes of violence or stealth—what better means than to round up all suspicious persons and imprison them, without worrying about such legal niceties as trials? He did have some qualms about this policy, since "strict and inflexible justice seems to reject" it;[24] but they were soon dismissed.

It is true, Bentham agreed, that a man is either guilty or not guilty: "if he is, punish him with the regular punishment: if not why punish him at all?"[25] But the point was—how could one form an opinion? Here Bentham invoked (not very effectively) the doctrine of mathematical probability. The probability of X's guilt may appear to be as one to infinity, infinity to one, one to one, or some intermediate variation.

> The question is then which is the greater mischief or danger of the two, taking the article of probability into account: the danger of a man's being made to suffer though not guilty by being made to betake himself

to this course [i.e., the workhouse] of livelyhood: and the danger of his betaking himself to similar enormities (upon the supposition that he was guilty) for want of such precaution.[26]

The greater the danger, the greater "the ratio of the apparent chances in favour of his guilt to the chances against that supposition."[27] The greater the ratio, the more reason to "convict."

But that is just the point: this was no ordinary conviction—there was to be no trial. Bentham's discussion may be a fair description of the process by which a judge or jury reaches a verdict; but the invocation of the doctrine of mathematical chance in fact added nothing to the argument that untriable (for lack of evidence) and indeed *acquitted* men could rightly be imprisoned in some form of workhouse.

The argument seemed even stronger with respect to convicts "whose terms of punishment have elapsed." In the first case "there is nothing but suspicion: in the other case there is perfect proof." (This assumed, of course, that only the guilty were convicted.) There was a chance that the prisoner may have been reformed; "still however it is but a chance"; and nothing should be left to chance. If discharged convicts would not willingly enter the House of Industry, it was only proof of their dishonest intentions and consequently all the more reason to force them into confinement.[28] Such reasoning was entirely contrary to Bentham's doctrine that no intention of itself was wrong: only coupled with the consequences of action—and here there was by the supposition no action—could an intention be culpable.[29]

What Bentham proposed in embryo in 1782 and carried to completion in his reform schemes of 1796–97 was nothing less than a variety of antiparasite laws of the most brazen kind. "No man," he wrote, "who has been taken up or examined on suspicion be it ever so faint," of a crime of indigence should be dismissed until he has explained how he has lived for a previous period, for example, six months. "If honestly, such an enquiry can not hurt him: if dishonestly, it is fit that provision should be made accordingly."[30]

Such an examination seems very much like what was required under the Vagrancy Act, or rather Acts. By an act of 1744[31] a vague class of vagrants was created, namely "persons wandering abroad and lodging in alehouses, barns, outhouses or in the open air, *not giving a good account of themselves*."[32] Indeed the general roundup of suspicious persons which Bentham proposed had first been sanctioned by a statute of 1495;[33] and the "privy search," as it was called, was a commonplace of eighteenth-century practice.[34] But Bentham abhorred the Vagrancy Act. In 1797 he attacked it for lumping together too many classes of persons, some pernicious, some not. And he made an even more telling argument: *"It violates justice for punishing, as for delinquency, without proof."*[35] Was this not precisely what he was himself proposing? At least under the Vagrancy Law one would have a trial.

By 1797 Bentham had found a way out of this glaring inconsistency. To do so he used one of the most potent weapons in his well-stocked arsenal: redefinition. Rounding up suspects—as well as those caught red-handed in the act of begging—and sending them to a "House of Industry" was redefined as no punishment at all. They were not being accused of a crime, and hence their treatment could not be described as punishment. The overriding *desideratum* of eliminating chance in society, of maximizing the security of expectation (in this case by snatching up "suspicious" persons whose future actions could not be calculated) had triumphed over all arguments for individual legal rights.[36]

Bentham's policy of winking at men's liberties when adherence to libertarian principles blocked what he thought of as men's *usefulness* was not entirely new to him in the 1780's, for he had defended just such a policy in his very first public utterance, a letter (signed Irenius) to the *Gazetteer and Daily Advertiser* in December of 1770. In that letter he championed the practice of impressment (the forcible taking of men for military or naval duty) as necessary for national defense. In reply to those who, like John Wilkes and his followers, attacked Press Warrants in the name of liberty, Bentham sarcastically remarked that every "vagabond, rescued from the danger of being useful, would be a fresh reinforcement to the squadrons of patriotism"; the "Aegis of Liberty" was merely being used to "dazzle the eyes of weak-sighted observers."[37] In his writings on poverty in the 1790's he was again to defend impressment, this time as a means of siphoning off the surplus of agricultural laborers which depressed wages.[38]

Bentham does not seem to have written specifically on the Poor Laws for several years after having put aside the characteristically uncompleted *Essay on Indirect Legislation*. Surely a concern for the poor was never far from his mind.[39] In the materials written in the mid-1780's that formed much of the basis for Etienne Dumont's edition of the *Traités de Législation civile et pénale* (1802), Bentham argued that "well-being" ("bien être"), the overall end of the state, is achieved through the pursuit of security, subsistence, abundance, and equality. A provision (which turned out to be a guarantee) for the minimal material existence of its subjects therefore ought to be among the first ends of any government.

The translation of Dumont's *Traités, The Theory of Legislation*, cannot be analyzed with any nicety as a Bentham text since, as a translation of Dumont's reworking of Bentham's rather unsatisfactory French, it is twice removed from the original. However, a comparison with the original manuscripts shows that the principal ideas in the discussion on indigence are Bentham's own thoughts and not an exegesis of Dumont's invention. In his manuscripts Bentham argues that the primary provision for subsistence that any state can make is through securing property: the physical sanction of hunger does the rest. "Subsistance . . . demande le moins attention de la part du legislateur";[40] ". . . it is by providing security in general and especially security in respect to property, the means of subsistence, that the laws make that necessary provision without which subsistence would, in spite of all laws directed to that particular object, be presently at an end."[41] However, in the case of those unable to provide for themselves, the state should gratuitously furnish subsistence. But for those able to work, an important qualification which was to assume great prominence in the Poor Law reform writings of the 1790's was added—work would be required in return for subsistence, for any law which offers security without industry undermines industry, or at least frugality.[42] On the other hand to those who thought misery and death the proper reward for prodigality, who maintained that "le catastrophe fatal de quelques-uns sera une loi et une leçon pour les autres," Bentham replied that this is fitting only if the object of the law is vengeance.[43]

Two further arguments against leaving the care of the indigent in private hands also look forward to Bentham's Poor Law reforms as they were expounded at length in the 1790's. Voluntary contribution as the sole support for indigence is unsatisfactory, first, because of its uncertainty, and secondly, because it represents a tax on the humane: "the avaricious," Dumont lets Bentham say in *The Theory of Legislation*, "calumniate the poor," whose care is left to "the more humane and virtuous," who may themselves be none too affluent. "Such an arrangement," the passage concludes, "is a favour granted to selfishness, and a punishment to humanity, that first of virtues."[44] Nor were the deserving poor necessarily the beneficiaries of charitable outpouring. Clearly, Bentham had already rejected those arguments which opposed any version of the Welfare State.

The rejection of such arguments is underlined by other remarks found in *The Theory of Legislation*, for at this point in his career Bentham chose to emphasize the conditions which dragged the working poor into the ranks of paupers without moral or prudential transgression. Some were those among the aged who, even with their best efforts, were unable to save for the years of decline; others were the young who were left parentless; and others still were victims of industrial stagnation, the weather, or similar circumstances.[45] That the indigent are not always or even usually responsible for their own misery was a justification for state intervention on behalf of the pauper that Bentham sometimes repeated in his tracts on poverty of the 1790's. But, as we will discover, he used the argument or ignored it as suited his purpose: when he needed a defense for scrapping virtually all home relief in favor of the onerous discipline of Panopticon, the 'innocence' of great masses of indigents was left conveniently unnoticed.

Another fragment of evidence from the 1780's gives further indication of Bentham's generally sympathetic view of poverty. In 1786 he evidently intended to compose a work on the poor, though of precisely what nature we do not know.[46] There is no mention of such a work or of the problems of poverty in general in his correspondence for that year; but there are several letters missing from the year, including one to James Anderson, which might provide some clue to his thinking—probably we shall never know. Whatever Bentham may have intended (or even written), all that has passed down to us is a manuscript of only a few pages entitled "Poor's Cry," some of whose ideas will be discussed later on. What concerns us here is the attack Bentham made in it on the Law of Settlement and its relation to his more extended treatment of Settlement made in the 1790's. Before discussing his attack, however, it would be well to understand what the problem of Settlement was.

Bentham and the Law of Settlement

The problem of Settlement stemmed from an act of 1662 ironically entitled "An Act for the Better Relief of the Poor of this Kingdom."[47] By this act, every person whose tenement did not have a rentable value of £10 a year, or who could not give security (attested by two Justices) for indemnifying the parish against poor relief expense, was liable to be forcibly removed to his place of "Settlement," usually his place of birth. Such removal had to be made within forty days of his arrival, and it was accomplished by the application of Churchwardens or Poor Overseers to two magistrates.[48]

The Act did not create the idea that every person 'belonged' to some parish; that notion had existed from time immemorial. Nor, indeed, was this the first provision for returning those who left their former abodes. In 1388, impotent beggars were directed to their birthplaces to be maintained;[49] in the next century they were told to return to their last dwelling, or, more vaguely, to where they were known; and in 1597 "Rogues, Vagabonds and Sturdy Beggars" were similarly treated (after being publicly whipped "until his or her body be bloody"). The vagrancy laws made many such restrictions on mobility against those deemed of criminal tendency, but there was no general prohibition against leaving one's own parish: properly identified by what amounted to an internal passport, the poor laborer could venture out of his parish in search of more stable work or higher wages.

Specific legal provision for transporting paupers from parish to parish until they reached their place of Settlement dated from the mid-sixteenth century when "aged impotent and lame persons" who were beggars were to be conveyed "on horseback, cart, chariot or otherwise to the next constable, and so forth from constable to constable, till they be brought to the place they were born or most conversant for the space of three years, there to be nourished of alms." Later sixteenth-century acts dropped beggars from the text, so that the law appears to have authorized the removal of the impotent poor, even though not actually begging or applying for poor relief. In any case, whatever the niceties of the law, regular attempts were made to clear parishes of those who might become chargeable to poor relief.[50]

Such attempts continued in the seventeenth century, but the legal situation was more confused. The Elizabethan poor laws of 1597/1598 (39 Elizabeth c.3) and 1601 (43 Elizabeth c.2) made no provision for removal, and some Justices, particularly during the Commonwealth, considered the earlier laws to have lapsed and refused orders for removal.[51]

If the Act of 1662 put an end to that particular confusion, it gave rise to others, usually with tragic and costly consequences. To avoid the expense of relief, parishes regularly tried surreptitiously to foist their paupers onto neighboring parishes. Bitter disputes broke out attended with costly litigation: over the next century and a half, parishes spent literally millions of pounds in legal fees,[52] and courts were choked with such cases. In 1735 a critic wrote that it was "notorious that half the business of every Quarter Sessions consists in deciding appeals in orders for removal."[53] And since the removal was effected *before* the appeal was decided upon, the already degraded pauper might find himself, having been transported from parish A to parish B, compelled to return to the first parish. Subsequent appeals could repeat the process several times.[54]

The operation of the Law of Settlement was extremely complex, and only a brief discussion can be given here. The Webbs estimated that it was enforced in tens of thousands of cases a year[55] and described the result as "the mournful and onerous 'general post' of indigent folk, men, women, and children, in all states of health and disease, perpetually criss-crossing the kingdom under expensive escort. . . ."[56]

During the first years of the Act's operation, many tried to evade it simply by secreting themselves in a parish for forty days, after which they acquired immunity. But Parliament remedied that by requiring written notice of arrival to be given to the Poor Overseer (later the notice had to be posted in the parish church) before the forty-day period could legally begin. Indeed, during the first sixty years of the Settlement Act's existence, Parliament passed successive laws to make Settlement in a new parish more difficult.

Moreover, parishes adopted a host of methods, some of them rather devious, to decant real or potential applicants from their borders. Some became matchmakers to reduce the number of single women; others used bribes to induce those with legal settlements to move elsewhere: no one who owned a freehold, however small, could be removed, and there is evidence that some parishes simply bought freeholds in other districts for unwanted families. Still others advanced the necessary £10 for the required minimum rent.[57]

Litigation was at times so absurd that it would be comic were it not for its oppressive consequences. There was, for instance, the doctrine of derivative Settlement, established by the Court of King's Bench. Children without Settlements were deemed to have inherited their fathers' Settlements; if they were unknown then they inherited their grandfathers' Settlements; and there were even cases where great-grandfathers' Settlements were given.[58] The result might mean the pauper's removal from his lifelong home to an altogether unknown place a great distance away.

The squabbling of the parishes reached bizarre heights in an 1815 case. A parish division ran through a pauper's home, through his bed in fact. A tribunal tried to determine where most of his body resided: the court held that the pauper was settled "where his head (being the nobler part) lay, though one of his legs at least, and a great part of his body, lay out of his parish."[59]

There was one great loophole that did allow mobility without liability to removal until one actually applied for relief. This was the provision for granting "certificates" (narrowly permitted in 1662 but extended in 1697), which gave immunity from removal for the holder until he was actually chargeable, that is, a pauper in need of relief. In practice, this system was often quite arbitrary. Some parishes granted them more, others less freely, others not at all. The Hammonds point out that, while it might seem in a parish's interest to give a certificate to an unemployed man, in practice matters might be otherwise: the man might wander far afield, and, should he become chargeable, the removal expense would fall on the home parish.[60]

In view of the obvious harshness of the Law of Settlement, it is hardly surprising that humane Englishmen protested vigorously against it. The attack took two main lines of argument. First, it was urged that the law was an outrageous infringement on personal liberty; secondly, it was argued that it impeded the mobility of labor with economically deleterious consequences. One writer attacked the 1662 Act soon after it was made as "a great imprisonment if not slavery"; the poor, he said, were "chained down to their wants, so they are deprived of means to mend their condition . . . by removing to places more proper for them. . . ."[61] Others, like William Hay, called attention to arbitrariness in granting certificates.[62] In 1791, Thomas Paine let out a mighty blast against the Law of Settlement in the course of proposing his own poor relief plan:

> By the operation of this plan, the poor laws, those instruments of civil torture, will be superceded. . . . The dying poor will not be dragged from place to place to breathe their last, as a reprisal of parish against parish.[63]

But the most famous and undoubtedly the most influential opponent of Settlement was Adam Smith. In the *Wealth of Nations*, Smith cited Richard Burn's *History of the Poor Laws* to effect in deriding the caprice of the certificate system;[64] and he denounced forcible removal as palpably unjust: "To remove a man who has committed no misdemeanor from the parish where he chooses to reside is an evident violation of natural liberty and justice." Smith was surprised that a people who prized their liberty would tolerate such "oppression"; there had been a general outcry against general warrants (he was thinking, of course, of the case of John Wilkes) but there was no "general popular clamour" against Settlement, which was infinitely worse. "There is scarce a poor man in England of forty years of age . . . who has not in some part of his life felt himself most cruelly op-pressed by this ill-contrived law of settlements."[65]

But it was Smith's further argument that accounts for his influence, namely, that the Law of Settlement restricted labor mobility. The conse-quences were a form of economic sin (that may not have been what Smith said, but that is how the matter came to be regarded) since wages were "artificially" raised or lowered, not according to the availability of labor in the larger area, but merely according to an artificial "obstruction," as he called it, erected by the Law of Settlement. That is, "the supply of labour" (or "hands,"[66] as he wrote later on) was paid more than otherwise if com-peting workers could not cross the parish line; and, *mutatis mutandis*, the principle operated in reverse. It was this artificial restriction, he argued—and on this point nobody ever answered him—that explained the "sudden and unaccountable differences in the wages of neighbouring places which we sometimes find in England. . . ."[67] Without any justification, one man earned more, another less; one employer paid more, another less, solely, Smith thought, on account of the parish boundary.

This argument was not novel; it had been argued as long before as 1670, as well as afterward. But such reasoning had never before been couched within a book as authoritative as *The Wealth of Nations*. Still, eighteenth-century readers did not passively accept Smith's conclusions. John Howlett for one, Frederic Eden for another, disputed his claims: if mobility was so restricted, Howlett asked, how could there have been so much growth in towns such as Birmingham?—not to mention the Metropolis.[68] And Eden, having cited Howlett's criticism of Adam Smith, went on to give both a backhand justification of Settlement and a refutation of the famous Scotsman: "Though man, in civilized society, loses much of his character, as a locomotive animal, I believe there is no country in Europe in which he changes residence so often as in England."[69]

There is a law of historiography that 'truth' consists in a compromise between two 'extreme' theories. Nevertheless, in this case, both sides can claim tactical advantage and neither side the victory. There certainly was some restriction of liberty, and therefore of movement of labor, but ex-actly how much cannot be determined. On the other hand, it was families (as well as single pregnant women) who were most feared by economical Poor Overseers, and it was they who were most liable to removal. Single men, so far as we know, were much less liable to fall afoul of the "general post" in human beings.[70]

However amiss Smith may have been, it was his case that seemed to carry the day in the court of eighteenth-century opinion. William Pitt, for one, accepted the argument, and he was Prime Minister in 1795 when the Law of Settlement was amended; and J. R. Poynter says bluntly that Smith's point of view on the law "became an orthodox tenet of [eighteenth-century] political economy."[71] As eighteenth-century men saw it (that is to say, those who influenced opinion), the worst evil was the provision for removing those who were merely *likely* (the term was vague) to become chargeable as opposed to actually *being* chargeable to the poor rates. The first reform came in 1793, when members of "Friendly Societies," insurance associations organized by the poor, became exempt from removal until chargeable; but the most important reform came in 1795 when nearly everyone (but not the feared class of pregnant women) was exempted from removal until chargeable. The language of the reforming act seems to suggest that it was not the restriction of individuals' liberty that was the strongest argument for reform but their lack of mobility as laborers: ". . . many industrious poor persons, chargeable to the parish . . . merely from want of work there, would in any other place, where sufficient employment is to be had, maintain themselves and families without being burthensome to any parish. . . ."[72] This may well be Smith's influence at work.

What position did Bentham take in these controversies? The answer is that he was in utter opposition to the Law of Settlement both in the fragmentary "Poor's Cry" of 1786 and in his writings of the '90's. In attacking Settlement, he used every argument that critics had marshalled and added novel ones of his own. Though he did not speak as the poor's advocate in the *Essay on Indirect Legislation* of 1782 or in his writings on poverty a decade and a half later, he did precisely that in the "Poor's Cry" and in the polemical pamphlets of the early '90's, *A Protest Against Law Taxes* and *Truth versus Ashurst*. This change in his legal brief, so to speak (and not very metaphorically), is important in understanding his systematic plan for the poor.

What the poor were 'crying' about in 1786 was the Law of Settlement. To Bentham, the law was an "injustice done to the Poor in respect of personal liberty." He echoed John North's protest of more than a century before when he described English practice as tyrannical: "The the poor, in this land of pretended liberty, the whole land is a prison. Englishmen are said to be free and they are taught to believe that no other people are so."[73] But the sort of liberty in which Englishmen believed was violated by a system that confined nine-tenths of the people to their parishes: "At this rate imprisonment in the King's Bench prison may be stiled liberty." He concluded that although only a part of the poor reap the benefit of the Poor Laws, "all the poor, all the working class are loaded with this grievous and unnecessary burthen."[74]

In 1792, Bentham added another ringing protest against the infringement of liberty imposed by the Law of Settlement. The occasion was the brilliant polemical pamphlet already noticed, *Truth versus Ashurst*. Justice Ashurst had claimed that English law imposed no other restraints on action than were necessary for "the safety and good order of the community at large." Obviously, the Law of Settlement made a mockery of such a claim, and Bentham made short work of his victim: "There is no employment for me in my own parish: there is abundance in the next. Yet if I offer to go there I am driven away. Why? Because I *might* become unable to work one of these days and so I must not work while I am able."[75] And at that rate, how was work ever to get done? Clearly, it was the mobility of labor argument that was uppermost in his mind.

Bentham's 1796–97 writings on the problem of Settlement are of a character different from these brief and spirited remarks. They are sober and systematic reflections designed to play an integral part in his arguments for sweeping reform of poor relief. Not surprisingly, there is scant reference to a lack of labor mobility, since that was largely a thing of the past: the 1795 reform had seen to that. Still, the Law of Settlement remained an evil: as soon as one applied for relief, he became subject to the humiliation of legal disputes and forceable removal. Bentham argued cogently that such treatment of those forced by circumstance to apply for relief was without justification. "Working hands," as he called them, were uniquely important: it was they who produced the wealth of the nation; it was they, in fact, who as a group produced the wherewithal of their own relief: "The very source and only source of relief is thus considered as a burthen." The very same persons, he continued,

> to whom in the first instance the country is exclusively indebted for its wealth are thus driven from pillar to post as if they were a nuisance. The notion proceeded upon is that the prosperity of the hive depends upon the extirpation of the working bees.[76]

This was the worst evil but not the only one. Naturally, Bentham was well aware of the mass of expensive litigation that squabbling parishes perpetually carried on; and there was the cost of conveyance as well. Moreover, under the Law of Settlement, relief could hardly be effective when need was immediate and the pauper's Settlement either undetermined or at a distant place.[77]

Nevertheless, the Law of Settlement *did* have a justification. Its object, Bentham said, "is or ought to be to prevent the overburthening of any Parish, by the sudden influx of a quantum of burthen disproportionate to its ability."[78] The problem was how to share a public burden as equally as possible, "that is, in as near a proportion as possible to the ability of those on whom it is imposed." We have already mentioned that Bentham had no quarrel with the local real estate tax; he believed (or professed to believe) that it was an accurate reflection of one's ability to pay. While it might be thought that he simply dared not propose an income tax (not to mention a wealth tax) in the belief that such proposals would be denounced as radical during the general panic over French affairs, in his *Proposal for a Mode of Taxation* written several years previously (1794) he had rejected a general income tax solely on grounds of economic justice.[79] (However, to finance the Napoleonic Wars, the government in fact levied an income tax between 1799 and 1816.)

The parish rate was an equable tax for Bentham, but the Settlement system was manifestly unjust. Yet if Settlement were simply abolished, some parishes might be unfairly swamped with paupers. The solution to this dilemma seemed obvious: pool the local rates in a *national* fund which could then be redistributed according to a plan. "In this case the occasion for ascertaining the settlements of individuals would in good measure if not altogether be taken away."[80]

Interestingly enough, Bentham did not contemplate a uniform national rate; rather, parishes would simply continue paying their usual rate. Since such rates varied considerably, his proposal clashed violently with his principle that the tax should be equal—in accordance with ability to pay. He offered two reasons to justify this inequality. The first underlines the crucial role that securing expectations played in his thought. Were the tax equalized, some would gain, others would lose: but, according to his usual rule of thumb, ". . . in operations of this sort the enjoyment of him who gains is not equal to the suffering of him who loses," and the result would be "a loss in point of national felicity upon the whole."[81] It was, perhaps, a rather glib remark—Bentham argued elsewhere that greater material equality yields a greater sum of happiness in society, though equality should be approached only gradually in order to avoid dashing expectations; and in this case he did not stop to consider the possibility of great suffering among the poorest ratepayers. However, he probably did not believe the issue to be of much consequence, since, as we shall see, he expected the poor rate to wither away completely if his reform plan was adopted. In any case, his second defense of the unequal tax was conclusive: proposing the fairer tax would raise such violent opposition that the entire reform would be endangered—"the zeal in defence of property may be expected to be more strenuous than the ardour for the augmentation of new advantages. . . ."[82] In other words, strategic considerations seemed to be dictating theoretical conclusions; otherwise the pain of the most heavily taxed might have weighed more heavily in the argument.

Finally, although he believed that the problem of Settlement would largely wither away, Bentham did not think requiring a Settlement could be abolished immediately: there would have to be some sort of interim law. He was not concerned with which criterion or criteria would be chosen as the means of gaining a Settlement, so long as the choice lay within certain guidelines. First of all, any law of Settlement must minimize the possibility of a sudden increase in paupers in a district and eliminate any ground for legal dispute.[83] Suppose, for example, place of birth remained a primary location of Settlement: how could the matter be put beyond argument? Bentham revived one of the vehicles for social control outlined in *Indirect Legislation*. Simply tattoo birthplace along with name on every infant—and call it a *"Birth-mark."*[84] Such a practice retained great significance to him —"This it is true is but one of a prodigious multitude and variety of uses to which an institution in itself so simple may be made subservient."[85]

Bentham mentioned a last guideline for a law of Settlement which really would have revolutionized the Settlement system, for it would have eliminated coercion. A place of Settlement should be "most likely to be accordant with the feelings of the individual concerned." The option between two places should "be given to the Pauper that he may not be banished from his connections."[86] This is one of the few times in the vast bulk of his writings on the Poor Law that one finds Bentham willing to respect the views of the pauper himself; many things might be intended for his benefit, but they had little to do with his *choice*. Bentham is a most perplexing and contradictory figure: he was capable of exquisite sensitivity to the privations and injustices inflicted on the poor; but he could be equally callous and manipulative. In this instance the feelings of the pauper would, he tells us, be respected; the pauper would have a choice. But what was that choice to be? He could choose which of Bentham's workhouses he wished to enter —workhouses where he would be held prisoner and in most cases under conditions of the most intense discipline.

2

The Poor Law in Crisis

The consequences of the Act of Settlement were perhaps the most glaring anomaly of poor relief, but for Bentham it was only one part of a situation which ought to be transformed at its roots. He was fond of distinguishing between the mere criticism and reform of "this or that" individual or problem and the overturning of what he called "the system." The former procedure was superficial treatment; only the latter had any chance of effecting a cure. Just as in his attack on the administration of justice, in the practice of poor relief the target was the "system" itself. That is one sense in which Bentham was a "radical" even in his anti-revolutionary days, long before anyone had heard of "Philosophical Radicals."

But as Bentham knew so well, it is rather ironic to speak of a "system" of poor relief in eighteenth-century England, since, so far from being systematic, apart from fundamental consistencies its operation showed little coherence. Poor Law administration had long since ceased to be centrally regulated: the measure of central control which the Privy Council strove to provide under Queen Elizabeth had collapsed during the Revolution and was not reinstated under the Restoration monarchy or afterwards.

The administration of that myriad of Acts which we know as the Poor Law was based primarily on parishes, most of which were quite small, and whose numbers increased from 12,000 in 1662 to 15,000 by 1834. The Webbs estimated that of these more than two-thirds dealt with populations of no more than a couple of hundred families, and that thousands of parishes had no more than a few hundred souls.[1] Responsibility in the parish for day-to-day poor relief lay, as provided in the Elizabethan Act of 1597–98, in Poor Overseers, who were usually appointed annually, two to a parish, by Justices of the Peace from a list provided by the parish vestry. In addition, the parish churchwardens, chosen annually by the vestry, were Poor Overseers *ex officio*. All were unpaid, all were amateur, and all were exposed to the temptations of corruption, to which not a few succumbed.

Control over the Overseers by parish vestries was usually irregular and uncertain. Overseers published no regular accounts, and critics argued that their primitive accounting methods defied all attempts to detect fraud.[2] It was with this in mind, as we shall see, that Bentham made strenuous efforts to incorporate strict accounting procedures into his poor plan.

In urban areas, parishes were especially open to corrupt control by oligarchies or even a single "boss."[3] Moreover, whether or not they were tainted, Overseers were accustomed to spending parish funds for elaborate feasts at the annual parish officers' election. One such event in the London parish of St. Martin-in-the-Fields in 1714 cost the princely sum of £49-13-6, enough to keep two families for a year.[4] Another in a small Hampshire town fifty years later included 37 bottles of wine (at a cost of £3-14) and liberal quantities of beer and punch.[5] Overseers were, however, legally accountable to the local Justices, who were often looked upon as protectors of the poor. The Justices themselves were overseen by County Bench at Quarter Sessions. Sovereignty was thus divided, with the Magistrates functioning as a kind of court of appeal.

In addition to parish organizations, there was a welter of autonomous administrative bodies which provided poor relief—municipal corporations, manorial boroughs, decaying manors, and the like. But the most important additional authorities which arose were the Incorporated Guardians of the Poor (various other names were also used). These were the officers of unions of parishes which were incorporated (before 1782) by the authority of Local Acts.

The main purpose of such corporations was the building of a common workhouse to which some of the poor could be sent in lieu of outdoor relief. Setting the poor to work had been enjoined by the Elizabethan Act of 1601 (as well as by earlier legislation of 1572–76); but in the seventeenth century, reformers such as Sir Josiah Child suggested a further idea: employing the poor to earn their entire maintenance. This idea never completely lost currency among reformers even after it had proved unworkable; the self-maintenance of the poor was, in the Webbs' phrase, the reformers' "golden dream."[6] And it was this dream that animated the reform plans of Jeremy Bentham.

One of the first experiments in the incorporation of urban parishes was carried out in Bristol at the end of the seventeenth century under the influence of a successful merchant, John Cary. Its workhouse was widely admired, and by 1712, thirteen towns had followed its example. An act of 1723 allowed parishes to build their own workhouses (but not to incorporate);[7] within a decade, more than one hundred had been built. By the 1830's, there were over four thousand.

Rural incorporation of parishes was both slower and less widespread. None at all, it seems, was carried out before 1758, when some enthusiastic squires and clergy of Suffolk, authorized by a Local Act, completed a House of Industry near Ipswich. The experiment was temporarily popular,[8] and other rural parishes followed suit, mostly in Suffolk and Norfolk. In all, 125 rural incorporations under Local Acts were carried out by 1834. But this was hardly scratching the surface of localism, since, as mentioned before, the number of parishes did not decline during the period of incorporation, but actually grew to 15,000 by 1834.

Still, the Incorporated Guardians had one theoretical advantage over the annually changing parish Overseers: to a much greater extent, paid officials were hired who might develop some degree of professional expertise by their permanence. Responsibility for oversight over them was vested in the hands of local notables, who made up the various governing committees of the district, and who were required to attend weekly or quarterly meetings. In practice, however, attendance usually dwindled away, and the paid officials were left ineffectively overseen: they sat in secret, published no regular accounts or reports, and were independent of outside inspection (as the parishes were not). Corruption and abuse of power were the inevitable results.[9]

The initial purpose of the workhouses of both single and incorporated districts was to make the poor self-maintaining. They were a dismal failure. By the time their failure was discovered, their principal *raison d'être* had become the deterrence of the poor from applying for relief at all. In the *State of the Poor*, Sir Frederic Eden listed case after case of poor relief costs initially dropping after the establishment of a workhouse, only to rise rapidly thereafter;[10] and by the time Bentham wrote his poor plan, disillusionment with poor self-maintenance was widespread. Small wonder, then, that he marshalled his arguments so energetically to prove that *he* could succeed where all others had failed.

A concerted effort to alleviate some of the evils of excessive localism was made by one of the most enterprising reformers of the day, Thomas Gilbert, M.P. In 1782, he succeeded in having a bill passed (he had failed once in 1765) which allowed (but did not require) parishes to incorporate to build a workhouse-cum-hospital, not for the able-bodied poor, but for the old and the very young. Those who were capable of working were to be found employment.

When adopted, the effect of Gilbert's Act (as it was known) was to remove poor administration from the hands of the discredited Overseers and transfer it to a professional Guardian. But it was not adopted by parishes, at least not to any significant extent. In all, by 1834 sixty-seven Gilbert Act unions were made, incorporating fewer than a thousand parishes. At the time Bentham set out to transform thousands of local practices into a single national policy, the means of curbing localism gone berserk were nowhere in sight.

The public workhouse was one of a variety of methods that parishes used in the attempt to employ the poor. Some maintained a primitive public works program (similar to Bentham's earliest suggestions for dealing with indigence), employing the able-bodied on roads or on farms which were specifically rented for the purpose. Others adopted the contract, or "farming out" system, according to which (in one of its forms) private individuals agreed to maintain the parish paupers in return for a stipulated sum. The contractor had the use of the poor's labor, from which he hoped to gain a profit. At times this method of relief had grotesque results: it was not unusual for indigent children to be more or less bought by manufacturers in the Midlands, transported far from their homes, and forced to work up to fourteen hours a day. Another form of "farming out" which often had gruesome consequences was the contracting for the insane, a practice which was often lucrative.[11] Without adequate accounting methods, the contract system was prey to corruption in the form of bribery; and without controls over the contractor, the pauper might find himself employed by a Simon Legree.[12]

Another frequently used though scarcely more satisfactory device was the "billet" or "roundsman" system. The unemployed "made the rounds" from house to house seeking work; if he was not employed, his wage was paid by the parish. In some parishes it was compulsory to employ the "roundsman": the employer was obliged to maintain the laborer but was permitted to pay whatever wage he chose, usually a pittance. Left in this way at the mercy of his master, the worker found himself frequently abused, especially in the form of underfeeding.[13]

Nevertheless, despite all the attempts to put the poor to work, the simple dole was a ubiquitous feature of eighteenth-century poor relief. Administratively, it was the simplest form of relief, and very often parishes found it the cheapest form as well, especially when they discovered the inefficiency of maintaining a workhouse. The Overseer could offer the pauper a choice: the horrors of the workhouse or a miniscule dole. The pauper often chose the latter.

One common practice in administering the dole was the "rate in aid of wages." Overseers were readily convinced that the poor could supplement relief with casual labor, although whether they actually could was another matter. A sub-subsistence allowance was given, and the pauper was expected to make up the deficiency himself. Allowances, however, tended to be below subsistence in any case, and were haphazardly bestowed as well. Given the unsystematic and inadequate nature of English poor relief, it is not hard to see why the near-famine conditions of 1795 produced a profound crisis in which the nature and mission of the entire Poor Law was called into question. It was this crisis that provided the setting for the far-reaching proposals of busy reformist pamphleters, including Jeremy Bentham.

1. The Crisis of 1795

The crisis of 1795 was a "double panic of famine and revolution," to use the phrase of a nineteenth-century writer,[14] occasioned by the dislocations of the war with France, by the deep sense of alarm among the middle and upper classes at the spectacle of the demands of the lower classes for political reform, and by soaring food prices. The winter of 1794–95 was exceptionally severe, and the price of food, especially of wheat, began to soar. The average price of wheat doubled between January and August 1795. In London it reached 108 shillings a quarter and in Leicester 160s. In April, complaints within the army over the cost of food were so vociferous that the government was forced to grant an extra food allowance.[15] There is little room for dissent from the observation of one of the most able contemporary writers on the poor that the condition of the ordinary laborer was one of "real, widespread, and increasing distress"; it was a simple fact that "the pay of the day-labourer is not adequate to his necessaries."[16]

The price rises were so acute that the common people took matters into their own hands. In the spring and summer, England (both North and South) was the scene of a series of "food riots," conducted mainly by women. In Carlisle, for instance, women accompanied by young children seized all available grain, brought it to the public hall, and formed a committee to decide its price. The incident was characteristic: the 'rioters' neither rioted in the ordinary sense nor stole, but rather forced the sale of food at prices they considered fair. Their actions were by no means revolutionary: at Bath, when the Riot Act was read to a group of women attempting to seize grain, they protested that they were no rioters and sang "God Save the King." Nevertheless, the riots naturally tended to increase the alarm of the upper classes, already badly frightened by the winds of change blowing from across the Channel.[17]

One inevitable effect of the tremendous rises in food costs was an inflation of the poor rates, for thousands of hitherto self-supporting working families were compelled to rely on public relief. Complaints about rising rates were a commonplace of eighteenth-century writing on the Poor Law, but the increases of 1795 must surely have been immense in many areas.

While there are no poor-rate returns for 1795, we do know that expenditures on the poor more than doubled between 1785 and 1803.[18] In Norwich the poor rate reached 12s. or 13s. in the pound in 1795, and John Thelwall, a leader of the London Corresponding Society, claimed that 25,000 workers in the city were applying for relief.[19] Whether or not he was exaggerating, the more painstaking researches of Eden give unmistakable clues to the extent of the crisis. In one Sussex parish, 25 percent of the inhabitants were chargeable to the rates and one-third of the rental went to maintaining them. In one district in Carlisle, a third of the population received relief; in Shrewsbury (whose population was estimated at 20,000) between 5,000 and 6,000 received charity in 1795 "exclusive of the regular poor."[20] There is small wonder that Bentham tried so assiduously to prove that his plan really could make the indigent self-maintaining and eventually eliminate the poor rate entirely.

Political unrest accompanied economic distress. In the eyes of the Pitt government, the chief culprit was the London Corresponding Society (L.C.S) and its provincial counterparts, who preached the seditious doctrines of universal manhood suffrage and annual Parliaments. The Society had been founded in 1792 by Thomas Hardy (a shoemaker, educated at the University of Geneva) and was quickly infiltrated by the first of a long series of government *agents provocateurs*, whose viciousness and utter hypocrisy could hardly be exaggerated.[21] Partly on the evidence of such men, Hardy, Thelwall, Horne Tooke, and ten others were arrested in May 1794, on charges of high treason. In October, Hardy was brought to trial, and, on Guy Fawkes Day, was acquitted amid a vast tumult among the

London mob. Thelwall and Tooke were subsequently acquitted as well, and the others were discharged.

Nevertheless, by March 1795, the L.C.S. had seriously declined and the provincial correspondence had fallen off, leaving the movement no national center. However, the fortunes of the Society began to revive in June when a great meeting, the largest reform demonstration London had ever seen, was held in St. George's Fields. Both L.C.S. membership and provincial correspondence grew from then until the end of the year. On 26 October, another huge gathering was organized by the L.C.S. in Copenhagen Fields, Islington, the organizers claiming an attendance of 100,000–150,000.[22] Three days later George III himself, on his way to open Parliament, was mobbed in the streets of London by a crowd shouting "No Pitt—No War—Peace, Peace, Bread, Bread."[23] The window of the King's coach was fractured, by what means no one knows—it may have been a stone—but the King believed he had been shot at. It was a day which, in E. P. Thompson's nice phrase, "if not sacred to liberty—most certainly scared authority."[24] Parliament was convulsed with fear and outrage. It decided to address the King, "so great had been the alarm and indignation created" by the attack. On October 31, a proclamation was issued offering £1,000 "for the discovery of any person guilty of those outrages."[25]

Pitt responded with his "Two Acts." The first made the incitement by speech or writing of hatred or contempt of the King, the Constitution, or the Government a treasonable offense; the second prohibited any gathering of over fifty persons without notifying a magistrate, who was given powers to stop speeches, arrest speakers, or disperse meetings. The "Two Acts" were given the royal assent in mid-December, but not before the L.C.S. called two more immense protest demonstrations.[26]

Only a handful in Parliament resisted such repression. One forceful opponent of Pitt's policy was Shelburne, now Lord Lansdowne, who accused ministers of sheer political opportunism. They intended, he argued, "to seize this opportunity to work upon the passions and fears of the people, and to lead their representatives into concessions derogatory to the public liberty . . . in order to confirm their own power at the expense of the constitution."[27] Be this as it may, such was the political atmosphere of London when Bentham sat down, probably at the end of the year, to propose a revolution in the practice of poor relief.

The response of the government to political turmoil (if that is the word) was simple: repression. The response to the economic crisis was more complex. One issue was the question of diet. The Rev. David Davies complained that critics of the poor's diet wished only to show them how "to live *worse* than they do."[28] From the point of view of the ordinary laborer in 1795, that was precisely what was expected of him. If wheat was scarce, bread mixed with barley and other grain should be eaten, and potatoes and oatmeal should be substituted for bread. To set an example, "ministerial people" agreed to cut their use of wheat bread by one-third.[29] However, heavy resistance to dietary change was encountered, especially among the southern laborers. Potatoes were considered a miserable food—"Erin's root fed hordes" might subsist on them, but many saw potatoes as no better than hog's food, and in any case not nourishing.[30] Brown (as opposed to white) bread was regarded with equal repugnance. In one instance, the charitable rich raised a subscription to sell the cheaper bread at a reduced price: many of the laborers, despite the enormous cost of white bread, refused the inferior substitute as too coarse and unpalatable.[31]

Oatmeal was another cheap food that could be substituted for wheat. But as the Hammonds remark, oatmeal with milk is a very different food from oatmeal eaten by itself.[32] Milk was plentiful in the north, and, as the researches of Davies and Eden show, formed a larger portion of the northern diet than in the south. In the south, thanks to the growth of enclosures (which drastically curtailed common grazing), milk was a scarce commodity. The poor could not afford the price of a cow (hence, as we shall see, Pitt's proposal for "cow money"), and, as for buying milk, as Davies put it, "it is not to be had for love or money."[33] And for the southern view of oatmeal, one recalls Dr. Johnson's famous barb in his *Dictionary*: "Oats: a grain which in England is generally given to horses, but in Scotland supports the people."[34]

Finally, the southern laborer was beset with one more difficulty, also occasioned at least in part by enclosure: a scarcity of fuel. If home-cooked foods were to be substituted for the baker's bread, how could the laborer, already on a sub-subsistence budget, afford expensive fuels in order to cook them? In fact, the southerner was already reduced to what has been called "fuel poaching," sneaking onto enclosed land and picking at hedges. In a word, the short-run effort at dietary reform was a complete failure. In the end, it was the potato that won the day; and it has been argued that it was the potato as much as any other factor that saved Britain from bloody revolution.[35]

Bentham's attitude towards the proper diet of the indigent will be examined later on; but one point which can be interjected here is important for understanding his deportment towards the poor: his tendency towards insensitivity and his tough-minded practicality. Bentham's copy of David Davies' *The Case of the Labourers in Husbandry* is preserved in the British Museum, complete with marginal comments. Davies gave well-researched and colorfully-presented evidence that the living standard of the common laborer "has geen going from bad to worse continually," and not, as some critics maintained, because of "mismanagement."[36] One of his points dealt with the accusation that tea drinking was an inexcusable luxury indulged in by the poor. If it were thought luxurious, he wrote, to drink

> fine hyson tea, sweetened by refined sugar, and softened with cream, I readily admit it to be so. But *this* is not the tea of the poor. Spring water, just coloured with a few leaves of the lowest-priced tea, and sweetened with the brownest sugar, is the luxury for which you reproach them.[37]

What were the poor to drink once milk became a scarcity? Small beer was once a necessity, but the price of hops put home brewing beyond the means of the common people. "The only thing remaining for them to moisten their bread with, was tea. That was their last resource." Bentham underlined the words "the only thing" and "tea." In the margin he wrote, "hydrophobia." Let them drink water. The comment speaks for itself.[38]

Little in the way of Parliamentary intervention in the crisis was attempted before the end of 1795. In mid-October the exemption of corn from import duty was extended for another year; and a bounty was placed on grain from the United States and the Mediterranean. However, the magistrates in many parts of England had already taken matters into their own hands. Some, as in Hampshire, merely admonished farmers to increase wages to a subsistence level. Others, as in Oxford, Buckinghamshire, and elsewhere, went further and ordered wages to be made up to a specified minimum level out of parish funds.[39]

But the most famous of the Justices' actions took place in Berkshire. On the 6th of May, magistrates and "other discreet persons" met at the Pelican Inn at Speen, in a district known as Speenhamland, to consider the disastrous condition of the poor. One suggestion, to regulate wages by law, was rejected. Instead, the Justices adopted what has since been known as the Speenhamland system, according to which the laborer's wage would be supplemented with parish funds. A scale was drawn up and published: total family income would vary with the price of bread and the number of children.[40]

The Speenhamland system (or "the rate in aid of wages") has been a matter of considerable historical controversy. The Hammonds flatly called it "the remedy adopted" for the crisis of 1795, but this view has been more recently challenged as oversimplified. That the allowance system was spreading is undoubted; how far it spread is another matter, if the bread scale is taken as the essential element.[41] There is historical agreement that, disregarding the bread scale, allowances to employed laborers, particularly during periods of distress, did become widespread in the three decades following 1795. But whether this amounted to a new 'system,' a last futile paternalistic effort to save the laborer from the status of a market commodity, is an unanswered question.[42]

The important issues of the extent and significance of allowances like the Speenhamland scale are beyond the scope of this discussion. More relevant is the fact that few, if any, influential contemporaries believed that a satisfactory solution had been found. In 1797, Sir Frederic Eden gave extensive treatment to Speenhamland in *The State of the Poor*,[43] and roundly denounced it in the name of the principles of classical economics. Eden was a devoted disciple of Adam Smith and dismissed the bread scale (as well as other allowances in aid of wages) as unwarranted and unnecessary interference with the functioning of economic laws. He insisted that Speenhamland was an aid to prodigality and idleness and an enemy to those cardinal virtues, exertion, self-help, and frugality. The laborer could live on less than the Berkshire Justices thought: the solution to the sharp rise in the price of bread was the substitution of cheaper foods. This was counteracted by Speenhamland; the laborer would have no inducement to change his food "though the substitute for it were cheap, obvious, and plentiful; and no less nutritious, palatable, and wholesome, than his ordinary food."[44] (This, of course, ignored the beliefs of the laborers themselves.)

Certainly at the end of 1795 ministers and MPs had no perception that a solution to the crisis had been found. On the contrary, panic over the spectre of revolution was an important element in the urgency that many felt towards ameliorating the lot which the great mass of ordinary laborers was enduring. Thus the *Annual Register* remarked that even during the long discussions over Pitt's Two Acts (which effectively stifled the L.C.S.),[45] the House was "not unmindful of the critical state of the country, through the scarcity of corn that had prevailed for some time."[46]

One remedy (if remedy it was) was offered by the would-be Poor Law reformer Samuel Whitbread, M.P., a Foxite Whig. On 9 December, he brought in a bill to empower magistrates (meeting in Quarter Sessions) to regulate wages. Now, wage regulation was hardly a novelty in 1795, for it had been practiced for more than four hundred years. A statute of Edward III spoke of a "great scarcity of servants" who "will not serve without excessive wages" and who would rather "beg in idleness than by labour . . . earn their living." Accordingly, a maximum wage was set, and the wages of skilled workers were limited to those of servants.[47] But, since an unvarying rate took no account of inflation, the measure was altered: a statute of Richard II added the notion that wages should fluctuate with prices and empowered Justices to make necessary changes ("for as much as the price of corn and victuals can not be put in certain").[48] A legal limit for certain categories of laborers continued into the eighteenth century, the law having been made uniform under Elizabeth and extended to further categories of workers under James I.[49]

These restrictions, as one would expect, ran afoul of the incisive pen of Adam Smith. Smith cited with obvious approval Richard Burn's conclusion that wage regulation "seems incapable of minute limitation; for if all persons in the same kind of work were to receive equal wages, there would be no emulation, and no room left for industry or ingenuity." It was true that as a general practice wage regulation had fallen into desuetude, but, Smith continued, particular trades in particular places were still subject to a maximum wage. For example, an Act of 1768 restricted the wage paid by master tailors in and around London. Such acts were blatantly discriminatory against workmen and were dismissed by Smith as inequitable. ("Whenever the legislature attempts to regulate the differences between masters and their workmen, its counsellors are always the masters.")[50] Smith believed that legal intervention in wage rates invariably had the purpose of lowering rather than raising them.[51] He was not quite correct, since the statute of James I did provide penalties for underpayment. However, this provision seems to have been generally ignored, and Smith's view of the earlier legislation was the one generally held in the late eighteenth century. In the debates over Whitbread's bill, both Pitt and Fox, as well as Whitbread himself, thought that the earlier law had provided only for maximum wages.[52]

Whitbread's bill sought to revive wage regulation and reverse its tendency. Justices, meeting at Quarter Sessions, would be empowered to set wage rates for agricultural workers (no other workmen were included) and, as under 5 Elizabeth c.4, to fix working hours. It would be unlawful to employ anyone (with certain exceptions) at a lower rate. Now, a fluctuating, locally-determined minimum wage was a policy that had some currency at the time, for it had been discussed at Suffolk Quarter Sessions and had gained the support of men like the redoubtable Arthur Young and the two able writers, Davies and Howlett. In the Commons, Whitbread's bill enjoyed some popularity, including the (somewhat half-hearted) approval of Fox, who spoke on its behalf.[53]

However, the bill was defeated on its Second Reading on 12 February 1796, having been crushed by a masterly speech by William Pitt. Pitt denied that the economic crisis was grave enough to warrant the interference of government by regulating wages; economic principles (that is the principles of Adam Smith) should be allowed to take their course. If Whitbread's remedy succeeded, "according to the most sanguine expectations, it only established what would have been better effected by principle"; and if it failed, it would be productive of either oppression or profligate idleness. "Is it not better for the House, then, to consider the operation of general principles, and rely upon the effects of their unconfined exercise?" Many of the present difficulties, Pitt believed, lay in abuses of the Poor Law; insufficient discrimination was made between the deserving and the undeserving in executing the law. The proper method of relief lay in providing employment wherever possible; what was required was the amendment of the Poor Law, not wage regulation.[54] Pitt promised to restore the Poor Laws to their "original purity," to remove those "corruptions by which they had been obscured" with a reform bill of his own. He admitted that his ideas were vague—"floating in his mind, though not digested with sufficient accuracy, not arranged with a proper degree of clearness." He attacked the Law of Settlement, which (to promote the free circulation of labor) should "undergo a radical amendment"; and he promised measures to encourage Friendly Societies, the voluntary insurance societies that proliferated among the lower classes, and to extend "schools of industry."[55] This was enough for the House of Commons: MPs were content to leave the matter in what they assumed to be the capable hands of the great Prime Minister.

They were to be rudely awakened from their complacency. The bill was not introduced until 22 December 1796, when it received the briefest of defenses from Pitt.[56] It passed quickly through Committee, where it was amended, and was printed before the end of the year. It was immediately the subject of violent public protest. A flood of pamphlets attacked it, including two from the London parishes of Bloomsbury and Kensington; petitions and individual letters urging its defeat descended on the Prime Minister.[57] Thomas Ruggles, the able author of *The History of the Poor Laws* (1793), and one of Pitt's advisors on Poor Law matters, wrote that "of all the Acts of Parliament I have ever read, I never knew one so difficult to understand, so confused in its order, and so incomplete in its enforcing sanction, not to say contradictory in its clauses."[58] (Ruggles was supposed to have helped Pitt with the bill, but was called in only after its main points had been drafted.) Perhaps one of the most moderate comments came from Sir Frederic Eden, who remarked that the plan would not be "either very alluring to the poor themselves, or very encouraging to those who maintain them."[59] In any case, the criticism, as Pitt admitted several years later, killed the bill, and late in February 1797, it was withdrawn, without so much as having been debated in Parliament.

Very briefly put, the principal features of the bill were as follows. A renovated parochial poor law administration was to be set up, including the offices of Wardens, Guardians, and Visitors. Magistrates, acting as Visitors, had powers of oversight, correcting any harshness of the Wardens (who were vested with day-to-day administrative responsibility). As promised, there was provision for a "School of Industry" in every parish or group of parishes (JPs were given power to unite parishes for the purpose); both children[60] and adults were to be employed at any trade without restriction. Although anyone refusing employment was to be refused relief, outdoor relief was not abolished, for Visitors had the option of relieving the pauper at home; and in certain cases extra allowances were given for larger families.[61]

Also as promised, the Law of Settlement was amended. No pauper could be removed for any relief given under the act; the cost of relieving the unsettled poor was to be reimbursed by the 'home' parish (thus setting the stage for even more litigation). The bill further provided that Settlement could now be acquired by five-years' residence. Another provision furthered Pitt's stated desire to encourage Friendly Societies. Old age and sickness insurance was to be dispensed from a Parochial Fund financed by individual subscription, charitable donation, and from the rates. The bill also gave sanction to the "rate in aid of wages." Those who were unable to earn the wage "usually given" in their parish could contract to work at a lesser rate, the deficiency necessary for subsistence being made up from the rates. Finally, there was the famous "cow money" clause, a clause designed to advance the cause of self-maintenance, that is, to keep the potential pauper off the parish relief rolls. Any poor person who could obtain the use of sufficient land could be given cash to buy a cow "or other animal yielding profit," provided that he was of good character and that further parochial assistance would be unnecessary.[62]

2. Bentham's Attack on Pitt's Bill

Such are the principal features of a bill which, it is sometimes supposed, was killed mainly by Bentham's criticism. He had first become acquainted with its provisions in May 1796. Pitt had drawn up (or had caused to be drawn up) the "Heads of a Bill . . ." in February and circulated it privately. In the beginning of May, the "Heads" reached Bentham's hands via George Rose. Bentham's reaction was immediate. On the same day that he saw Pitt's intentions, he wrote to his half brother Charles Abbot, "Rose has just given me the Heads of the Poor Bill—what stuff!"[63] Perhaps it is surprising that he did not immediately set about writing a critique (without awaiting a more definitive draft) as he had done in 1778 in his *View of the Hard Labour Bill*. However, in 1778 his object was to *improve* the bill; in 1797 it was to *kill* it. 'Improving' Pitt's reforms would be mere tinkering with a system that should be scrapped altogether.

Whatever his reasons, Bentham waited until the bill was printed, and in January and February 1797 wrote his *Observations on the Poor Bill*,[64] which was circulated in manuscript form. It is very difficult to know precisely how influential it was. Edwin Chadwick, who discovered the work among Bentham's papers in 1838 (when it was printed for private circulation), thought that the work "powerfully contributed to the abandonment of the measure in question";[65] and the Hammonds remark that Bentham "is often supposed to have killed the Bill."[66] But the evidence seems to be singularly flimsy. Chadwick based his belief on Bentham's correspondence by "which it appears that he was in communication with some of the influential members of the legislature." His correspondence, however, does not substantiate this claim sufficiently. His letters to George Rose and William Wilberforce during February both (there are only two) concern Panopticon. He was in contact with the Duke of Portland's office, and in mid-January mentioned his intention to make a "thorough description" of the Poor Bill,[67] but no other correspondence on the subject seems to exist.

Other letters do give some small credence to Chadwick's claim. Bentham met George Rose on 12 February on the subject of the poor.[68] Exactly what they discussed is not known, but Pitt's bill must surely have been a topic, if not *the* topic, of conversation. Bentham also sent a copy of the *Observations* to A. P. Buchan, who replied: "Wood's[69] pamphlet is much the best I have seen and comes nearest yours. I have no doubt that such general reprobation will force Pitt to abandon his plan."[70] Nothing else in Bentham's correspondence indicates the influence of his *Observa-*

tions. It can probably be safely assumed that he had some influence in high places, but it is hardly warranted to infer that it was he who killed the bill. Surely Buchan must be nearer to the truth in saying that "such general reprobation" would force Pitt to abandon his bill. Evidence does not appear to exist which would enable us sufficiently to disentangle Bentham's influence from the inevitable effect of widespread opposition and pronounce him the executioner of Pitt's proposal.

Bentham's *Observations* was, for Bentham, quite brief. At the beginning of February time was running short; Pitt's mastery of the House of Commons (as demonstrated by his demolition of Whitbread's Bill) was a force to be reckoned with. If Pitt's plan was *in*, Bentham's was *out*. "I am not only counsel against this Bill," he wrote in mid-January, "but I am counsel for another system. . . ."[71] His brief was summary.

There were but two faults with Pitt's bill: its form and its content.[72] The bill's prolixity and confusing language could not but deeply offend the author of *The Promulgation of the Laws and the Reasons thereof*, a work (first published by Dumont in the *Traités de législation* . . . of 1802) which among other things demanded legal clarity. Before embarking on his indictment, Bentham pretended, with mock self-effacement, to be apprehensive of "doing unintentional injustice" to the bill by misstating its meaning. His interpretations of the bill had to be corrected by "stronger minds."[73] In other words, the bill was shot through with ambiguity.

The form of laws in general and Pitt's bill in particular was not merely a peripheral issue to Bentham. It was not accidental that when he set out his initial thoughts on the proposed legislation early in January, he turned immediately to a discussion of "form"; this was a continuation of his long-standing concern with the conciseness and clarity of law as well as with the method of its promulgation. As seen from his correspondence,[74] Bentham distinguished between the form and matter of law at least as early as the 1780 "Prospectus" for his "Plan of a Penal Code." It was this distinction which led him in the mid-1780's to write two separate "essays," the *Projet Forme* and the *Projet Matière*, whose titles referred respectively to the form and matter of law. (The manuscripts for these essays provided much of the material for the work we know as *The Theory of Legislation*.)

Sensitive to the issues of the form and clarity of law, Bentham complained bitterly in 1797 about the "disorder" and "obscurity" of Pitt's bill and argued that an explanatory pamphlet should have been published.[75] (In fact Pitt had commissioned Thomas Ruggles to write such a pamphlet a year earlier.)[76] For Bentham, the proper form of legal writing was an essential ingredient in controlled social change. "Reform in the legal stile," he wrote, is "the most important of all reforms—because a preliminary *sine qua non* to every other." And, as he had done so often in the past, he lashed out at "Judge and Company" for usurping the role of legislator: courts could interpret ambiguously written statutes almost as they pleased. In every other corner of English law "there is a secret history contradicting and overruling that which is aboveboard." The legislature might write the laws, but "there is a power superior to the legislature . . . : this autocrator is I know not what clerk in the Court of King's Bench."[77] Thus did courts have it in their power to foil attempts at reform.

One of Bentham's criticisms of Pitt's bill included all other Parliamentary bills and acts as well: the sections were unnumbered. Adopted from natural science, the use of quantification was a longstanding implement in Bentham's drive to make the social world knowable. The persons and objects of that world must be weighed and counted, marked out and identified, subjected to the brightness of the public light, the better to be seen by the public eye. Only then could they be controlled and security made possible; and only then might the mad reign of contingency be brought to a close. Given that aim, who can deny that Bentham was correct? In the state within the state that was his "pauper kingdom," the very trees on its grounds would be numbered and counted.[78]

As for Pitt's bill, Bentham argued that the absence of numbered sections made it that much more difficult to become an object of knowledge, and so he numbered them himself. "This privation of the physical possibility of becoming the subject-matter of reference," he wrote, "this prolific cause and certain pledge of uncertainty, disorder, and inconsistency, each in the extreme; this privation of one of the many helps to intellection, the exclusion of which is peculiar to that species of composition in which the importance of the qualities of order, precision, and conciseness, stands at the very highest pitch . . . is not the particular fault of *this* Bill or of any one concerned in it. It is the fault of *everybody*, and thence *nobody*."[79]

Bentham singled out one allegedly ambiguous phrase in the bill for a special and prolonged flogging.[80] He professed to be unable to determine who, precisely, was eligible for the benefits of the act. If that was unclear in the language of the act, then the matter would be settled by the judiciary, and Parliament would have effectively handed over its power to decide who should be relieved. The bill spoke of "the persons entitled to the benefits of this Act," who seemed to be defined as—"the persons entitled to the benefits of this Act."[81] Bentham's caustic remarks, however, were partially carping. It was clear enough in the bill that those entitled to relief were those unable to earn their own subsistence. Nevertheless, he seized on the phrase "All persons wanting relief" as a possible definition of the intended beneficiaries and ridiculed it by choosing to interpret "wanting" as "desiring"; but this was purely gratuitous since "wanting" obviously meant "needing."[82] He was nearer to the mark in suggesting that the complexity and confusion of the bill would guarantee that few if any paupers would understand it, and its purpose would therefore be undermined. "A man must have got the Act by heart to have found out all the benefits of it."[83] More than that, the confusion of the bill might also guarantee the necessity of court action to reap intended benefits. Bentham sarcastically suggested that after months or years of legal haggling, the poor, "such of them as have more money than they know what to do with, may know by a knock at the noble interpreter's great gate, which of them this and that benefit was intended for. . . ."[84]

So much for form. The content of the bill fared little better. Bentham chose several of the bill's provisions for analysis and directed much of his criticism to one general accusation: the "waste" of public money. Pitt's bill would result in an appalling system of public profusion in which "public money is scattered without being weighed or counted."[85] Profusion, he confessed, frightened him, and he could see "no bounds" to profusion under Pitt's system. "Figures of arithmetic, and not of speech," he wrote, "are the figures that govern me."[86] Nevertheless, Bentham was not (on this occasion as on so many others)[87] beyond using highly colored language to evoke the proper reaction in his audience: relief under Pitt's proposals he termed "pensions," and those receiving it were on "pension-lists."[88] Worse yet were pensions in the form of cows.

> The pension *during pleasure* is instantly converted into a pension *for years* or *during life*, and that pension *at the same instant* bought out by a *gross* sum, leaving the demand for a *fresh* pension to recur at any time, to be again bought off, and so *toties quoties*. The spigot was *there* opened, *here* the *bung-hole*.[89]

Bentham foresaw an unnecessary flood of public money as a consequence of the clause which gave extra relief to large families. Families with more than two children (or, in the case of widows, more than one child) were to receive not less than one shilling a week for each extra child until they "can and shall maintain themselves by their labour." Why, Bentham demanded, should an entire shilling be paid, when in some places a child might be kept for less?[90] Obviously the intention of the bill and Bentham's obsession with eliminating every grain of public waste were at loggerheads. This clause sought to ensure a minimum *quality* of subsistence for the child; Bentham was far more concerned with a minimum *cost* of maintenance. And, for the sake of extra money, he believed, parents, forever watchful for a means of cheating, would keep their children idle. This part of the bill was therefore completely inadequate in achieving an essential *desideratum: forcing* the poor to diligent labor.

Again, the "Apprenticeship Clause" was a source of potential waste. Those who attended Pitt's proposed "Schools of Industry" would be found apprenticeships, a fee being paid to the master concerned. Would the fees be well spent? The dark spectre of contingency suddenly loomed. For apprentices of the lowest classes, Bentham could see but "an uncertain chance of improvement, in point of morality" (morality was industriousness, immorality idleness) "bought at a certain expence"; he was uncertain whether "the chance purchased will be worth the price." Perhaps the master would have employment for the money but none for the apprentice.[91]

There were other difficulties with the apprenticeship clause. For one thing, there was the accusation (which Bentham undoubtedly gleaned from *The Wealth of Nations*)[92] that the whole system of apprenticeship was an oppressive monopoly of trade. Still, it was a system that did have two important functions, first as a source of instruction, and more importantly as a *"a security for good behaviour."*[93] And this was a public benefit. In questioning the usefulness of apprenticeship fees for producing good behavior, Bentham was quite literally calling for a cost-benefit analysis. His analysis of another difficulty was more revealing. If pauper children were bought apprenticeships in highly paid occupations, would the number of apprenticeships actually be increased? If it would, the monopolistic character of the trade would be microscopically reduced. But if, as he thought likely, the number remained stable, then the pauper child would receive a benefit which would otherwise accrue to another—another who was more likely to be of a "superior" class. And this Bentham believed to be unfair:

> For no reason can be assigned why the superior class should not in the way of natural increase be as capable of keeping up its numbers as the inferior class; and the offspring of the superior class has better opportunity of an introduction into his own superior class than is likely to fall to the share of a member of the inferior class.[94]

It was unfair that, to give the poor child "a lift," the child of a trades-man received "a fall." Bentham was quick to point out that he was not advocating a caste system, but rather "a system of equal and unexpensive liberty" in which no law set up an artificial barrier to class mobility. Merit on one hand, fortune on the other—this was one of the few instances that Bentham accepted the role of chance in social life—would determine who would rise, who would fall from his station.[95] The expectations of the "superior" classes that they would remain "superior" ought not to be meddled with by law. Of course, he was not thinking of the aristocracy when he spoke here of "superior" classes: they were among the few who did not owe their position to diligent labor. Only later, in 1816 (when he published *Chrestomathia*) did he suggest that they too should be forced to useful action to retain their social influence. But in 1797, in the midst of the French Revolution, Bentham could hardly contemplate such a politi-cally suicidal and heretical policy.

In his speech on the poor law in February 1796, Pitt promised to abolish the law which forbade giving relief where any visible property remained.[96] A clause in his bill fulfilled the promise. Bentham attacked it. No person was to be excluded from relief who held visible property up to £30 in val-ue: Bentham called this the "Relief-Extension, or Opulence-Relief Clause." Now, the use of the term "opulence" was purely propagandistic, for £30 was hardly great wealth in 1797. What he was in fact objecting to was the degree of security which the provision would provide, for one would not have needed to be utterly ruined in order to receive relief. Bentham argued that this was as much as guaranteeing men a minimum status. "We com-miserate *Darius*, we commiserate *Lear*, but it is not in the power of *parishes* to give kingdoms." To guarantee every man a subsistence, he continued, "is *practicable* and *practised*; to guarantee to every man the perpetuity of his station in the scale of opulence would be altogether impracticable, the very *attempt mischievous* and *perserverance ruinous*."[97] Of course, as he knew very well, the clause was certainly not guaranteeing *every* "station in the scale of opulence," only a certain *minimum*. But for Bentham, men must be forced through fear to diligent labor, and the "opulence relief" clause undermined the threat of total ruin, of relegation to the lowest class in society. A system of poor relief necessarily must include deterrence. That was precisely the problem with "home provision"; it was not un-pleasant enough to deter. Men must feel their decline in status and feel it acutely. In this respect Bentham retained much of the common eighteenth-century notion that poverty is the fault of the pauper. He was willing to provide small temporary loans (they formed a part of his own poor plan), but if they could not be obtained and if private charity refused its aid, "the presumption, though not absolutely conclusive, is at any rate not weak, not only that extraordinary merit, but that ordinary good conduct, has been wanting; and that the pangs of falling prosperity are but the just and *useful* punishment of improbity or improvidence."[98] Mend your ways or go to the poorhouse.

To some degree (on rare occasions acutely), Bentham felt the conflict between the claims of common humanity and the ruthless course of sheer impersonal calculation which in the case of poor relief meant the calculation of pounds and pence. In his attack on Pitt's bill, he praised its author for his humanity, and described the "excruciating" scene of a blameless family reduced to penury being commanded to "Come in and give up your all, or stay out and starve."[99]

It is difficult to know how sincere Bentham was in depicting this heart-rending prospect; he may well have been crying crocodile tears. His initial (unpublished) thoughts on the bill included several "Topics of Praise" for the bill which were at best partially bogus and are probably completely so. In a passage headed "Praise A Excuse," he wrote, "Whatever be the fate of the Bill"—that is, when it was thrown onto the garbage dump of history— "the several virtues on the part of the Patrons of it will be written in indelible characters."[100] In other words, Pitt's well-meaning but foolish supporters would have a consolation prize. In his own case, the claims of compassion were admitted into evidence only to be dismissed from court in a single sentence: compassion was laudable, indeed it was "unavoidable," but "compassion is one thing; relief, efficacious and unmischievous relief, a very different thing. . . ."[101]

Bentham seems to have engaged in a kind of all-or-nothing reasoning. Either humanitarian concern would utterly suffuse a relief system (and therefore run the risk of rendering it unpractical), or it must be removed entirely, replaced with a muscular and unbending pragmatism, rule-governed to the last, typically unwilling to allow exceptions in exceptional cases. There was no middle ground. For Bentham sentiment had no standing in a system whose soul was a set of preestablished rules; to allow it a role would open a floodgate of precarious emotion: but human feelings were wayward, turbulent, and irrational—incalculable sources of insecurity and of pain. One recalls Bentham's youthful distrust even of brotherly love.[102]

The "cow money" clause was yet another source of public profusion. Since the poor were always liable to cheat, since the most "natural" and common alliance was between indigence and vice,[103] who could trust them actually to buy a cow with the public capital provided? Any fool knew that many of the poor were drunkards, and so to Bentham the clause might as well be called the "Gin-money" clause: "The capital is to be advanced, not in the shape of the *cow*, but in the shape of *hard money*, with which the object of this extraordinary bounty is left perfectly at liberty to lay in a fund either in *milk* or *gin*, according to his taste."[104] Elsewhere he was still more graphic in denouncing the policy of giving *anything*—either money or goods—to the poor.

> In the hands of Midas every thing turned to gold: in the hand of the drunkard every thing turns to drink. In the laboratory of Midas weight was got for weight: but in the laboratory of the Pawnbroker, 50 percent goes off in *service*.[105]

If the poor had bad habits, so did cows. Some died, others gave little or no milk, others still were stolen, and all of them took up valuable space on already overcrowded (not to mention diminishing) commons. They had another bad feature; they did not demand great diligence in their care. Once again Bentham suggested that poverty was the fault of the poor: they were lazy. Poor relief ought to engrain "the habit of industry"; obviously, he assumed that it was lacking: "A *dairy* of cows *would* do this. Attendance upon a *single* cow is a species of industry, if industry it can be called, which is, if anything that *can* bear that name, the nearest of kin to idleness."[106]

This criticism, like the last, ignored the plain language (in this case) of the bill, language which Bentham himself cited. He argued that drunkards would sell cows to buy liquor; but the bill specified that two poor administrators attest to the good character of the recipients before money would be advanced. Again, he complained that attendance on a single cow fails to ensure real industriousness; but the bill made it quite clear that the purpose of "cow money" was to supplement the incomes of those already employed and who would otherwise be forced to turn to the dole.[107] Unsatisfied with these barbs, Bentham went to special lengths to snare his quarry. The bill spoke of a cow "or other profit yielding animal." "A rattle-snake," he retorted, "is 'profit yielding' to the hand that shows it, and no *common* is surcharged by it."[108]

As always, the wiles of caprice were not far from sight. Bentham spoke of "cow money" as itself a kind of lottery for the poor; the pauper would "take his chance for getting the cow-money."[109] And his remarks on the mortality of cows also suggested that natural contingencies were allowed unnecessary influence: "the resource presented by a *loom* is a *permanent* one"; and better yet it might be made an "unfluctuating" one. "A loom eats nothing; is not apt to be sick; does not sink in value by underfeeding; has no legs to be driven away upon; and is not exposed to sudden death." The banishment of chance and the consolidation of certainty is what Bentham's work is all about. Thus a proper method of poor relief ought to rely not on blind Fortune but on that foundation of civilization, foresight. "The system to be sought for," Bentham argued, "is a system which shall make the supply of means keep pace with that of wants, and that by a pre-established chain of causes and effects, whatever be the rapidity . . . of the progression."[110] As will be seen later on, this demand could only be met by placing the poor relief system (and it was systematic with a vengeance) on a footing radically different from that of the paramount source of social discontinuity, especially in the fortunes of the poor: the market economy. The remedy to the fluctuations of the market was a thoroughly independent preplanned pauper economy, an alternate economy within an economy, existing symbiotically with market society.

There was one more clause of Pitt's bill which found itself under the sharp edge of Bentham's analytic scalpel, the clause that allowed for "deficient" wages of the poor to be increased from the poor rate. Now there was no doubt in Bentham's mind that wages were deficient in many cases, particularly (thanks to the work of David Davies) among agricultural workers. The question hinged on the proper method of raising them. Bentham tried to dispose of the two principal ways of increasing wages which had been proposed since the crisis of 1795, the minimum wage (Whitbread's Bill) and (using the term broadly) the Speenhamland system, a variety of which Pitt's bill had in mind.

As for a minimum wage, Bentham thought that its effect would be ruinous—"you *exclude* from employment many persons who might have otherwise obtained it." If the value of a man's labor did not reach the prescribed minimum, he simply would not be employed, at least not in many circumstances: "An employer *may* give 9s. a week, for example, to a labourer whose labour is worth but 8s. or 7s., but he will not give the 9s. to a labourer whose labour is worth 3s. or 4s."[111] Here Bentham may well have been correct; certainly many twentieth-century economists agree with his conclusion that a minimum wage can have the effect of reducing employment. Of course, this hardly settles the question of minimum wages, since one might well decide that in the long run society is better off if some forms of undesirable work are eliminated or reduced, residual workers being more highly compensated than otherwise. But that is the long run, and here we are dealing with an immediate crisis, a crisis for which a minimum wage would surely have been at best an inadequate palliative and would more probably have done actual harm.

However, Bentham's critique of the "Under-Ability or Supplemental-Wages Clause" (as he called it) is another matter altogether, for a large part of his criticism was predicated on a breathtaking misreading of the clause, a misreading which amounts to an extraordinary mental lapse on his part. What the bill proposed was as follows. Any poor person who was unable to earn the "full rate or wages usually given" in his parish and who would "contract and agree" to work at a lesser rate, "which wages shall not be sufficient for the maintenance and support" of the person and his or her family, would be eligible, if the poor overseers so decided, ("with the approbation of one or more" of the Justices of the district) for his wages to be supplemented from the rates "to make up such deficiency as may be necessary for the support of such poor person, and his or her family, (regard being had to the earnings of such family). . . ." The receiver would not be required to work in the local "school of industry."[112]

Now, we should be clear about what this does and does not say. First of all, anyone working at a sub-subsistence wage would not necessarily have his pay supplemented. The act simply said that "it shall and may be lawful" for overseers to make an addition: they were not *compelled* to do so. Secondly and more important, the amount added from the rates would not necessarily make the total income equal to the "full rate or wages usually given." What the "full rate" was was quite irrelevant: the object, very clearly stated, was to allow the pauper and his family a subsistence income.

Bentham professed not to understand this. He spoke as if the bill sought to force poor authorities to "make up" the deficient wage to the "full rate": "*Full* is a word not only of precision, but of *energy*. The '*full rate*', that and nothing less, is the rate without which the legislator has declared he will not in *future* be satisfied; and whosoever presumes to give less than that full rate *disobeys*."[113] It is astonishing that a man of Bentham's analytic power and legal training could write such nonsense, especially when it is so easily exposed. Several circumstances may have contributed to this *faux pas*—his haste in writing this *pièce d'occasion*, his overbearing self-confidence born of his complete disdain for the bill, and most of all his desire to leave it in hopeless ruins so that his own plan could be considered in its place.

A further explanation for this 'misreading' is perhaps more plausible than any other. It is that Bentham quite deliberately misrepresented the bill. To do so would be strategically apposite: if his readers accepted his version of the clause, then so much the worse for the bill; if they did not, then it must be poorly written indeed if such a legal mind as his misconstrued it so utterly. His introductory note explaining how "sincere" his efforts had been to understand the bill, how he feared doing an "unintentional injustice to the Bill by mis-stating from time to time the intended import of it," and how his interpretive forays into its dense verbiage "must be understood to be submitted all along to correction"[114] strikes one as slightly *de trop*—an ill-contrived effort to conceal from his readers what he knew all along to be true, that the bill didn't say what he said it said. If so, the mystery of Bentham's palpably fallacious misreading vanishes.

3. Bentham on Wages

If the methods of raising wages suggested by Pitt and Whitbread were inappropriate, how should they be increased? Bentham did not address himself to this question in the *Observations*, but he did discuss it in his manuscripts. "To raise the wages of any class of hands," he wrote, "there are but two methods: one is to lessen the number of such hands; the other is to encrease the quantity of employment offered to them."[115] The quantity of employment could be increased by the influx of new capital into any given industry; wages would rise as employers of new capital bid for labor, driving up its price. (Bentham did not consider the case where a Marxian "reserve army of the unemployed" was drawn upon by new employers.) Likewise, with a given amount of capital in a particular industry, a reduction in the labor force would increase wages.[116]

What, then, ought government policy to be in order to alleviate the condition of the most distressed class, as Bentham believed, that of "labourers in husbandry"? One suggestion, put forward by David Davies, was summarily discarded—placing a limit on the size of farms. Bentham argued that such a policy would draw large capital away from agriculture and, in the short run, create more distress. True, in the long run, small capital might be attracted, but a "wound," as Bentham described it, would nevertheless be inflicted: "To all this as to all other political wounds, time would afford a cure. But till the cure were affected, what would the body be the better for the cure?"[117] He might have added that in starvation conditions, in the short run we are all dead. After all, half a century later that is precisely what happened in Ireland.

Bentham did not develop a detailed policy for increasing agricultural wages, but he did outline some semblance of a general strategy. For one thing, the mobility of labor should be increased.[118] His own plan called for an "Employment Gazette," a national periodical, filled with what some call "want ads." For another, the army and navy might decrease the rural work force by taking recruits (and men were *taken*) from the countryside.[119]

Armies, as statesmen have long since found out, are good for the unemployment problem. Daniel Defoe, however indirectly, had advertised that fact decades before Bentham wrote, when he implied that armies siphon off the young and desperate. (In fact they siphon off only a portion of them; other 'occupations' absorb the rest.) In 1704 Defoe argued that there was no great dearth of employment, and therefore no need for semi-public companies (like Bentham's "National Charity Company") to provide it. Lives there a man, he asked, with pride so shattered that he would not "carry a Musquet rather than starve, and wear the Queens cloth, or any Bodies Cloth, rather than go Naked and live in Rags and want. . . ?" Unemployment feeds the ranks: if a man could otherwise earn a pound a week, he must be "Drunk or Mad when he Lists for a Soldier, to be knock'd o' th' Head for 3s, 6d. *per* Week. . . ." But, Defoe continued, if the indigent

> had not Bread to eat, nor knew not how to earn it, thousands of young lusty Fellows would fly to the Pike and Musquet, and choose to dye like Men in the Face of the Enemy, rather than lye at home, starve, perish in Poverty and Distress.[120]

For Bentham as for Defoe, the poor were the potential stuff of armies. One function of his poor plan was the training of the poor for military service; and, indeed, his language in speaking of the potential inmates of his workhouse suggests that he thought of them in military terms: he called them "classes mustered."[121]

Another proper government policy was the attraction of capital into agriculture. Bentham did not spell out what policies should be positively pursued, but he did indicate that government should at least "abstain from attracting capital from it by encouragements given to other branches: by encouragements given, and given at a vast expence, to the remaining modes of employing capital to a productive purpose—to manufactures, to the carrying trade, and above all, to colonization."[122]

But the most important immediate means available for increasing wages was the adoption of his own plan, for, with compulsory admission of the indigent into poorhouses, the labor force would be immediately reduced. This was one way that Bentham's "National Charity Company" worked hand in hand with the market economy. Depleting the supply of labor in this manner was especially effective, he believed, in the case of children. What else were they but tomorrow's competitors in the race for employment? He consciously intended his poor plan to serve the same purpose that higher education inadvertently serves today: the young are kept off the labor market. "The keeping them up under the Company's management on the Company's farms in a situation where they can do no work but for the account of the Company, and for their own maintenance, creates a proportionate *vacuum* in that supply [of labour] : that vacuum must therefore be, and therefore will be supplied from the stock [of] the self-maintaining Poor." Considering both young and old, "the first effect of the deduction thus made from the natural supply of hands will be to raise the wages of labour. . . ."[123]

Besides the increment in the "wages of labour," the formation of the National Charity Company would lead (or so Bentham hoped) to another highly attractive consequence: the diminution of the rates. This was only just, for as we saw earlier, he believed it wrong to deprive a man of the fruits of his labor (fruits determined by his place in the market) without overriding necessity (for example, that otherwise another man *might* starve).[124] And, if the rates were cut, "so much money is left free in the hands of the rateable inhabitants to be spent in the gratification of their own desires of all kinds, instead of being taken from them to be spent in the satisfaction of the necessary desires of other people: viz.: the indigent poor. . . ."[125] Moreover, savings on the rates would create employment. The money might be either spent or saved, but "spent it cannot be, nor hoarded[126] (if put out to interest) without giving employment to a proportionable stock of fresh hands; nor consequently without creating a proportionable demand for a fresh supply of such fresh hands."[127]

This brings us to the question of Bentham's attitude toward wages: ought they to be as high as possible or was it more desirable that they be kept low? Eighteenth-century opinion varied from the argument that high wages encouraged consumption and therefore production, to the injunction that, since the poor would be idle unless spurred by necessity, all wages ought to approach subsistence. "When Men shew such an extraordinary proclivity to Idleness and Pleasure," wrote Mandeville in *The Fable of the Bees*, "what reason have we to think that they would ever work, unless they were oblig'd to it by immediate Necessity?" Men who could earn their subsistence in four days would not work on the fifth; and thousands of laborers "tho' they can hardly subsist, put themselves to fifty Inconveniences, disoblige their Masters, pinch their Bellies, and run into Debt, to make Holidays." It would be easier, he thought, to live without money than without the poor, "for who would do the work?"[128] Later in the century, Arthur Young expressed a similar sentiment: "Every one but an idiot knows that the lower classes must be kept poor, or they will never be industrious!"[129]

Bentham's attitude was ambiguous if not confused. Certainly it is far too simple to say, as one historian has done, that "Bentham thought high wages desirable."[130] Now, Bentham does say precisely that. "The wages of the poor," he wrote, "are the patrimony, the only property of the poor. The number of the Poor being given, the rate of wages therefore can not be too high." The wealth or poverty of nations should be judged according to the condition of the majority of their inhabitants, and these were the poor, that is, "those who depend on their labour for their subsistence."[131] Acts of government which had the effect of reducing wages (for example, by causing an influx of workers into a particular industry) had the effect of a tax: "a partial and oppressive" tax, altogether useless.[132] Moreover, subsistence being given, "a given mass of wealth produces more happiness the greater the number of individuals among whom it is divided, so long as the parcels in which it is divided are not too minute to produce a sensation in any individual."[133]

However, having said this, Bentham offered material qualifications which becloud his position considerably. Wages could not be too high "except in as far as the superfluity happens to be expended in the purchase of the means of drunkenness or other means of procuring present satisfaction at the expense of lasting welfare."[134] Government measures which reduced high wages might be pernicious from one point of view, but they could nevertheless "in relation to the *superior interests* of good morals be useful, and that to such a degree as to be eligible upon the whole."[135] Two conditions in particular made high wages morally pernicious: where the rate fluctuated and where the receiver of high wages lacked a "suitable" education. In both cases, the key issue was drunkenness. If a man's wages fluctuated, when they were high so would he be also: he was dizzy with success (intoxicated, to be exact), celebrating his new-found prosperity. On the other hand, when they were low, he was confined to a rank which prevented the personal cultivation which could prepare him for the benign use of the leisure time which a high rate would afford. "The course of his life is thus divided into two tracks, each of which has drunkenness at the end of it: the one for joy, the other for consolation."[136]

Bentham's concern at the connection between "excessive" wages (as he put it in the *Observations on the Poor Bill*)[137] and excessive drinking had its origins long before his writings on the Poor Law, for he had commented on the dangers of affluence at least as early as 1782. In the *Essay on Indirect Legislation*, he had said that those whose labor bears a high price can afford to make "considerable sacrifices to sloth and drunkenness." And it was not only the lower orders who were culpable. Laborers might fall victim to that demon, drink, but "so may the class of proprietors when arrived at a certain degree of opulence spare their whole time to the same purpose."[138]

However, in his writings of the '90's, Bentham makes no mention of the middle ranks of society. His world seems to have become sharply bifurcated, divided into the educated and opulent on one hand, and the ignorant and poor on the other. Only education could make society safe for affluence. For Bentham the absence of the necessity to work creates a dangerous vacuum of time and a vacuity of mind: but the devil need not find work for the idle fingers of the cultivated man, for he could occupy himself with innocent amusement "pure from future pain and inconvenience"[139] (like cirrhosis of the liver). On the other hand, it was widely assumed, and Bentham agreed, that given half a chance, the British worker would drink himself silly. Without the means of providing himself with "innocent amusements," one yields to deleterious temptations, among which drunkenness is "at the same time the most generally alluring and the most uniformly pernicious":

> With a full purse and an empty head nothing [is] more difficult than for a man to avoid falling into the abyss of drunkenness. Hence the connection so intimate, so well known, and so much and so justly lamented, between drunkenness and high wages, that is excessive opulence in the lower lines of life, opulence raised above the level of education.[140]

Obviously, all of this was in direct contradiction with the initial assertion that the rate of wages "can not be too high": how could the two positions be reconciled? The answer lay in the recreation of the laborer in the image of Utilitarian Man, which is to say, in the adoption of Bentham's own Poor Plan. For a fundamental purpose of it was the re-education, the "utilitarianization" (to coin a barbarous but very Benthamite term) of the indigent. (Better yet, to etch the virtues of the work ethic on the *tabula rasa* of youth.) Withdrawn from the corrupting influences of working-class life into the sanctuary of Bentham's monastic Panopticon, the indigent could be inured with the "united virtues of the two [*sic*] branches of the united kingdom: English efficiency on the one hand, [and] Scottish . . . frugality and temperance" on the other. Bentham argued that, were his plan adopted, the public would gain "a superior sort of population in exchange for an inferior" one. It was a population ingrained with a perpetual postponement of present pleasure for the sake of greater future satisfaction, for it was "enured to . . . producing much and consuming little." It would be, finally, a "population which by its habits of temperance and frugality adding to the quantity of stock laid up, diminishing the quantity dissipated, goes on laying up . . . fresh funds of population for periods yet to come."[141] Here was more than a hint that Bentham's proposed reform would meet the objections of Malthusians; his more inclusive rebuttal will be examined later on.

3

Panopticon "in Both its Branches"

For the whole of a working life that stretched for more than sixty years, Jeremy Bentham is known to have written nearly every day. He is also known to have urged a myriad of social and legal reforms—composed, revised, and forged again in the course of his daily labors. But it is less well known how deeply involved he was in the practical campaign for their enactment. These two activities, intellectual creation and political struggle, proceeded simultaneously for long periods of his life, though more than once the bright road traveled so hopefully in theoretical exposition became an obscure labyrinth leading only to bitter frustration when theory was translated into action.

During the period 1796–97 Bentham was involved in several of these ventures and at the same time connived at introducing himself into British relations with France. While he drew up his poor plan he was still deeply entangled, as he would be for years to come, in his epic struggle with the British bureaucracy to save the project that for two decades was the consuming passion of his life: Panopticon prison. It was to become his trail of tears.

Panopticon prison was a particular application of a general principle of social discipline in an institutional setting. Discipline was achieved in establishments governed by the Panopticon principle by means of circular architecture at whose center was a tower, or inspector's "lodge," surrounded by cells at the circumference. Inspectors could peer into all the cells by the simple expedient of turning round and round; but, watching through slits, they could not be observed by those occupying the cells. Since they could never be sure they were unseen, and since punishment for the infraction of rules was swift and automatic, those watched, Bentham believed, would be effectively deterred from illicit behavior.

Bentham had adopted the architectural principle from his brother Samuel in 1786 while the two were living in Russia, where Samuel was employed by Prince Potemkin. Samuel had first utilized the idea in the building of a workshop, but Jeremy seized upon it as capable of a more universal application, provided it with a distinctive name (from the Greek "all seeing"), and gave it its meaning by spinning out a complex of system of management designed to fuse architecture and ideology. While the initial focus of Bentham's writing on Panopticon and the bulk of his efforts for its practical adoption lay in its incarnation as penitentiary, the Panopticon idea was intended from its inception as a paradigm for a whole series of further institutions, for schools and factories, for hospitals and lazarettos, and, not incidentally, for pauper workhouses. In fact, of these further uses, Panopticon poorhouse was decidedly uppermost in his mind. That is why he later referred to Panopticon in "both its branches," meaning prison and poorhouse. The opening of the Preface to his tracts on Panopticon published in 1791 suggests that he had already formed the expectation that the application of the Panopticon principle to poorhouses was capable of the general reform of poor relief: "Morals reformed—health preserved—industry invigorated—instruction diffused—public burdens lightened—Economy seated, as it were, upon a rock—the gordian knot of the Poor Laws not cut, but untied—all by a simple idea in Architecture!"[1]

Panopticon poorhouse borrowed important features from Bentham's original prospectus for an "Inspection House" prison, several of which should be mentioned here. Both prison and workhouses were to be run on the contract system, and from both he expected to reap substantial profit —he was to be sole contractor for the former and an investor and paid official in the latter. The system of pauper workhouses would also mesh with Panopticon prison, for Bentham had proposed a "subsidiary" institution to receive and employ—at lower wages than the market rate—discharged prisoners who were otherwise unemployed. A poorhouse suited this need perfectly and was accordingly substituted for the subsidiary institution. "Discharged" prisoners unable to find immediate employment would journey from one variety of Panopticon to another, though perhaps the difference between prison and workhouse might be lost on them.[2]

More important was a modification of Bentham's prison regime for inclusion in the scheme of pauper workhouse management, for it appears to have been the origin of the "less eligibility principle," the principle that was incorporated into the Poor Law Amendment Act of 1834 and into the administration of poor relief throughout the remainder of the nineteenth century and abandoned in practice only in the twentieth. In his *Panopticon Postscript* of 1791 Bentham proposed a "rule of severity" according to which the "ordinary condition" of a convict "ought not to be made more eligible" than that of "the poorest class of subjects in a state of innocence and liberty." The "less eligibility principle" seems to be an extension of the "rule of severity"; from conditions which were to have been not "more eligible" than those of the worst-off outsiders, it was but a short step to propose those conditions to be *worse*—"less eligible."[3]

But as we have said it was Panopticon prison that was the object of Bentham's efforts in the practical world during the years that he theorized about the Poor Law. Working with phenomenal energy and persistence, he continued his years'-old barrage of messages to the government, urging, pleading, even demanding action; and he lost no opportunity to seek out new allies or to enlist the services of his friends in aid of this great "engine" of moral reform. It was, in retrospect, as if he had marched into quicksand; the more furiously he thrashed away at the procrastination or stubbornness of those involved, the more futile his efforts seemed to become.

One difficulty lay in finding a site for the new prison. A succession of possibilities in or near London was considered but for one reason or another ultimately had to be discarded. Two were near Woolwich (Hanging Wood and Plumstead Heath), and another was at Barnes Common near Battersea Rise. The latter tract was owned by Lord Spencer, who proved singularly unaccommodating: he wouldn't sell. That is, without legal coercion, he wouldn't sell to Bentham. Bentham tried his best. In April 1796 he heard that Spencer objected to the sale because land adjoining the proposed prison would be rendered unrentable. Bentham offered to take over the leases. Next, Spencer declined to part with a portion of the land Bentham wanted and offered only a marshy area to the east of Battersea Bridge. But, as Jeremy wrote to Samuel, there was, in fact, "no way of fixing him to anything"; and Spencer was personally abusive in the bargain. Finally, after more pleas from Bentham, Spencer let it be known that he was unwilling to sell Bentham anything.[4]

A similar fate awaited a fourth site, Tothill Fields. Frustrated by Spencer as well as by an owner of one tract at Woolwich,[5] by September 1796

Bentham had fastened his hopes on this last possibility. To secure it, he needed the approval of the Bishop of Rochester together with the Dean and Chapter of Westminster, and it was abundantly clear, as Bentham discovered, that they would not easily give way to the practical progress of Moral Reformation. In fact, they were far more interested in cricket than Panopticon, for they allocated part of Tothill Fields as a cricket pitch for the use of the scholars at Bentham's old *bête noire* Westminster School, and they were loathe to relinquish a sufficient part of the land for the sake of a prison.[6]

Bentham knew he had a struggle on his hands, and he set out with every resource at his command to win the day. In November he wrote to Samuel that he was "intriguing like Lucifer."[7] It was not an overstatement. The list of allies with whom he plotted strategy and who acted on his behalf is long and impressive. Some, like Henry Dundas at the War office, Charles Long and George Rose at the Treasury, and Evan Nepean at the Admiralty, were within the government itself. Others, such as William Wilberforce (who more or less acted as Bentham's chief liaison officer with the Prime Minister) and W. Morton Pitt were influential back-benchers. Others still, like Samuel Romilly, were outside of Parliament altogether.

Such men had long been associated with Bentham's efforts to secure government approval for Panopticon. Others were new recruits. At the beginning of December 1796, at the bequest of George Rose, Bentham visited James Wyatt, surveyor to the Board of Public Works, in search of his support. His mission was successful, for the following day he could write to his brother and his wife, "Animals, Wyat, [sic] the formidable Wyat is our own."[8] At the same time, Bentham was in the process of acquiring another valuable friend and associate, Patrick Colquhoun, the London police magistrate and author of the famous *Treatise on the Police of the Metropolis* (1795). Colquhoun, who had tried unsuccessfully to meet Bentham more than a year earlier, had a lively interest in Panopticon, and wrote to him early in December suggesting that they meet to discuss the subject. Bentham responded with an invitation to an "unceremonious dinner in a Batchelor's house" preceded by a visit to Tothill Fields.[9] The meeting was an evident success. The two reformers struck up a friendship, and Colquhoun set about using his personal prestige and his political connections to help Panopticon clear what proved to be insurmountable barriers.

By the end of 1796 Bentham was faced with two intractable problems. One concerned the necessity for a new Act of Parliament so that part of Tothill Fields could be appropriated as a prison site. The act, which Bentham had cajoled through Parliament two years earlier (34 George 3.c.84), authorized the Treasury to buy individually-owned land, but Tothill Fields was not individually owned, falling as it did under the category of "Wastes and Commons." A second act, as Bentham told George Rose, would "explain and amend" 34 George 3.c.84 "by extending the powers from lands in severality to Wastes and Commons."[10] Early in December, Bentham was optimistic enough to think that such an act would be passed before the adjournment of Parliament the following February.[11]

The addition of Patrick Colquhoun's name to the rolls of his supporters could only have strengthened Bentham's sanguine expectations. Colquhoun put Bentham in touch with William Baldwin, a confidant of the Home Secretary (the Duke of Portland), who was entrusted with the "Chief Superintendances of Convicts Pardons etc.," and who, Colquhoun assured Bentham, would be happy "not only to accelerate but to assist in promoting such legislative Regulations as may yet be necessary. . . ."[12] Baldwin did, indeed, give what aid he could. He was every bit as enthusiastic about Panopticon as Colquhoun and took the matter up with the Duke of Portland. The Duke, in turn, became sufficiently interested in the project to accompany Baldwin to Queen's Square Place to see the models of Panopticon which Bentham kept on display for prominent visitors.[13]

Still, however promising such maneuvering was, it was not producing the enactment of Bentham's bill. William Wilberforce had assured Bentham that Pitt was agreeable to Tothill Fields[14] and the bill had been drafted, but by the end of February it was nowhere in sight. The bill seemed stuck in the unmovable bowels of bureaucracy, in this case in the office of the Attorney General. Bentham was quite understandably beginning to show signs of pique. "The next time you happen on Mr Attorney General, in the House or elsewhere," he wrote to Wilberforce, "be pleased to take a spike, the longer and sharper the better, and applying it to the seat of honour, tell him it is by way of *memento*, that the Penitentiary Contract Bill, has, for I know not what length of time, been sticking in his hands. . . ." "A corking pin," he added, "was applied yesterday by Mr Abbot."[15]

Bentham and his friends kept up the pressure on the Attorney General to produce the bill. At the end of March, he had not only not considered the draft, but even denied to Bentham that he so much as possessed it—it was the Solicitor General (Mitford) who was the source of delay. But this was false, for Mitford himself found the document among the Attorney General's papers.[16] Such were the tribulations Bentham had to endure. At the end of March he fired off an almost imperious letter to the Attorney

General, saying that if he had to write again about the matter "it would be impossible to me to treat it in any other than the most serious light."[17] He had to wait nearly a month before hearing from Samuel Romilly the bittersweet fruit of his labors: the Attorney General had at last considered the bill. He had, in fact, considered it so carefully that he had found numerous objections. It was "the most unlike an Act of Parliament he ever saw"; and, Bentham learned from another friend, he insinuated that "the Plan of it was romantic." Moreover, the Solicitor General didn't approve of it either.[18] In the end, the draft-bill had to be scrapped altogether, and a new one substituted. So, by the close of 1797, Bentham was no closer to securing the Tothill Fields site than he had been the year before.

The other interminable problem over Panopticon lay in signing a contract for the prison with the government. Bentham expected that that would be completed soon after the Penitentiary Bill received the royal assent. That was the summer of 1794. The following May it was still not signed, although on 15 May Jeremy told Samuel that he hoped it would be signed the next day.[19] It was not. More than another year passed, and it was still unsigned in July 1796 when Charles Long of the Treasury sent it for engrossing.[20]

Bentham pleaded for an end to the delays, to no avail. In February 1796, he wrote a rather devious letter to Pitt in order to humor the great man into action. Pitt, it will be recalled, had promised "Schools of Industry" as part of his Poor Law Reform, outlined in his speech against Whitbread's bill. Now, Bentham, as we know, despised Pitt's "Industry-Houses." But after all, if worse came to worst, and Pitt's plan *was* adopted, why not persuade him to take up the Panopticon principle? Bentham's real concern in writing, however, was the delay of the contract; the rest was merely a ploy. He told Pitt that six months had elapsed since "everything was understood to be settled but legal form"; and that had been long since settled. "A single word only is wanting—how much longer will it be withholden? or is it never meant to be pronounced?"[21]

The following year Bentham hit on a further scheme to influence the Prime Minister. Although there is no evidence that he actually carried the plan out, he intended, in any case, to send Pitt a copy of his paper "On the Loss by want of Dispatch in Public Works—and on the means of avoiding it"—but he would conceal the author's true identity. He drafted a letter to Pitt pretending that he had merely found an official paper which he was transmitting in the hope that, should its contents meet with Pitt's approval, it would restore "that place in your remembrance which for above these four years the want of which I have been experiencing so severely."[22] Bentham may well have decided that such strong language would be counterproductive; no copy of this letter survives in Pitt's papers.

If the procrastination of government offices was one source of Bentham's agony, there was another practical circumstance of at least equal importance without which no contract could be signed: the question of land. In 1798, a committee of the Commons investigated Bentham's project and gave a highly favorable report (drawing heavily on the testimony of Patrick Colquhoun). Why had no contract been executed? They were informed that although the "Lords Commissioners of His Majesty's Treasury" were willing enough, "the Contract intended to have been entered into has been delayed, because an essential part of such Contract was to be the giving possession of the Land upon which the Penitentiary House was to be erected. . . ."[23] As we have seen, in 1796–97, none of those concerned would willingly part with the necessary ground, and Parliament, especially Pitt, did not seem much inclined to override their opposition.

Such is the barest outline of Bentham's Panopticon negotiations of 1796–97. Without following in detail the dozens of meetings in Government offices, the scores of letters on the subject, and the intricate plotting with Samuel—such an exercise would require a volume in itself—perhaps enough has been said for one to see the enormous energy which Bentham expended on Panopticon during this period. Nor was dealing with the government his only concern: there was also the supervision of elaborate preparations for building the prison. Plans had to be drawn up and materials gathered and tested. In addition, he was intimately involved in various inventions (pumps, valves, and the like), some of which were probably intended for use in Panopticon, that Samuel was busily working on.[24] And all of this required so many thousands of pounds in expenditure—testing cost £1,500 for iron alone—that Bentham was kept in debt and constantly fretting over money.

Bentham was not only worried about his own personal affairs: there were also those of his country, in particular the war with France. His correspondence is lightly sprinkled with comments on all the latest developments, but in September 1796 there was a flurry of activity when he hit upon an extraordinary idea. He and Wilberforce would negotiate peace with France. It was a grandiose pipe dream which took Bentham by storm. He had read an extract from a speech of the Genoan envoy to France, to which the French in their reply expressed satisfaction at the envoy's selection as a "Citizen who has acquired the reputation of being a friend to humanity and to the liberty of the French Republicans." Didn't that description precisely fit himself and Wilberforce? At any rate, wasn't that what the French thought of them? After all, both had been made honorary citizens. An excited Bentham wrote to Wilberforce proposing the mission, describing in detail his own "French Connection." The second French Assembly had printed a sketch of the Panopticon plan, and Talleyrand, in the name of the then Department of Paris, had asked him to set up "Panopticons of different sorts *there.*" Extracts of his *Judicial Establishments* had appeared in France; and he was a friend of Brissot as well as of the Duc de la Rochefoucault.[25]

Bentham admitted that if the French ever read his *Anarchical Fallacies* he would at once become *persona non grata*; but then the essay was not in Paris but lying unpublished on his shelves at Queen's Square Place. And there was no need for him to divulge his views, for "no man is bound to get his own head broke to no use." It was also true, he admitted, that if Wilberforce's "great *Friend*" (i.e., Pitt) saw the suggestion (as he would have to) he might smile, "but there are times, in which for a *chance*, how *faint* soever, of being of use, a man may be excused for *exposing* himself to a *smile.*"[26]

Wilberforce, for his part, had misgivings about the project, and so Bentham turned to his friend, the sometime diplomat Lord St. Helens. With grace and urbanity, St. Helens argued that Bentham's status as honorary citizen, so far from enhancing, actually detracted from his fitness for such a mission; but if it were offered, he (St. Helens) would be inclined to accept.[27] This was enough of a straw for Bentham to grasp at. He nearly begged to accompany St. Helens, should he be appointed to a post at Paris. Bentham would disguise himself as a sober, honest but very ignorant John Doe, and gather intelligence on the sly: he would be a secret agent of sorts.[28]

Nothing came of this affair (or rather non-affair), and we hear no more of it after mid-September. Once again, Bentham seemed willing to suspend the multitude of his activities (even Panopticon!), to run "from a good project to a better." The 'Paris Mission' episode underlines as well Bentham's deep desire to leave his mark on the world, to play an active part in practical politics. But one suspects a deeper impulse, namely, that he had messianic ambitions. Certainly he dreamed of the day when he, as lawgiver, would rule (even if he were dead) like Moses and Solon before him. But more than that, he seems to have wanted not only to rule men but to save them. He would bring peace: "We must sooner or later, have done fighting Pandemonium," he wrote in his long proposal to Wilberforce, "and upon that occasion may find it advisable to look out for some sort of a *Candle* to hold to the *Princes of the Devils*," in order to "smooth the approach of Peace."[29] Was it perhaps a "Prince of Peace" who held out a candle amidst the darkness presided over by the "Princes of the Devils"? There is something more than a little suspicious (if that is the word) in Bentham's description of himself to Wilberforce as "your obscure and humble *would be follower*, who has the *prophet-like* property of being still more unknown in his *own* country than in the *next.* . . . "[30] The scarcely veiled pretense of humility was a mask which hid far-flung ambition, a burning will to power. One notes Bentham's reference to his "prophet-like Property." He seemed to be seeking fulfillment not through the love of individual human beings—this was denied to him—but through the love and gratitude of all mankind, the universal acclaim accorded to the Great Man.

The theory of Bentham's messianic self-image helps to account for an otherwise enigmatic aspect of his character, that is, the *particular manner* in which he interjects biblical allusions into his writings. Instances of this span decades of his working life—there are several, for example, in the *Essay on Indirect Legislation*,[31] as well as during the short period we are discussing. In September 1797, Bentham wrote to the Society of Agriculture proposing the consideration of his poor plan. "Now that your Treasury is opened," he wrote,

> . . . I should be sorry, mortified I confess, not to be admitted to throw in my mite: and the only mite I have to bestow has the name of project stamped upon it. My heart is with you—my purse should be, if I had one. The cause of my having none—a cause which I am not ashamed of— . . . is not unknown to some of you nor has it been altogether un-merited. Silver and Gold then I have none: but what I have—a project that I give unto you . . . I do not mean silver and gold alone: but deeds done—deeds done for the relief of human wretchedness, for the reforma-tion of human wickedness . . . such as you have had the satisfaction of proclaiming to the world—with the implied exhortation—Go and do thou likewise.[32]

Leaving aside the question of 'good works' ("Deeds done"), there are four obvious biblical allusions in this passage, all from the New Testament. Two are from the parables which Luke reports were spoken by Jesus of Nazareth himself; a third, from the *Acts*, refers to Peter and John. A fourth is drawn from Jesus' Sermon on the Mount as reported by Matthew. In the first, Bentham identifies himself with the poor widow whose gift of a pittance was greater than all the wealth of the mighty, for it was her all.[33] The gift of the humble, obscure, not widowered, to be sure, but unmarried Bentham was greater than that of any other. If this is humility, there is no such thing as pride. Silver and gold he had none, for he had virtuously spent it on Panopticon; and, like Panopticon prison, Panopticon poorhouse was a vehicle of moral regeneration, a great engine of resurrection from wretchedness and wickedness. Here he likened himself to Peter ("on this rock I will build my church"?) who commanded the lame beggar to become a whole man: "Silver and gold I have none; but such as I have I give thee: In the name of Jesus of Nazareth rise up and walk."[34] By implication, Bentham's ideas were carriers of messianic healing power. Next, he saw himself as following Jesus' injunction in the parable of the good Samaritan to "Go, and do thou likewise." And finally, alluding to Jesus' "For where your treasure is, there will your heart be also," he says he ought to have contributed his treasure to the Society of Agriculture, since his heart belonged to their common cause, the Progress of Mankind.[35]

Somehow, this good samaritan worked out his 'salvation' for the poor while immersed in the welter of activities just described. Ordinary men could hardly have found time or summoned energy enough after such intense negotiations and maneuvers to attempt simultaneously a formidable project of research and intellectual creation; but then Bentham was no ordinary man. As mentioned before, he had intended the Panopticon idea to be applied to poorhouses as well as other institutions from its inception, and it was purely fortuitous that the "inspection principle" was being applied in the 1790's only to prisons rather than to other institutions as well. In fact, one of the earliest glimmers of interest in Panopticon was for the building not of prisons but of poorhouses. In 1790, Jeremy wrote to Samuel that "Poor Inspection House is taken up by the Government of Ireland; they have ordered it to be printed, and given me what money I have a mind for" to waste it upon architects.[36] And two years later we find Bentham plotting strategy with a friend to convince the Overseers at Welshpool, who were in the process of planning a poorhouse, to adopt Panopticon architecture.[37]

But if building individual Panopticons for the poor had long been in Bentham's mind, the complete remodeling of the English Poor Law was quite a different (not to mention more complex and demanding) task. It is possible that, in the face of the growing crisis, Wilberforce or Morton Pitt was instrumental in turning Bentham's attention to the problem of poverty. In 1796 he wrote to them that the "commands of one of you" occasion "this little work." (The "little work" is unidentified.) Not very modestly he described his work as "searching the uttermost depths of the subject"; and with his accustomed humility he hoped that his plan would earn him the accolades of future generations: ". . . if it be good for anything, it must live: and to visit posterity in such company, is a pleasing thought."[38]

By February 1796 he was fully immersed in the new project. ". . . *Poor Provision* goes on swimmingly," he told Samuel, "—rich in *sens*, and bidding fairer for engaging attention than ever *Safeguard* to which it cannot be refused the preference."[39] In accordance with his usual procedure, Bentham undertook a prodigious program of research side by side with his writing. Items in the press dealing with such relevant topics as the mortality rates in foundling hospitals, prisons, and workhouses were carefully noted.[40] A plethora of books was read; how many we do not know, but most probably it is no exaggeration to say that they ran to scores. There were the works of Ruggles, Burn, Colquhoun, and Davies, as well as those of lesser lights such as John MacFarlan.[41] Bentham scoured the massive volumes of Eden's *State of the Poor*, taking copious notes; and he gathered what information he could on the state of existing poorhouses, such as the famous House of Industry at Shrewsbury.[42] The workhouse at Bradford responded to inquiries with a good deal of helpful information. Bookkeeping, diet, rules of the house, expense of maintenance, and the value of the work done were all described in detail. He learned, for example, that on Wednesdays the inmates breakfasted on milk, oatmeal, and bread; lunched on cheese, bread, and beer, and supped on oatmeal and bread (meals on other days were given as well); that all of the paupers in and out of the house were compelled to wear badges; that theft within the house was punished by a year of menial labor; and that, needless to say, the value of the paupers' work did not cover expenses.[43]

The search for data, one of Bentham's great passions, was extended to include the earnings of agricultural workers. He was evidently less than satisfied with the incomplete returns reported by David Davies. Great tables were drawn, listing all the counties of England and Wales, comparing the earnings of men and women during summer, winter and harvest.[44] Other information which he acquired was of a different nature. To learn more of the kinds of work that might be required in a system of poorhouses (it should be borne in mind that Bentham's workhouses were to be collectively self-sufficient), he wrote to more than three hundred tradesmen from every corner of England and Scotland (but concentrated, not surprisingly, in the industrializing Midlands) inquiring about the nature of their work, which ranged from pin making to diaper weaving.[45] Unfortunately, the replies of those who responded have not survived.

Bentham also canvassed his old patron Lord Lansdowne for both information and ideas on the poor. Lansdowne, who was staying at his town house at Berkeley Square, sent what books he could—"Everything else I have regarding the poor is at Bowood, where Mr. Townsend has had the [librarian] ransacking them, but I believe there is nothing that applies"— and added his own cursory notions of poor law reform. He did not think that anything effective could be done "till the municipal government of the country is revised and invigorated"; but he offered several suggestions in the interim. For one thing, Friendly Societies should be "enforc'd" to include both manufacturing and agricultural poor.[46] (Whether Lansdowne was actually proposing some variety of compulsory social insurance is unclear.)

Now, Friendly Societies almost universally met in Public Houses; in fact, part of their *raison d'être* was the social occasion which such meetings provided. How Lansdowne expected them to function is obscure, for his next suggestion was that pubs be abolished, except those necessary for travellers: "Public houses and Poaching you may depend on it are the root of every evil." Such talk was revolutionary in more than one sense. Scarcely less so was the former Prime Minister's final point. The poor rate should be limited "without delay, and finally abolish'd, unless the administration of it can be totally chang'd."[47] Lansdowne did not elaborate on what he meant by a totally changed administration of the poor laws. Perhaps his desire to limit the poor rate and eventually eliminate it was influenced by the man who was ransacking his library in Wiltshire, Joseph Townsend, whose very similar views we will examine later.[48] In any case, such brief and obviously hastily composed ideas had no discernible effect on Bentham, and there is no evidence that he pursued the matter with his former mentor.

At the same time that Bentham sought information, he was composing his reform plans; and, with an equal intensity, he was searching out political support for their adoption. This was, as we have said, proceeding simultaneously with Panopticon prison, and the two lines of influence tended to overlap. But this was not always true. In May 1796, he sent a batch of his papers to Thomas Powys, M.P. for Northhampton, whose good opinion Bentham evidently thought would be a valuable recommendation. Powys found the papers "interesting" and asked to see more.[49] For Bentham even such a small success was gratifying:[50] and no wonder, given the state of Panopticon negotiations.

By the middle of the same year, Bentham was cultivating a figure whose ideas on the proper treatment of the poor were attracting public attention: Benjamin Thompson, Count Rumford. Rumford was an American (a Massachusetts schoolmaster) who remained loyal during the Revolution and emigrated to England. In 1784 he was knighted, and in the same year he entered the service of the Elector of Bavaria. For some years he concentrated his attention on the reform of the army—improving the pay, providing cleaner barracks, setting up free schools for soldiers and their children. He tried, he tells us, "to make soldiers citizens and citizens soldiers."[51]

Faced with the question of what to do with an army during peacetime, Rumford hit upon an intriguing, if unorthodox answer: they could be used as a domestic police force. The towns of Bavaria, he said, were swarming with beggars who were worse than a public nuisance. They were "monsters."[52] Accordingly, in Munich on New Year's Day 1790 (New Year's Day was the traditional almsgiving day in Bavaria), having informed the magistrates of his intentions, Rumford had the first beggar he met arrested and handed over to the army; and within the hour (or so he claimed) the entire town was purged of these heinous creatures.[53]

Thereafter, the poor of Munich were treated according to Rumford's own peculiar ideas. The route to the reformation of the poor, that is to industriousness, discipline, and docility, lay not through harsh treatment but mild. Instead of trying to make the poor happy by making them virtuous, the order should be reversed. "My hopes," he wrote, "that a habit of enjoying the real comforts and conveniences which were provided for them would in time soften their hearts, open their eyes, render them grateful and docile, were not disappointed."[54] A workhouse was opened where paupers made uniforms for the army. If Rumford is to be believed, its regime was a model of cleanliness (a virtue on which he placed great emphasis), orderliness and benevolent discipline, although the claim that its handsomely painted walls lent an air of "elegance" seems rather farfetched. Nevertheless, there is no reason to doubt that there was some effort made to make the pauper *"really comfortable."*[55] For one thing, unlike English practice, no one lived in the Munich workhouse: Rumford believed that compulsory living-in reduced paupers to the level of prisoners. The poor were lodged instead near the house and were disciplined for late arrival. As one would expect, the keynote of the house was assiduous labor. Rumford looked especially to the young to create the habit of industry. Children too young to work were seated around a hall where older children performed their tasks. Restless with inactivity, they cried to join in the fun. "How sweet these tears were to me," he remarked, "can easily be imagined."[56]

For Rumford, the greatest difficulty in instilling industrious habits was the frequent dullness of work: how could the poor's labors be made interesting? Wages were an insufficient tool; the desire to emulate, the love of "glory" (by whatever name it went) was far better. Praise, distinctions, and rewards were the order of the day. For Rumford, the will to excel was among the "secret springs of action of the human heart." "The machine is intrinsically the same in all situations. The great secret is, *first to put it in tune*, before an attempt is made to play upon it."[57] Like other eighteenth-century writers such as Beccaria and Bentham, Rumford believed that rewards and punishments are "the only means by which mankind can be controlled and directed,"[58] but, at least in the treatment of the poor, unlike Bentham and Joseph Townsend (among many others), Rumford clearly opted for the use of reward. However, his ideas were not systematically pursued. If the policy of eschewing the threat of punishment was humane, Rumford's attitudes toward the poor folk of Munich not only betray the usual eighteenth-century ambience of patronizing paternalism, but in many places fairly reek of sentimentality as well. (Neither Bentham nor Townsend could be accused of *that*.) On one visit to the workhouse, as Rumford tells the story, the poor recognized him as their benefactor, "and with tears dropping fast from their cheeks, continued their works in the most expressive silence." Asked what was the matter, they were supposed to have said "nichts" with affectionate regard "so exquisitely touching as frequently to draw tears from the most insensible of the bystanders."[59]

Rumford's recommendations for the general administration of poor relief were rudimentary and tended to be little more than the universal adoption of the Munich plan. An unpaid council for poor relief should be established in every city; a respectable citizen chosen as inspector; the poor set to work in a Rumford-style workhouse, their goods sent to some "good market"; and a voluntary poor subscription opened. All of this, he believed, would lead to the end of poor rates.[60] But none of this proved very impressive to English ears. We have already seen that by the 1790's there was widespread disillusionment with the workhouse as a means of making the poor pay for their own maintenance. Rumford's scheme was no panacea for that problem; the Munich house could never have survived on its own resources, depending as it did on both donations and government money in the form of special taxes and tolls.[61]

More attractive to the English public was Rumford's penchant for applying technology to the everyday practice of poor relief, and it was in this direction that his influence was felt. He is best known for his experiments on heat and light, for which he earned himself a minor place in the history of science. Like Bentham, he set out to use science in the service of social reform; and occasionally he suggested that society should be understood in terms analogous to scientific principles such as the laws of mechanics. Just as "no mechanical power can be made to act," he wrote, unless "a force be applied to it sufficient to overcome the resistance not only of its *vis inertiae*, but also of friction, so no moral agent can be brought to act to any given end without sufficient motives. . . ."[62]

Rumford applied the experimental technique to food for the poor, in particular to its preparation. He hoped that his plans for feeding and employing the poor would bring forward "into general use, new Inventions and Improvements, particularly as relate to the management of *Heat* and the saving of *Fuel*."[63] The institution of the public soup kitchen (financed by subscription) was the perfect vehicle for the economical feeding of paupers. Soup was one of Rumford's great passions: he concocted special recipes and wrote glowingly on the pleasures of eating it. He succeeded in popularizing soup for the hungry in the mind of many an English philanthropist, and today it is still administered in nightly doses to the dossers of London.

Rumford was embarked on one of his innovating projects when Bentham contacted him in July 1796. The Count was building, or rather rebuilding—his instructions had been madly misunderstood—a kitchen for the Foundling Hospital of London, the asylum for abandoned children that had been established by a retired sea captain, Captain Thomas Coram, in the 1740's.[64] Anxious to impress Rumford with his ideas, Bentham sent his "Essays on the Poor Laws" and asked for an opinion. For the moment, Rumford was too pressed for time to read the essays carefully, but he assured Bentham that "if you do justice to my opinion of your merit as an author you will be persuaded that I am really very glad to see the subject in your hands."[65]

Bentham, who had been in contact with Rumford at least as early as December 1795,[66] unquestionably saw little merit in Rumford's comprehensive plans for poor relief. (Neither did William Wilberforce, though Lord

Lansdowne was more enthusiastic.)[67] One reason was that Rumford's ideas were a far cry from the single, self-enclosed, centrally administered network of poorhouses on which Bentham lay such heavy emphasis. On the other hand, Rumford's policy of a general roundup of beggars must have set Bentham's heart aglow. We have already seen him propose precisely that in 1782, and we will find him setting a similar idea afoot in 1797. And Rumford's proclivity, however commonplace, to the strict enforcement of discipline among the poor was another subject close to Bentham's heart. But what united the two men most was their mutual desire to apply technological innovation to social problems. (In this respect, what separated them was Bentham's application of technology to *moral* problems, as opposed to economic ones. The 'efficiency' of Panopticon and the efficiency of better kitchen arrangements are obviously very different.) Rumford's concern with providing the poor with a cheap diet which was also nourishing—such was the order of priority—was mirrored in Bentham's comments on food for paupers in *Pauper Management Improved*;[68] and in their different ways both men were equally insistent on using the experimental method to draw up a menu for the destitute.[69] Finally, there was one other possible avenue of Rumford's influence on Bentham. In *Pauper Management Improved*, Bentham listed fifteen "Pauper Comforts," together with a special section on comforts for apprentices.[70] These were to be the sweet fruits plucked by the indigent from the benevolence of the "National Charity Company." One cannot be entirely certain, but this sounds very much as if Rumford's pleas that the poor be well treated had reached Bentham's ears. On the other hand, Bentham needed no Rumford to remind him how imperative it was to convince his readers that the filthy and chaotic conditions that often suffused the eighteenth-century workhouse would not obtain in those he proposed to build.

Rumford was one of a vast array of influential contemporaries whom Bentham sought out for both support and information. Another was Patrick Colquhoun, who, as we have seen, approached Bentham early in December 1796 full of warm feelings toward Panopticon. By the end of the month Bentham took advantage of this good will and was pressing his plans for the poor upon his new ally. Batches of manuscripts were sent from Queen's Square Place to Charles Square, where Colquhoun greeted them enthusiastically[71] and proposed a mutual exchange of ideas. The two men became collaborators of a sort—the lines of influence were a one-sided affair, Colquhoun borrowing from Bentham—and when Bentham took the initial steps to open a subscription for a National Charity Company, Colquhoun lent his name to the project.[72] And even as Colquhoun was lobbying for Panopticon prison, he was using his good offices to bring Bentham's Poor Law plans to the attention of the Duke of Portland.[73]

Similarly, Bentham struck up a lively association with Sir Frederic Eden, whose volumes on the Poor Law he so admired. More bundles of manuscripts, together with scarce books and documents, traveled through the streets of Westminster to Eden's rooms in Lincoln's Inn Fields, where they found a very favorable reception.[74] Eden's acquaintance was potentially of great value, for through his many contacts in the country he was well placed to render (or at least to attempt to render) considerable aid in an intelligence mission which Bentham considered essential to the success of the proposed Company. This was nothing less than a detailed census of the paupers of England and Wales receiving public assistance—a project that reflected Bentham's longstanding interest in sociological statistics of every variety.

To take such a census, Bentham drew up an elaborate "Pauper Population Table" listing more than twenty categories of paupers, broken down according to age and sex. These were first circulated in handwritten copies and later, after being published in the *Annuals of Agriculture* at the end of 1797, in printed form. The information was crucial: how many poorhouses had to be built? The number of paupers had to be known for that to be determined. And how many could work? What sort of work would they be capable of? Were there enough able-bodied "hands" so that the system of houses could be collectively self-maintaining, or would it be overloaded with the very old, the very young, and the disabled? In other words, could it be shown that Bentham's plan would work? "The stock of information here in question," Bentham wrote, "constitutes what will be found to be an indispensable groundwork to every well-digested plan of provision that can be framed in relation to the poor." No general plan could "rationally be attempted" without something like an estimate of the *"mouths* to be fed, as well as the pauper *hands* to work with."[75] Frederic Eden had attempted a pauper census in thirty-one parishes, but of course this was far too incomplete to be relied upon as representative. As Bentham pointed out, what was needed was a general census; population estimates such as those of Richard Price were notoriously undependable.[76]

Bentham mobilized his army of acquaintances to secure the vital data. Besides Eden, he called on such men as George Rose, Samuel Romilly, and Dr. Samuel Parr to aid in the quest; and he tried to enlist the services of

Caroline Fox (who conveniently lived in the country at Bowood) to arouse the interest of Lords Lansdowne, Holland, Warwick and Ossory: each was to extract the pertinent information from the authorities within his sphere of influence.[77]

The extent and intensity of the campaign can be gleaned from the long list of those who received the "Pauper Population Table," once printed copies were available from the *Annals of Agriculture*. Among the more than one hundred names, there were prominent MPs, Lords, Ladies, clerics, reformers, and periodicals—even Mrs. John Lind, widow of Bentham's friend of the 1770's. The Lord Mayor of London was sent a copy, as was Sir John Sinclair, founder of the Board of Agriculture.[78] But it was all to no avail. The Poor Overseers, ever zealously guarding their little kingdoms, jealous of any intrusion, suspicious of 'foreign' eyes, could not be induced to deliver up their innermost secrets. Bentham's own experience was typical. A manager of the poor in a large London parish had consented to a general request for information: "I sent him a pair of the Tables, and . . . he returned them with an excuse."[79]

While this search for information and influence was proceeding, no one was more willing to be of service to Bentham than the influential editor of the *Annals of Agriculture*, Arthur Young. Young had long been a collector of agricultural statistics and other intelligence, and, when Bentham peppered him with inquiries, he responded with alacrity.[80] At the end of the summer of 1797, Bentham, chafing under the delays of Panopticon prison and anxious to make his weight felt in public affairs, applied to Young for space in the *Annals*. Young was quick to see the originality of Bentham's thought on poor reform and went so far as to give him precedence over other manuscripts vying for publication.[81] The result was the successive appearance of Bentham's "Table of Cases Calling for Relief," "Pauper Population Table," and his (characteristically unfinished) "Outline of a Work entitled Pauper Management Improved." Once again a grandiose scheme had been launched. Before examining the nature of that scheme, however, in the following chapter we will discuss Bentham's defense against critics of the very existence of a Poor Law, that is, of the Welfare State itself.

4

In Defense of the Welfare State

1. Christian Virtue and Social Cohesion

Eighteenth-century critics of the English Poor Laws often worried about their effects on social stability; in particular, it was argued that the Poor Laws' incorporation of a legal right to relief made the poor less dependent on their superiors, thereby undermining social subordination. Moreover, with public relief so widespread, private charity was left an inferior role to play, and the incentives and opportunities to exercise the virtue and duty of Christian charity were unduly limited. Certainly this position was nothing like a consensus—witness the many writers who argued for the "independence" of the poor through voluntary relief societies funded by the contributions of the poor themselves.[1]

Still, the belief in the importance of private benevolence was prevalent enough that Bentham felt compelled both to reassure his audience that benevolence could still be practiced under his plan and to attack those who placed undue value on private benevolence. To see what he had in mind, it is worth examining in some detail the arguments of his 'opposition,' believers in 'traditional' society, an ordered hierarchy knit together to a significant extent by the bonds of Christian charity on the one hand and gratitude on the other. We will turn, then, to the thoughts of two such 'opponents,' first those of a little-known Scotsman, and then to those of a better-known Englishman, the Reverend Joseph Townsend.

Among Bentham's papers there is a long letter on the subject of the poor laws in England written by a Glasgow clergyman, the Reverend Dr. William Porteus, to Bentham's friend, Patrick Colquhoun.[2] Porteus was a perspicacious and obviously sincere man who had spent much of his life administering private charities and who was well acquainted with the literature on the English Poor Law; when he wrote to Colquhoun he had just spent a fortnight poring over the three ponderous volumes of Eden's *The State of the Poor.* He unquestionably disliked the compulsory poor rate in England, but he realized that he could add little to the debate simply by suggesting abolition, and he instead oriented his arguments to the English context rather than to Scotland (where there was no poor rate).

Writing in 1797, Porteus, like so many of his contemporaries, was undoubtedly worried by the influence of Thomas Paine, whose *The Rights of Man,* of which over 200,000 copies had been sold from 1791 to 1793,[3] was largely responsible for the dissemination of 'pernicious' French ideas in Britain. To Porteus, "subversive" men, like those of the London Corresponding Society, seemed to be everywhere: "the present state of society," he wrote, "is in a very high degree alarming, [and] our hopes are not founded on its progress, but on its retreat. . . ."[4] It was necessary therefore that in relieving the poor, social connections not be weakened nor the influence of religion lessened.

Porteus admitted that every man "of whatever character had a Just title to be supported in a healthy state" when he could not obtain subsistence from his own labor or from "the justice, gratitude or favour of his relations." But this public relief was to be absolutely minimal: Parliament had no right to assess ratepayers for more than this minimum; and if cheaper methods of keeping body and soul together were discovered, rates should be reduced accordingly. (He was probably thinking of the cheap soups invented by Count Rumford.) Porteus reasoned that if government must "in a particular state of society interfere in behalf of the poor, such interference ought never to invade the territory of Benevolence, but confine itself entirely to the narrow field of Justice and necessity." The distinction, he added, was of "radical importance."[5] Parliament should somehow make a precise estimate of what a bare subsistence cost and limit the poor rates accordingly.[6] At this point Porteus got himself unwittingly into a difficulty. He admitted that the gifts of the benevolent might be "uncertain, irregular and insufficient," but since the necessities of life were legally provided, "the danger cannot be great." But what if inflation pushed the cost of minimal subsistence over the Parliamentary limit? Porteus' answer was not reassuring: ". . . for though the sum assessed may be too low of providing even the necessaries of life, the deficiency can be easily supplied out of the pocket of beneficence"—that is, from a fund that might be "uncertain, irregular and insufficient."[7]

As opposed to Bentham, Porteus was a staunch advocate of outdoor relief, and it was here that his concern for the cohesion of society became evident. It was mere "theory" that recommended sending the aged and the wholly disabled to hospitals or poorhouses; experience had confirmed the tragic consequences of this policy. "Their connections with society are dissolved"; and natural affections were uprooted: "They enter into a new world," he wrote, "in which they have no interest and no friend;—A prison inhabited by disease and sloth and vice—The sense of shame and of honour are speedily lost."[8] The pauper was deprived of the "child who lived with him or even the neighbour who visited him. . . ." Instead, relatives should be assisted with his maintenance, or a situation resembling his usual one should be found.

Similar arguments were given in the case of the orphan—placing an infant in an orphanage leaves him "estranged from his natural connections."[9] Relatives should be found to rear him, or if worse came to worst, he could be farmed out. Again, it was the preservation of social connections which made rent subsidies desirable—"This preserves an attachment to home, to domestic relations and objects. . . ."[10]

Above all, Porteus was anxious to give the freest reign to the virtue of benevolence. With public relief scanty, "men would recover the habits of Benevolence, which are at present discouraged by the Laws." A precarious existence on the one hand, the possibility of aid from one's betters—if one behaved himself—on the other, cemented a characteristic of traditional relationships that Porteus badly wanted to preserve: subordination. "The poor would be less tempted to sloth, they would depend more on their character—The link which connects master and servants together would be rivetted. . . ."[11] The security of the poor might be lessened, but this was a good thing, for they would be "more contented and thankful, much more industrious, Oeconomical and virtuous."[12] The operational word here was "thankful"; it was *gratitude* that provided the crucial link between Christian charity and the ordered subordination of the poor, kept deliberately insecure. Gratitude was the glue, so to speak, of social cohesion. Porteus made it quite clear why he considered benevolence so fundamental. Political men, he insisted, "ought to consider its influence on the lower ranks who are dependent on their superiors—*How are these two classes of men con-*

nected together?" The answer was simple: "acts of favour on the one hand, and gratitude on the other, by kind attentions and gratefull returns on the other."[13] Acts of justice—conforming to the law—would not suffice to create gratitude: justice is one's due, benevolence is not. The poor laws created that most hateful of objects, a monopoly[14]—a monopoly on relief that dried up gratitude:

> Gratitude is the best sweetner of the human temper, it is the parent of contentment and the foe of democracy. But if the law continues to provide not only the necessarys—but the conveniences and comforts of life, it will expell both beneficence and gratitude and . . . one of the strongest bonds of society will be broken.[15]

Porteus added that benevolence was not the exclusive property of the rich, but existed "with a simple glory" among the poor to an even greater degree; but the instances he gave ("the friendly visit, the cup of cold water in time of need") were conspicuously lacking in expense; and as such were an afterthought to his argument, having little to do with the vexed question of the poor laws.

Similar arguments (though far less subtly put) were made by Bentham's friend, the Reverend Joseph Townsend, in his well-known tract, *A Dissertation on the Poor Laws,*[16] a work best known for arguments prefiguring the thesis of Thomas Malthus. Townsend, writing twelve years before the publication of *An Essay on the principle of Population,*[17] urged that since population tends to outstrip food supply, some check on population is necessary. "Prudent, careful, and industrious citizens" refrain from marrying when they are too poor; but the English poor laws encourage the slothful to reproduce.[18] Public housing, with few exceptions, was an obnoxious intrusion into the natural order since it encouraged the unproductive to marry and reproduce.[19] The limitation of marriage together with emigration were "natural" remedies for overpopulation; if these were rejected, the "unnatural" remedy would have to be employed: ". . . it can remain only for the poor to expose their children the moment they are born," which was a "horrid practice."[20]

With a population greater than one can feed—and Townsend made quite clear that he thought this was true in England[21]—some additional check was "absolutely needful," the sexual appetite being so strong. And that check could only consist of one thing—fear of hunger.[22] This was not to be hunger directly felt by the pauper but as feared for his immediate offspring. (Townsend roundly attacked such deterrents to sloth as the work-house.)[23] Fear of hunger would force men to persevering industriousness and an uncompromising frugality. The one thing needful was to impel the poor to these ends, to put *"pressure"* on them. "Unless the degree of pressure be increased," Townsend wrote, "the labouring poor will never acquire habits of diligent application, and a severe frugality."[24] The means of turning up the heat was turning down to a trickle (to mix a metaphor) the gushing flood of legally enforced public assistance. The poor should depend on the rich for relief, relief which must be "limited and precarious."[25] Townsend advocated reducing the poor rate by one tenth every year for nine years ("better yet, eliminate it entirely"), and putting its administration entirely in the hands of Poor Overseers, Ministers, and Churchwardens without the interference of Justices of the Peace.[26]

Townsend's proposals had other purposes than the reduction of the poor rate and the limitation of population. Principal among them was social subordination. "Hunger," he remarked, "will tame the fiercest animals, it will teach decency and civility, obedience and subjection, to the most brutish, the most obstinate, and the most perverse."[27] Indeed, at times Townsend seemed to value the subordination that his plan would produce more than the limitation of population: a good system of poor relief must "in the first place, encourage industry, oeconomy and subordination; and, in the second place, regulate population by the demand for labour."[28] In any case, under Townsend's plan, "the subordination of the poor would be more effectually secured. . . ."[29]

What then, of Christian charity? Townsend was, after all, a clergyman and professed to be a Christian. The gospels gave a positive injunction to charity ("for God loveth a cheerful giver") and should "never have been forgot." Christians were given the highest encouragements to give and were "under the strongest obligations to be liberal in their donations"; still, "strongest obligations" or no, they were left "at liberty to give or not to give, proceeding upon this maxim, that it should be lawful for a man to do what he will with his own." There was emphatically no obligation for *indiscriminate* giving; the frugal, not the profligate, should be given the primary attention of charity; others might share the leftovers, if any.[30] Townsend seemed very close to saying that some would—and should—be left to starve; his entire argument seemed to point to that conclusion.

What would be the effect of this increase in benevolence brought forth by the near elimination of the poor rate? Townsend's answer was similar to that of Porteus. Benevolence in the rich would induce "love, reverence, and gratitude in the poor." Gratitude was once again seen as the glue of social cohesion. "When the poor are obligated to cultivate the friendship of the rich, the rich will never want the inclination to relieve the poor." The present system was a disgrace; "Nothing in nature can be more disgusting than a parish pay-table" with its "snuff, gin, rags, vermin, insolence, and abusive language. . . ."[31] By contrast, Townsend waxed eloquent (in a rather nauseating way) in describing the idyllic scene of the benevolent ministering unto the needy. Nothing can be more beautiful, he wrote,

> than the mild complacency of benevolence, hastening to the humble cottage to relieve the wants of industry and virtue, to feed the hungry, to cloath the naked, and to sooth the sorrows of the widow with her tender orphans; nothing can be more pleasing, unless it be their sparkling eyes, their bursting tears, and their uplifted hands, the artless expression of unfeigned gratitude for unexpected favours.[32]

Townsend was correct to speak of "unexpected favours"; it is difficult to form secure expectations of sheer charity. Indeed, it was the essence of his plan to maintain the insecurity of the poor, forcing them not only to toil unremittingly and consume sparingly but also to "cultivate the friendship of the rich." The deferential society would rest on safe foundations.

Such, then, are the kinds of arguments that Bentham was obliged to answer. His replies took various forms. In the first place, he insisted that the poor were a collective, community responsibility. A community's burdens should be borne equally by its members—equally, that is, in proportion to the ability to pay. Now, it was mentioned before that it is surprising that Bentham considered rates levied on the rental value of habitable dwellings and their land to be equitable, as opposed to an income or a wealth tax. Neither of these seems to have occurred to him. However, in 1796 he no longer considered the rates as the most equitable tax that could be devised, as he had in the '80's, for now he believed that a tax on the consumption of "superfluities" would be a more equable tax. Still, he thought that the rates distributed the burden in a tolerable fashion.

What, then, would be the effect of providing for poor relief exclusively by private charity? Bentham argued cogently that it would amount to a tax on the humane. With the present system, "the hard hearted as well as the humane are pressed into the service of humanity." Provision by private means alone "would leave the hard hearted untouched, whatever were their opulence: it would bear exclusively on the humane, and that with a degree of severity in exact proportion to their humanity."[33]

Moreover, the "tax" might be even more unequal, because it might be the poor themselves, Bentham thought, who would feel compelled to pay more. It was they who were closer to the condition of indigence; they were closer in physical proximity and closer in social condition: the poor would feel the *pain of sympathy* more acutely and pay accordingly.[34]

Of equal importance was Bentham's attack on private benevolence as the plaything of contingency. In *Pauper Management Improved* he argued that the funds of organized private charities were too often open to misuse and mismanagement: "What is every man's business being no man's business, funds bestowed for this purpose are universally and notoriously exposed to depredation." Private trustees, being accountable solely to the Court of Chancery, could be sued only at great expense (quite possibly greater than the amount of alleged misuse), and then only for "the *chance* of obtaining . . . satisfaction."[35]

Townsend had claimed that relief would come almost automatically to the deserving indigent—an assertion for which he offered no solid evidence whatever. For Bentham it was intolerable to give so free a reign to chance as a system of private charity inevitably would; and the whims of benevolence might bestow too much as well as too little: "The union of the two extremes of excess and defect is inseparable from the state of things which commits the relief of the indigent to the chance medly of private charity."[36] And after all, what was the guarantee that relief would be forthcoming in any case? Here Bentham made use of his old analysis of the determinates of any action: knowledge, inclination, and power. In rural areas, there might usually be knowledge of distress, but not necessarily inclination or power.[37] As for the cities, Bentham made the telling point that their cohesiveness could hardly be relied upon; the poor were far too anonymous. Men might be desperate, but would anyone necessarily know of it? Hardly, "for vicinity creates no acquaintance," especially between the wealthy and the poor. Again, it was a question of "what is everybody's business is nobody's":

> Each uncertain in what degree others will think fit to share with him in the burthen, grudges to give under that uncertainty, what, were he sure of a proportionable contribution on the part of the others, he would be satisfied to give.[38]

Far removed from the cozy country village which Townsend had in mind and placed in an urban setting inevitably less cohesive, the arguments of men like Townsend hardly mattered; but, then, men like Townsend hardly seemed to care.

Against this anarchy of contingency, this potential hell of anonymity or brazen will, the situation of the pauper in a "House of Industry" of Bentham's design could hardly form a more perfect contrast. In *Pauper Management Improved*, he sang to the virtues of perfect control. "Every circumstance," he wrote, "by which the condition of an individual can be influenced, being remarked and inventoried, nothing . . . [is] left to chance, caprice, or unguided discretion, everything being surveyed and set down in dimension, number, weight, and measure. . . ."[39]

Bentham had another salvo to fire off at the extollers of voluntary charity: "voluntary" charity was not, in fact, voluntary. To call it that is a confusion of terms, for it is really a form of extortion practiced by those who prey on what Bentham called the "pain of sympathy." "It is extorted by painful sensations, not drawn forth by pleasurable ones. There is a pleasure attending the relieving one's self from these sensations—true—and so is there in relieving one's self from a tooth-ack: but this does not make it better for a man to catch a tooth-ack than to be free from it." It is one thing to give a child money for candy, quite another to give bread to a starving man. The first act is voluntary; the second "is voluntary but in name: it is only to relieve myself from pain that I give it. . . ." No pain, no gift.[40] Most often, Bentham argued, men will not go out of their way to inflict the pain of sympathy on themselves; consequently it is absolutely necessary for starving men, say, to beg in the most public manner: ". . . and the beggar who by any means whatever can contrive to produce most pain will fare the best." The successful beggar therefore is the best actor, an actor who, by his very success, might operate as a lure for those who otherwise had no need to beg.[41]

As for the 'Christian argument,' the notion that it is wrong to minimize the opportunities for acts of benevolence, Bentham was scornful indeed. This was a misplaced idea of virtue: "instead of employing a remedy to keep out or drive out the disease" of poverty, the 'benevolence maximizer', as we might call him, "is for introducing the disease to find business for the remedy." One might as well allow or even foster gin-drinking, sedition, war, plague and famine, or any source of misery, "for the better promotion of sobriety, patriotism, courage, medicine and benevolence."[42] In a fit of pique perhaps, Bentham went even further in his tirade against private benevolence. If the "business" of benevolence could be done without the "trouble" of benevolence, "benevolence might go and join a visit to Astraea and the earth be ne'er the worse for it."[43] Bitterly sarcastic, he continued: "Shut up the Temple of public charity to promote benevolence!—"Shut up the Law Courts then, to promote Justice!"[44]

Finally, there was the matter of gratitude. First of all, the calls for an effusion of gratitude from the poor were themselves tainted. In his *Protest Against Law Taxes* of 1793, Bentham pointed out that benevolence is not necessarily all that it seems. "We think of the poor in the way of charity, for to deal out charity gratifies not only benevolence, but pride."[45] A similar point was made several years later: "The poor ought not to be taxed with ingratitude. . . . An accusation of ingratitude is a confession of selfishness."[46]

Bentham's main objection, however, was that gratitude simply cannot be depended upon as a secure source of social cohesion—it was for him too much in the realm of contingency, particularly during the turbulence of the French Revolution. The poor should not be trusted; no secure expectations could be founded on a class whose capricious emotions made their future actions uncalcuable: "nothing but the worst, especially in a case like the present, ought in prudence to be expected. For benefits conferred nothing of gratitude ought ever to be looked for: for hardship imposed . . . resentment and violence ought to be regarded as certain."[47] He went on to attack the poor as more than merely untrustworthy. "As objects of tenderness and beneficence," he wrote, "they ought to be regarded as children: but as instruments ever ripe for mischief they ought to be guarded against as enemies."[48]

However violently opposed to the "Christian argument," Bentham knew he had to go some way in calming the fears of those who wished to practice charitable virtues. Those who thought as William Porteus did saw the poor laws, ideally, as a backstop to private relief: Bentham reversed this priority, giving charity the role of adding certain amenities to the minimal existence provided by public law. In *Pauper Management Improved* he urged that charity furnish the superfluities, the "extra comforts" for the deserving inmates of his poorhouses.[49] Special boxes, some for general use, some for specific applications, would be placed in each house. The "National Charity Company" would act as trustee, publish accounts, and guarantee that the funds would be used in their entirety (no corrupt trustees skimming off the cream) in accordance with the givers' intentions. So far from char-

itable inclination being diminished under his plan, he argued that it would
be readily elicited in the form of pity. Pity, he said, is strongest when excited by *specific* impressions—"It is the observation of some particular
want . . . that gives birth to that *pain of sympathy*," which can only obtain
relief "by the idea of the cessation of the suffering thus witnessed or imagined."[50] Since painful impressions would obviously be experienced by visitors to this "utopia," charity (he claimed) would be preserved *better* than
at present.

There are several implications to these proposals. Through the distribution of such donations, the poorhouse administration would acquire an additional sanction in controlling its wards. Recipients among three categories
—"special merit, or past prosperity, or particularly afflictive infirmity"—
would be chosen by the Company, not the donor. Bentham vigorously
defended the creation of such a hierarchy of privileged paupers who com-
peted for the extra comforts supplied by private charity by highlighting
the homogeneous equality of existing workhouses: "Everything lies pros-
trate upon the same dead and dreary level: the virtuous and the vicious, the
habitual beggar and the man of fallen fortunes, the healthy and the agoniz-
ing—all are confounded together, in the poor-house as in the grave."[51]

There was a more subtle point. The "poor boxes," for the reasons Bentham gave, would be located in the house itself rather than in another
place, say a church. To a great extent (just how much will be shown later
on), Bentham intended the "House of Industry" to usurp the place of the
church. After all, there is the obvious point that the entire plan put the
parish very largely out of the charity business (and at the same time made
it literally *into* a business). Here we simply note a minor harbinger, but
a harbinger nevertheless, of the surreptitious but conscious plotting of the
decline of the church and the rise of a more Utilitarian institution. In all
but name the parish church poor-box would move to the local branch of
the National Charity Company.

2. Poverty, Population and the Movement
to Abolish the Poor Law

What is poverty? The question is complex, and the answer is by no means
obvious. In the first place, poverty may be considered either as an absolute
or as a relative condition. If it is absolute, in what sense can one justify
calling 'poor' those who, by the standards of a previous age, would be

considered wealthy, indeed even fabulously wealthy? Had the 'poor' of eighteenth-century England the economic wherewithal of many whom we consider impoverished in twentieth-century America or western Europe, they would have rejoiced at the extraordinary generosity of their maker. And secondly, if most men receive twenty times my income, am I necessarily poor? It is not obvious that I live poorly, that I do not live well, however much better my neighbor lives. (On the other hand, it is also not obvious what it means to 'live well.')[52]

Bentham avoided these difficulties by distinguishing between poverty and indigence, vastly expanding the latter category. In 1786 he embraced the biblical definition of poverty, a definition which had by then gained a measure of acceptance. All those are poor who must live as Adam and Eve were obliged to live after their expulsion from the Garden of Eden: "Taken in the gross to live by the sweat of his brow has always been man's sentence, and is become man's nature."[53] To labor from necessity is to be poor. Bentham formally drew up the distinction between poverty and indigence in his "Essays relative to the subject of the Poor Laws" of 1796. "Poverty is the state of every one who, in order to obtain *subsistence*, is forced to have recourse to *labour*." Indigence, on the other hand, is the condition of one who is altogether destitute of property (or of property with sufficient liquidity) and consequently lacks the means for the "immediate satisfaction of the particular want by which he happens to be pressed"; and at the same time is either unable to labor "or unable, even *for* labour, to procure the supply of which he happens thus to be in want." Indigence is an evil but poverty is not, for poverty is the "natural, the primitive, the general, and the *unchangeable*, lot of man."[54] It is impossible to make all men rich, that is to unchain them from the yoke of the necessity to labor, for in such an event the means of subsistence would soon be exhausted, and labor is the sole source of those means.[55]

It is clear from Bentham's language that he regarded the acquisition of the necessities of life not as a communal activity, but first and foremost as an activity of particular individuals. The emphasis which Adam Smith placed on the importance of the division of labor—a point later taken up by Marx and Durkheim, among others—seems to have passed Bentham by entirely. "The *natural* and *only natural* source of the subsistence of every man (who has it not in the shape of property in store)," he wrote, "is obviously his *own* labour, at least in as far as it is adequate to the purpose."[56] It is also natural that men *individually* receive the produce of their labor; it is not only natural, but it is *just* (Bentham seems to suggest that it is just *because* it is natural); and finally, to clinch the argument, it is more than natural justice, it is critically important in a practical way: "But if the fruits of his labour were not secured to him, who is there that would labour? And even were it possible would it be just that the fruits of labour should be the reward of idleness?"[57]

"He who does not work shall not eat." This Pauline moral revelation was a guiding beacon through everything Bentham wrote on the relief of poverty. Even in the garb of his secularized Protestantism, it is shot-through with the psychology of sin. Idleness was an evil on its face, a *malum in se*; and we will see over and over again how seriously he took the adage that "the devil finds work for idle fingers." But if it is wrong *prima facie* to take from producers the hard-won prizes of their toil, how can taxation (which is involuntary), rather than charity (which is not), be justified to provide for the indigent? To answer this paramount question, he systematically developed a variety of arguments.

Bentham set out to demolish the position of the "abolitionists," the growing coterie of men like the Rev. Joseph Townsend, soon to be joined by the stern figure of the Rev. Thomas Malthus, who urged the complete elimination of the poor laws.[58] One argument was simply prudential: poor relief was necessary to avoid the violent uprising of the hungry. In Scotland the impoverished might be starved with impunity—" . . . *because*, (as the man said) *they are used to it*." But in England they were decidedly *not* used to it and would, Bentham implied, fight.[59]

What men were "used to" led to another consideration involving a principle which without exaggeration one can call—aside from the utility principle itself—the foremost notion of Bentham's thought: *security of expectation*. This is but another form of his overriding passion to eliminate contingency in social life. Now, although Bentham had scant use for custom, beginning, of course, with customary (common) law, the point was that, whatever one might say of them, customs *create expectation*. And that was precisely what the Poor Law did. Just as a man of the propertied class was born with "a rightful expectation" of enjoying his property, "so in the labouring class every man is born with the equally rightful expectation of coming into the enjoyment of a maintenance, charged upon the estates of proprietors, upon the contingency of his falling into indigence. . . ." Why should the title of paupers to their subsistence be any weaker than that of the rich to their property?[60] If sixty years' possession of property rendered good a title originally bad (as it did under English law), the contention that the poor could justly be divested of their right to relief, having endured for more than three times sixty years, and originating, as it did, not in a bad title but in a good one (namely, 43 Elizabeth c.2), was very shaky indeed, to put it mildly.[61] Such was the argument, so to speak, from prescription.

Other arguments came more directly from the fount of utility itself. The injunction against dashing expectations is itself Utilitarian: the violation of expectation creates *pain*. The desirability of the amelioration of suffering (a first principle which Bentham states without defending) and the prevention of class war were foremost among the others. "In a civilized political community," Bentham began his essay "Necessity of relief," "it is neither consistent with common *humanity*, nor with public *security*, that any individual should, for want of any of the necessities of life, be left to perish *outright*—Or *gradually*, to wit through *infirmity* or *disease*."[62] The lower orders could not themselves cope with the problem: they were excluded by their poverty, their lack of ability, "and their ignorance from even the desire of doing it for themselves." (In view of the widespread existence of "Friendly Societies," this latter assertion was hardly well grounded.) The duty of governments and their advisors to concern themselves with the sheer survival of the poor classes rested on the superiority of the numbers and the superiority of the need of those affected—"The poor are the materials of which the far greater part of the fabric of society is composed."[63]

There was a more urgent reason why poor relief ought to be legally established as a public responsibility rather than left to the hazards of private charity. We have already examined many of Bentham's arguments against exclusive private charity. But in the *Essays* of 1796–97, a fundamental consideration was added: by itself, private philanthropy would leave the very lives of the indigent the plaything of contingency. Starvation cannot "to any sufficient degree of *certainty*, be prevented, but by means of a *certain* fund of relief, appropriated to the purpose." No private fund, no fund depending on voluntary contributions, could "to any sufficient degree of *certainty*, be so much as *kept up* to any certain standard . . . much less predetermined to *encrease* in exactly the same *degree*, and exactly at the same *time*, with every encrease in the *demand*"; only a public fund could be permanently adequate to the purpose. Moreover, contrary to what some critics were advocating, obviously no "fixed" fund could suffice.[64] And for the ghastly peril of those left unprotected by legally established relief, he noted elsewhere, one need look no farther than Scotland, where "in the reign of King William 80,000 persons of all ages died by famine in the compass of one year." Bentham estimated that more than six percent of the population perished.[65]

However, none of this went sufficiently far in answering a standard charge of the abolitionists: that public relief actually created pvoerty, expropriating the independent laborer (thereby impoverishing him) for the benefit of the lazy, profligate, and improvident.[66] Bentham's solution to this alleged problem was of the greatest importance, for it was here that he formulated the so-called "less-eligibility principle," which, thanks to the efforts of his young former secretary Edwin Chadwick, was actually incorporated into the Poor Law Amendment Act of 1834. We have already seen how emphatically Bentham agreed with the proposition that each individual ought rightfully to retain the fruits of his own labor. The question was whether and in what respect "this natural and primitive order of things ought, from [the standpoint] of general utility to be broken in upon. . . ."[67] Certainly, were it more attractive to live from the produce of another's work, disaster would follow:

> If the condition of persons maintained without property of their own, by the labour of others, were rendered more eligible than that of persons maintained by their own labour, then in proportion as the existence of this state of things were actually ascertained, individuals destitute of property would be continually withdrawing themselves from the class of persons maintained by their own labour, to the class of persons maintained by the labour of others: and the sort of idleness, which at present is more or less confined to persons of independent fortune, would thus extend itself sooner or later to every individual, . . . on whose labour the perpetual reproduction of the perpetually consuming stock of subsistence depends: till at last there would be nobody left to labour at all for anybody.[68]

In short, economic production would be at an end. The solution to this dilemma followed logically: place the recipient of public relief in less desirable (less "eligible") circumstances than the worst-off independent laborer; reduce relief to life's barest necessities, and those of the cheapest and most vulgar sort.[69] It was a restatement of the old deterrence theory of the workhouse; at the very least, Bentham took it as a principle of common sense that relief "ought not . . . put receivers into a better plight than givers."[70]

It was quite another matter to suggest, as did the Reverend Joseph Townsend, that the improvident and lazy ought to starve. Bentham granted that there was a duty to avoid indigence at all costs; but the existence of a duty, he argued, "is no sufficient reason for refusing to save men from the consequences of transgression." If there ought to be "no hospitals because men ought to live prudently," there should also be "no gallows because they ought to live honestly."[71] A further argument was made in several places, including the *Pannomial Fragments* of the 1820's. Allowing men to starve is equivalent to inflicting capital punishment (which he opposed in any case). "A slow death," he wrote, is "too severe a punishment for even the highest degree of improvidence, which in many instances is a constitutional and incurable disease."[72] In the Poor Law Essay "Definitions and Distinctions" he laid it down that "ill desert" detracts not at all from the exigencies demanded in the state of indigence. If a man is to be punished, he had better be a criminal. If he really is so worthless, "it must be on account of this or that *act* of worthlessness, that he has *committed*." If it is a criminal act, he should be punished; but if it is not, "it will be too much to punish him more than a man is ever punished for a crime, even for the *highest* crime, that is to *starve* him, to leave him to *perish* by a *slow death*."[73] (It must be recalled, however, that Bentham intended to imprison without trial or other legal recourse beggars, suspicious persons, and many others, justifying the practice by redefining the terms "crime" and "punishment.") Moreover, if one objects to the consumption of the fruits of others' labor by non-producers, why select the poor? Which class in society is it, in fact, that continuously lives from the labor of others without themselves laboring? For Bentham the answer is obvious—it is, of course, the rich. The poorest class, he wrote, are the "hardest working" and the "most productive": "the defalcation from the class of consumers in a country is no defalcation from the absolute wealth of a country, and is an actual accession to the sum of relative wealth."[74]

There was, however, a further objection to the existence of the Poor Laws which required a reply, for the spectre of Malthusianism had already begun to haunt Europe, or rather it was beginning to haunt a few Englishmen. Malthus may not have published his first *Essay* until a year after Bentham set pen to paper in reply; but, no matter, Joseph Townsend had in essential respects more or less done it for him more than a decade before (a fact, among others, that led Karl Marx to brand Malthus's entire first *Essay* a "school boyish superficial plagiary").[75]

In his *Dissertation on the Poor Laws* of 1786, Townsend attacked the pervasive eighteenth-century attitude that a growing population is desirable. ("The cry is, Population, population! population at all events! But is there any reasonable fear of depopulation?")[76] Since population inevitably outstripped food supply, privation was inexorably the consequence;

and the only question was "who is most worthy to suffer cold and hunger, the prodigal or the provident, the slothful or the diligent, the virtuous or the vicious?"[77] While the prudent wisely refrained from marriage when their means were inadequate, profligate pleasure-seekers indulged their appetites and fell back on the Poor Laws to support the offspring they themselves could ill afford. "The farmer breeds only from the best of all his cattle," Townsend wrote, "but our laws choose rather to preserve the worst, and seem to be anxious lest the breed should fail."[78] Townsend illustrated his argument with a delightful vignette from a volume by Dampier, the account of Juan Fernandes' South Sea island. There, it was said, were planted a pair of goats, which lived in abundant pasture and happily obeyed the first Commandment to be fruitful and multiply, until by-and-by wealth yielded to penury through overpopulation, whereupon the weakest starved to death. But through such revolutions, the fortunes of goats (and of men) come full circle, and the state of abundance was restored. The moral was inescapable: "Thus, what might have been considered as misfortunes, proved a source of comfort; and to them at least, partial evil was universal good."[79] Arguments from positive law, arguments from natural justice, arguments from humanitarian impulse: none of them could have the slightest relevance in the defense of "public charity" when there was simply not enough to go around. How could the Poor Law possibly be justified when it promoted on a larger scale the very catastrophe (starvation) it sought to avoid?

Bentham never did give an extended, complete, and fully reasoned reply to the challenge to any sort of Poor Law which was made by the haunting portrait of a world starving through overpopulation. Nevertheless, his position is tolerably clear. First of all, the "Malthusian" argument against the existence of a Poor Law could never cut any ice with Bentham so long as the means of subsistence could be had. The burden of proof was on the opposition, for reasons already given, to show why food ought to be denied to the starving when food was available: "So long as any particle of the matter of abundance remains in any one hand," Bentham wrote in the *Constitutional Code* (1830), "it will rest with those, to whom it appears that they are able to assign a sufficient reason, to show why the requisite supply to any deficiency in the means of subsistence should be refused."[80] *

---

*This did not mean, however, that Bentham believed either governments or individuals to be under an obligation (as one might have expected) to feed the starving beyond their own political community. He nowhere discusses the question—an omission which is perhaps in itself significant; but in any case such an obligation cannot be inferred from his version of Utilitarianism. His philosophical position was not, as

But if there was going to be a burden of proof, surely Townsend-Malthus came staggering into court, or so it appeared to many in the early nineteenth century.

Although he was not always consistent, Bentham's answer to the prospect of overpopulation, briefly put, was this: in the short run colonize, in the long run practice birth control and remove criminal penalties from "irregular" sexual appetites, that is, those which did not involve procreation. (In fact, such penalities serve no useful purpose, he thought, and ought to be removed, with or without overpopulation.)[81] In his *Defence of Usury*, he argued that the quantity and value of capital is decreased by procreation,[82] and elsewhere he agreed with the weight of eighteenth-century opinion that population is limited by the means of subsistence—cheap food, on the other hand, induced marriage and procreation.[83] But there was no cause for alarm. In *Supply without Burthen* (1795), he thought that even though per capita wealth in Britain would be greater with a smaller population, it was demonstrable that "relative wealth" had nevertheless been increasing. But in the same tract, he opposed positive encouragement to marriage on the ground that it would result in the influx of more drones into the social hive. The drones, however, were certainly not the poor, who never showed any reluctance to marry.[84] As for the opposite policy, that of limiting marriage, if any class needed discouragement, it was the rich.[85] A more cautionary note was sounded in *The True Alarm* (1801), where Bentham advised against increasing population at the expense of relative wealth.[86]

Bentham does not seem to have given any thought to the prospect of future overpopulation before 1796–97.[87] When he did consider it, he attempted to turn the whole question to his own advantage. The adoption of his poor plan, so far from exacerbating the scarcity of food, would on the contrary, he said, aid in its amelioration. The "National Charity Company" would operate in the first instance as a sort of internal colony, siphoning off excess population, putting it to work cultivating wastes, making it self-sufficient in food.[88] "This is not a plan for a day," he wrote, "—it looks

---

Professor Lyons has shown, a universalist Utilitarianism; that is, the obligation on the part of the legislator or private citizen to maximize pleasure and to minimize pain extended no farther than the borders of his own political community: his position was parochial rather than Universalist. See David Lyons, "Was Bentham a Utilitarian?", in *Reason and Reality*, Royal Institute of Philosophy Lectures, Vol. 5, 1970–71 (London, 1972) pp. 196–221; and see his *In the Interest of the Governed* (Oxford, 1973) pp. 19–105, *passim*.

onwards to the end of earthly time. Sooner or later, should government have gone on improving with other arts, or even though it should be but stationary, sooner or later, the yet vacant lands in the country will have been filled with culture and population."[89] In 1797 he thought that time was "remote but surely not altogether ideal," but after 1800 he believed it would come long before the end of the century.[90] And then, "the company will have turned its thoughts to colonization: and the [?] rising strength of these its hives, will by art, as in other hives by nature, have been educated for swarming." The point was that, since the exportation of excess population was an inevitable necessity, there was a pressing need for an institution that would function as social planner: "The difference is that without the company it will be performed without appropriate preparation, and only under the pressure of distress." With the planning agency, on the other hand, "the want will have been prepared for, the mode predetermined, and hope instead of fear the form given to the impelling principle."[91]

The problem of overpopulation left Bentham's attitude toward colonies somewhat ambiguous. In the manuscripts of the late 1780's which formed the basis of the *Principles of International Law*, colonies were viewed negatively as sources of military conflict and therefore of expense. This negative view was expounded unequivocally in his well-known tract *Emancipate Your Colonies!* (1792). By 1797, however, the looming prospect of future population pressure had obviously given pause to unambiguous condemnation; and after the turn of the century quite a different attitude had emerged. In the *Defence of a Maximum* (1801), there are passages in praise of Empire worthy of Rudyard Kipling himself. Here Bentham argued that although colonization is unprofitable when domestic resources are still available, the situation is reversed with overpopulation: ". . . in this already impending, if yet scarcely so much as imagined, state of things, colonies, though still a drain, are notwithstanding, and even because they are a drain, a relief." If emigration there must be—"and emigrate ere long the hands must do or be starved"—better that men emigrate within the British Empire than without: untaxable colonies, he said, "are all loss."[92] With a new-found vision, Bentham mounted a radiant patriotic peroration, probably unapproached in anything else he ever wrote:

> The retribution for the past expence is a scene from *Paradise Lost*— a prospect such as the angel shewed to Adam: men spreading in distant climes, through distant ages, from the best stock, the earth covered with British population, rich with British wealth, tranquil with British security, the fruit of British law.[93]

This was said in all seriousness, without a touch of irony. The fruit of British law indeed! British law was the law of the reviled William Blackstone, of "Judge & Company," and of "Matchless Constitution," under which "though your right is as clear as the sun at noonday, you lose it by a quibble"; it was the law that denied justice to the poor, and it was the law whose impenetrable jungle of tangled nuance formed a "labyrinth without a clue." It was the law, finally, whose most tenacious, implacable, and outspoken critic was none other than Jeremy Bentham.

Bentham's attitude toward colonies did not remain in its guise of 1801. Both in a preface for a new edition of *Emancipate Your Colonies!* written in 1818, and in the uncompleted *Rid Yourselves of Ultramaria!* (1820–22), he reaffirmed his old position of 1792 and earlier.[94] Nevertheless, when the population question arose, he waivered. In *Pannomial Fragments* written in the latter part of the 1820's, he reiterated the necessity for emigration at the direction of government to an uninhabited part of the globe —another way of speaking of colonization. And the scenario he drew up was of desperate, Malthusian proportions. There was no immediate prospect for the abatement of population growth, and "this augmentation thus produced will proceed with much greater rapidity than any addition that can be made to the quantity of the matter of subsistence. . . ."[95] As a consequence he foresaw all the world divided into three parts: those possessed of the means of subsistence, those on their way to death by starvation, and those who "to save themselves from impending death are occupied in waging war upon the rest." Even colonization would eventually fail since sooner or later the habitable part of the earth would be fully populated; and the prevention of such a catastrophic dénouement was therefore the order of the day:

> Human benevolence can . . . hardly be better employed than in a quiet solution of these difficulties, and in the reconciliation of a provision for those otherwise perishing indigent, with this continual tendency to an increase in the demand for such provision.[96]

The suggestion of "a quiet solution of these difficulties" brings us to another of Bentham's expedients for ameliorating the population 'problem' without falling prey to the attacks on the Abolitionists—birth control. (This was undoubtedly included in his "quiet solution"; it was also thoroughly disapproved of by Malthus.)[97] By the 1820's, several of the inner coterie of Philosophical Radicals—men such as Francis Place and John Mill —were openly espousing contraception; and, although Bentham never said so publicly (surely because he feared prejudicing the cause of reform and tarnishing his name), he was in complete agreement.[98] By the 1820's he had been aware of the eventual need to limit population for decades; he had hinted at contraception as a means of combating poverty in a passage discreetly written in Latin (as he was wont to do) in the 1790's in his *Manual of Political Economy*.[99] Most probably it was Joseph Townsend who first broached the subject to him as a remedy for overpopulation. In *Situation and relief of the Poor* (published in the *Annals of Agriculture* as a preface to his writings on Poor Law reform), Bentham spoke of the desire of "an illustrious friend of mine" to limit the poor rates:

> When I speak of *limitation*, do not suppose that limitation would content me. My *reverend* friend, hurried away by the torrent of his own eloquence, drove beyond *you*, and let drop something about a *spunge*. I too have my spunge; but that a slow one, and not quite so rough a one. Mine goes, I promise you, into the fire, the instant you can shew me that a single particle of necessity is deprived by it of relief.[100]

The "reverend friend" who "let drop something about a spunge" is unquestionably Joseph Townsend. Bentham is not, however, as one commentator thought, himself recommending contraception in this passage. *His* "sponge" was his poor plan: by gradually making the poor pay their own way, the National Charity Company would slowly soak up the rates.[101]

A further, somewhat cryptic, reference to the population problem is found among Bentham's 1796–97 manuscripts. Here, evidently, he felt that the day that a population crisis would overtake the earth was far distant, for he said that sooner or later a prolonged period of "maturity and repletion" would come to the world "if the play of the planets suffer it to last thus long." "Then," he continued, "will the policy of the statesman be directed to the arrestment of population, as now to its increase: and what is now stigmatized as vice will then receive the treatment, if not the name, of virtue."[102] One writer remarked that "[n]o doubt Bentham here referred to birth control."[103] Now, the term "vice" covers (as it were) a multitude of sins, and it may be that he indeed had birth control in mind. But that is not altogether clear, since we do not know that eighteenth-century men (however unanimously they praised a growing population) usually included contraception in their standard catalogue of "vices." But even if Bentham did have that in mind, it was not all he had in mind, nor even what he had principally in mind.

This leads us to the last of Bentham's vehicles for limiting population: legal toleration for the relevant "vices." Much of his argument appears in the section entitled "Population" in his *Institute of Political Economy*, part of which was written after the publication of Malthus' second *Essay* (1803), and all of which was written after the first *Essay* had appeared. This is curious, for Bentham seems to have regressed to the usual eighteenth-century view of population. "Encrease of population," he said, "is desirable, as being an increase of 1. the beings susceptible of *enjoyment*;[104] 2. the beings capable of being employed as *instruments of defence*."[105] (This is an odd argument—it is hard to believe that cannon fodder for the Napoleonic Wars would be susceptible of very much enjoyment.)

Bentham divided what he thought ought to be appropriate government policy for the support of population into an agenda and a non-agenda. The agenda included the care of curable and incurable sick through hospitals and, of course, establishments for the maintenance of indigents. But it is the non-agenda that interests us. Government policies which had as their end the increase of population were ridiculed, not for being irresponsible under Malthusian conditions, but because they were entirely unnecessary. Bentham compared such policies with such absurd parallel policies as punishing men for not eating, or for eating food not sufficiently nourishing, or rewarding them with premiums for eating the most and the most often. Of exactly the same caliber were laws which forbade infanticide (!), abortion, and most importantly, "irregularities of all sorts in the venereal appetite."[106]

In defense of this position, Bentham's first point was that it was ridiculous for government to punish sexual practices which did not produce offspring as if there could conceivably otherwise develop a shortage of fecund sexual intercourse. It took but one act of intercourse per couple per year to produce a year's maximum number of offspring: and the propensity for sexual relations could be considered, for example, a daily occurrence:

> On these assumptions, the disposition to sexual conjunction in the regular way is 365 times as great as it need be to the production of the maximum of effect in the way of population. Halve the ratio or double it, the conclusion will be the same. Before any the least decrease of population could have been produced by the uncontrolled indulgence of irregular appetites, the regular gratification of the regular appetite must have become *unnatural* in the extreme.[107]

So much for penal restrictions in conditions of underpopulation; clearly, this *reductio ad absurdum* would operate with even greater force with society stalked by the great shadow of the Malthusian bogey-man.

Bentham's next barb was precisely on target. "For penal laws of this class," he argued, "an anxiety about population has never been any thing but a pretence." Such laws were instituted under the tyrannical sway of the principles of asceticism and antipathy—the principles against which Bentham had been doing battle since the days when he scribbled the first pages of what was to become *An Introduction to the Principles of Morals and Legislation* (1789). Years later he wrote that "nature has given to man two cups of physical sweets"—one by which the individual is preserved and the other by which the species is perpetuated. But "blind antipathy" (and religion in particular) had attempted to turn "the cup of sweets into a cup of bitterness" (and, he might have added, for some individuals succeeded rather well).[108] In the *Institute*, he sarcastically charged that if the ascetic were really consistent, he ought to forbid sexual relations between married persons incapable of offspring and following conception, until the end of childbirth convalescence; "as likewise to desserts following a full meal, and to the use of tobacco in every shape, &c. &c.." The consistent antipathist should follow a similar bent, *mutatis mutandis*; those who chew betel nut "should mutually extirpate, and be extirpated by, the chewers, snuffers and smoakers of tobacco." "Expressions of abhorrence for opinions not his own," he went on, "is a price which no man need grudge, and which the most worthless never grudge, to pay for the praise of virtue."[109]

What Bentham had foremost in his mind when he advocated legal toleration of "irregularities of all sorts in the venereal appetite," and when he spoke of the future toleration of "vice" as a check to population, was homosexuality. He had first argued for the removal of legal penalties for homosexuality in the 1770's while working on the legal code he intended to submit to the Berne prize committee, and he specifically labelled homosexuality a vice:

> Another spectacle amusing enough is, to observe the distress men are under to keep the peace between two favourite prejudices that are apt cruelly to jar: the one in disfavour of this vice; the other in favour of antiquity, especially ancient Greece. . . . Sometimes they will dissemble and shut their eyes against the fact—sometimes they will attempt to question it.[110]

At the same time, he dismissed the detriment-to-population argument as simply not factual.[111]

When he again turned his attention to the subject in the 1780's, he used the same argument that we found in the *Institute of Political Economy*, namely that the origin of punishment for homosexuality was antipathy: physical antipathy turns itself into moral antipathy. But not the physical antipathy of the actor: he is doing it for the pleasure.[112] Anyway, he thought, a ribbon or a ringlet is a much better way to attract "the affections of a lover than the hangman's rope."[113] Antipathy was again identified as the culprit when in the 1820's Bentham considered the question of punishing what he now termed "sexual eccentricities." (Previously, drawing on the tradition of toleration for religious nonconformists, he had usually spoken of "sexual non-conformity.") It was only a question of conflicting tastes: "You like oysters: I do not: therefore you ought to be killed, and I ought to do my utmost to have you killed."[114] Too late for his own benefit, the old radical Bentham then announced that the banning of sexual pleasure was nothing less than an act of tyranny. "By the physical appetite of the tyrant has the standard been fixt: from that standard every other appetite has been regarded as an aberation: and for the crime of aberation the penalty is death." Moreover, with the influence of Malthus rife in the land, detriment to population could no longer serve as a pretense for outlawing homosexuality. If previously fears of population decline were expressed, "since the publication of Mr Malthus the apprehension of the public has been to take a contrary direction. Overpopulation not underpopulation is now seen to be the great cause" of world catastrophe.[115] But Malthus condemned "unnatural passions" along with "improper arts" as means to limit the growth of population.[116] This was too much for the Hermit of Queen Square Place:

> Yet of those antidotes to this evil, what he calls *vice* is one. . . . But in so far as the practice is free from worry to third persons, virtue rather than vice should be the appelation of [such] a practice, . . . [and he should] recommend the use. But Mr Malthus belongs to that profession to which acknowledgement of error is rendered impossible.[117]

In the Poor Law manuscripts of 1797, Bentham had predicted that when population became a threat, the practitioners of sexual "irregularities" ("what is now stigmatized as vice") would receive the treatment if not the name of virtue. More than two decades before he had remonstrated with the persecutors of homosexuals, arguing that "their physical disgust, worked up by exaggerated epithets into a pitch of fury . . . makes them mistake an object of physical disgust for an object of moral disapprobation"; and, pleading for "indulgence for a fellow-creature who neither injures thee nor any one," he became passionate—"Say, are there not miseries enough upon this earth without thy heedless cruelty adding to the heap?"[118] But in 1825, the angry old philosopher ceased pleading; homosexuals, he now argued, should be given the name as well as the treatment of the virtuous.

Here, then, with the various means we have been considering to stem the tide of the onrushing flood of humanity, Bentham rested his case against the Malthusian advocates of the abolition of the Poor Law.

Finally, we will consider an ingenious argument against providing for the poor, an argument couched in purely Utilitarian terms. So far as one can tell, it was first made, a decade after Bentham wrote on the Poor Law, by Richard Lowell Edgeworth, father of the novelist Maria Edgeworth. Edgeworth and his daughter were both close friends of Bentham's most important editor, Etienne Dumont, and carried on an extensive and lively correspondence with him. (Neither seems to have met Bentham himself—on at least one occasion Bentham refused to see Richard Edgeworth—and in any case both were biased against him; they implied that Dumont possessed the superior mind—a doubtful proposition to say the least—and resented his subservient relation with his master.)[119]

In a letter to Dumont in 1806, Edgeworth retailed several standard Abolitionist attacks on the Poor Law. Giving to the poor was a bounty to idleness; the poor were too dependent on the Parish—instead they should depend on their children. There were no poor laws in Ireland, and in the Emerald Isle filial affection was very great. This is, perhaps, a variation on the 'Cohesion of Society' argument discussed earlier: public provision for the poor loosens the interdependence of the family.[120]

Among other thoughts on the subject, Edgeworth presented a novel point of view: public relief might very well run counter to the utility principle itself (depending on how one conceives of that principle). Edgeworth defined "the universal principle of public utility" not as "the greatest happiness of the greatest number" (as, of course, Bentham thought of it for most of his life), but rather as "the greatest sum of happiness." (In fact, it has been argued, in my view incorrectly, that whatever Bentham may have *said*, "greatest happiness"—rather than "greatest happiness of the greatest number"—is what he always *meant*.)[121] Edgeworth reasoned as follows:

> Ten thousand people *may* during an existence of ten years enjoy more pleasure in the aggregate, than twenty thousand others *can* with the same means of subsistence in the same period. The legislator ought therefore to prefer the smaller number to the greater: I therefore see no reason why the attainable comforts of one class of men should be lessened by any forced contribution for the support of the improvident and selfish.[122]

There are some difficulties with this argument. Quite apart from the question whether it was the poor rather than the rich who were the more selfish members of society, Edgeworth's logic is not exactly impeccable. On the contrary, it involves a glaring *non sequitur*. If a smaller group *"may"* derive more pleasure from a given lot of goods than a larger group, it does not follow that there is "no reason" why the larger group should retain the goods: the question is, which group is more likely to derive more benefit? And if no precise measurement is available (and none is), what sort of reasoning is involved in making a decision? Moreover, Edgeworth speaks in the passage just cited of the "means of subsistence," not of resources beyond mere subsistence. This seems to imply—anyway it can not logically be excluded—that some, indeed the *larger* group, could in accordance with the utility principle be left without the means of subsistence for the sake of "the attainable comforts of one class of men." Surely it is morally hideous to consider that even the most ecstatic pleasures of one group could outweigh the pain of an equal, let alone a larger, group starving to death, even if it were true (as Edgeworth gratuitously assumes) that the poor were selfish and improvident.

It cannot be said with any certainty whether Dumont informed Bentham of Edgeworth's argument or whether he learned of it (or something similar) from another source. Nevertheless, in writing his *"Pannomion"*[123] in the late 1820's, he quite explicitly contradicted Edgeworth's reasoning. He began by distinguishing, as he had done for decades, between the "matter of subsistence" and the "matter of abundance," the former being included in the latter. The matter of subsistence is necessary for existence, and existence is necessary for happiness. Bentham imagined the situation in which a legislator controlled the resources for the subsistence of 10,000 persons, already in existence. How could happiness be maximized? By dividing the resources equally among the 10,000, or by giving double the amount to each of 5,000, leaving nothing at all to the rest? In the first case, there would be abundance for no one; in the second, some modicum of abundance would exist for half the population. The answer for Bentham was simply axiomatic: the first choice was preferable since on the other supposition "the 5,000 thus left destitute would soon die through a lingering death."[124] It may be objected (and here we assume the darkest implication of Edgeworth's letter) that Bentham has done nothing more than answer an assertion with an assertion. And that is quite true since axioms are no more than premises laid down and agreed upon so that conclusions can be logically derived. Obviously, Bentham assumed agreement to the notion that, all other things being equal, it is morally repugnant that one man starve so that another might be happier. (We have already seen Bentham's argument in the case where all other things are *not* equal, and the indigent are called worthless.) One must leave it to subtler and abler minds to show why Bentham's axiom should be discarded.

But there was a further case which Bentham considered. Suppose the existence of 10,000 persons, and suppose that the resources of society could support double the number, each at bare subsistence. Suppose also that the legislator had it in his power to give or to deny existence to the second 10,000—clearly a question of birth control.[125] To state the obvious, this was a case altogether different from Edgeworth's, in which resources were to be divided among those already living. Here happiness is maximized by eliminating population growth altogether and doubling the wealth of each individual.

Bentham gave a number of reasons why he did not consider it desirable to maximize the number of souls called to what has traditionally been described as "the feast of life," most of which flowed from the effort to loosen the iron grip of public enemy number one, contingency. For one thing, life at the level of bare subsistence is by definition anything but a feast. But more than that, thanks to chance and the caprice of nature, one can never form the secure expectation that the so-called "feast of life" will not turn literally into famine: "for supposing the whole 10,000 having each of them the minimum of the matter of subsistence on any given day, —the next day, in consequence of some accident they might cease to have it, and in consequence cease to have existence."[126] The situation is otherwise where society possesses resources beyond those necessary for survival (which is what Bentham meant by abundance), for "the abundance possessed by some is . . . a stock, a fund, out of which matter is capable of being taken applicable to the purpose of affording, whether immediate or through exchange, subsistence to the others."[127] But there was one critical condition that had to be met—the "matter of abundance" must be "capable of being by the legislator so disposed of as to be made to constitute the matter of subsistence" for those who would otherwise starve.[128] In other words, not only had the *wealth* of nations to include food, but also that food had to be at the disposal of government. To defeat contingency (to maximize happiness), provision for indigence must necessarily be a matter of public policy.

In summary Bentham's defense of the Welfare State amounted, first, to the reiteration of his prior and primary contention that the alleviation of suffering is an end in comparison with which all other ends are properly subordinate, and, second, to the derivative contention that the suffering which results from indigence ought properly to be a responsibility of the community as a whole and not of individuals. He was adamant that private means, organized or not, are undependable as buttresses against the rigors of distress, especially in an urban setting where anonymity forms an invisible barrier to an awareness of both need and desert. As a substitute for the Welfare State a system of private means is also undesirable because it unfairly taxes the most humane and morally sensitive members of the community, whose gifts to those in need are only formally voluntary. That the fruits of a man's labor are properly his own is indeed a moral truth, but it is not an absolute truth; more good is produced by taxing the selfish for the sake of the destitute than is produced by the slavish adherence to a principle which if applied universally would amount to a variety of mere sadism. All of this tells us that Bentham's social theory had quite impressive limits to its individualism and that it would be mistaken to label him a "possessive individualist" *tout court*. Moreover, where the Welfare State is already an established institution its abandonment is morally forbidden as a violation of one of the central pillars of any society, the security of expectations. Finally, the potentially catastrophic circumstance of runaway population growth should be dealt with through rational planning well in advance of its approach—dealt with through internal and external colonization, through contraception, and through the decriminalization, and even the encouragement, of non-fecund sexuality, especially homosexuality.

5

The National Charity Company:
Benevolence Incorporated

The essence of the idea of a Welfare State lies in a single proposition, namely that the *State* (rather than any lesser association or the citizen himself acting in his own behalf) assumes the responsibility of providing the means which assure the general well-being of its subjects. There is a sense, it is true, in which all states are "welfare states," for every state is committed to ensuring the primeval ingredient of well-being—the physical protection of all within its borders, citizen and alien alike, from internal and external attack. But if the state as such is committed to protection from force and fraud, it is committed to little else. The sick need care, the hungry nourishment, the homeless shelter: that state is still a state which assumes no burden to succor its weakest members and leaves their fate instead to the mercy or indifference of nature and charity. Historically it has more often than not been true that the officers and authorities of the "mortal god," as Hobbes so justly characterized the modern state, were content to leave attendance to the helpless in the hands of the organized followers of that other God as well as in those of municipalities and private philanthropists.[1]

In England, however, it was otherwise. There, from the end of the sixteenth century onwards, thanks to the Poor Law, it was a matter of universal public responsibility, in law if not always in deed, that the idle be employed, the sick tended, and the aged given relief, all at public expense. We should not, therefore, find it greatly astonishing that the most radical and comprehensive revision of the English Poor Law ever proposed—Bentham's—took on the guise of a full-blown Welfare State more developed by far than the practice of its day. The revision which Bentham propounded was an intricate blending of reform and revolution (revolution from above) whose special character and flavor we are about to investigate. The 'House that Bentham built' is very peculiar, and to know it thoroughly, we need to survey its main pillars, tour its chambers, and crawl through its small places, all the while feeling its textures and smelling not only the aromas of its kitchens but also the stenches of its sewers.

It is striking that in his writings on the reform of the Poor Law, as in his philosophy generally, Bentham saw no ultimate or overwhelming moral conflicts. Thus many thousands would be imprisoned without trial under his regime, but that denied justice to no one. And child labor would be exploited to the hilt, but this was neither cruel nor unjust. Indeed, children, those "living treasures" on whom Bentham founded his claim that the National Charity Company would be profitable, could be used as collateral for loans to the poor: no payment, no child—until he reached his maturity the child would be co-opted into the involuntary servitude of the "apprentice" population of the "House of Industry." This arrangement too presented Bentham no moral conundrum. On the contrary, the proposed system represented so complete a resolution of practical and theoretical difficulties, moral and economic alike, and was so closely knit together into a fabric of such perfect harmony, that he was pleased to call it his "Utopia." Professor Himmelfarb is surely right in thinking it more than a little odd that a poor house of *any* description be called Utopia:[2] if a poor house is Utopia, what is Inferno?

1. The Constitution

First things first: what was the "National Charity Company"? The short answer is that it was a joint-stock company designed to supplant the existing motley conglomeration of poor laws, assimilating all of their essential functions and adding a number of others as well: ". . . nothing less than the whole field of the existing Poor Laws," Bentham argued, "can with any tolerable degree of advantage be taken for the subject matter of the proposed system."[3] Its internal constitution was modeled after that of the East India Company, a body with which Bentham had been intimately familiar since the days of the early 1780's when he pored over the massive volumes of Parliamentary reports on its operations, prior to writing *The Influence of Place and Time in Matters of Legislation* (1782). A Board of General Direction would sit in London; and the qualifications for directors, for voting in elections of directors, and for voting in assemblies of stockholders were to be carbon copies of those of the East India Company.[4] The joint-stock company form was chosen for a number of compelling reasons, one of which lay in the greater possibility of honest and efficient management: it was this that government could not provide. By this time, Bentham had had enough years under his belt of dickering with Pitt's administration over Panopticon to believe that "the race between the individual and government exertion in the line of economical improvement is a race between the greyhound and the sloth."[5] Another reason for forming a joint-stock company lay in the question of finance, for in raising a public subscription, the burden would be transferred from the unwilling to the willing.[6] Nevertheless, in case of a shortfall, the public treasury would be obliged to make up the difference.[7] The existing poor rates would continue to be levied for the time being (at a uniform national rate rather than at the wildly varying local rates which then prevailed), but Bentham fully expected that they would in time be reduced and finally eliminated altogether.

The heart of the work of the National Charity Company was the operation of an integrated system of some two hundred and fifty workhouses ("Houses of Industry") spread at equal distances across the entire landscape of England and Wales (Scotland was prudently omitted) and managed "upon a plan in most points exactly the same."[8] The name "National Charity Company" was a misnomer—no charity was distributed; food and shelter were *earned*, not given. To these refuges from penury Bentham expected some half a million souls to drag themselves or else be dragged within the first days of the Company's existence, and he believed that another half-million, all of them children, would be added within 21 years, after which growth would cease.[9] All this was the subject of his extensive pleading and planning.

Secondly: how were the "Houses of Industry" to be managed, and by what personnel? We will look more closely at Bentham's ideas on management in due course and confine ourselves here to a general view of a complete system of management. First of all, this *was* a system of *"management"*—by *personnel*. The idea of modern management is by no means simple, but the essential ingredients are present in Bentham's writings, in particular, in his discussion of the control, planning, and coordination of an extensive enterprise. Bentham was one of the small coterie of men who, before the nineteenth century, consciously sought to elucidate rational principles of management: and well he might, for it was the decided weight of eighteenth-century opinion that salaried managers, especially managers of joint-stock companies, were preordained to inefficiency and peculation. At mid-century Josiah Tucker argued that chartered companies were invariably less efficient than individual entrepreneurs—" . . . it has been *always* found, that if private Adventurers shall be *permitted* to *engage* in the *same* trade, they will infallibly carry it away from the Company."[10] In 1769 the Abbé Morelett (with whom Bentham had become acquainted after 1789) listed 55 joint-stock companies established after 1600 which, in Adam Smith's words, "according to him, have all failed from mismanagement, notwithstanding they had exclusive privileges."[11] Smith himself was similarly disposed, for he thought that the affairs of joint-stock companies governed by salaried managers ("being the managers of other people's money than their own") would forever be badly administered unless it was an enterprise "of which all operations are capable of being reduced to what is called a routine, or to such a uniformity of method as admits of little or no variation."[12]

Such "routine," such "uniformity of method" was precisely what Bentham's rules of management were designed to identify and control. These rules formed the legal code, so to speak, of his domestic colony, his little commonwealth; they were a *Constitutional Code* (1830) writ small.

Populating the bureaux of the Company's poor-Panopticons was a standard set of personnel, the *dramatis personae* of a vast tableau whose scenes and roles had been predetermined by a master playwright. Like the old Globe Theatre, the stage was round for maximum visibility; but this was not traditional theater—it was a topsy-turvy, modern form of audience participation: the stage was circular to enhance the players' view of the 'audience' (the better to direct them) rather than the other way around. Indeed, the unruly mob summoned to participate in this tragi-comedy was for the most part deliberately impeded from seeing the cast of their directors, and if any theatrical analogy is apt, it must be some version of absurdist theatre.

Each officer of a "House of Industry" was allotted circumscribed "functions" (the word is Bentham's) for which he would be accountable to the Company. The Governor's power was to be nearly absolute; he would oversee the chaplain, doctor, schoolmistress ("for the younger part of the female apprentices"), foreman and forewoman, head nurse, and others. An organist, music master on Sundays, doubled as a clerk on weekdays; the schoolmaster, for reasons we will see later, would have time to be secretary as well.[13]

The keynote of the internal government of this system was the protection of everyone from everyone else through maximum visibility and therefore responsibility. The alternative title to Bentham's first book on Panopticon was "The Inspection House." Obviously the title referred primarily to architecture, every nook of the circular structure being visible from the center; but "inspection" applied with equal force to management, particularly to the management of Panopticon poorhouses. Every decision, every action would be recorded for the world to see; even governors could keep no decision secret from subordinates, some of whom were empowered, *in extremis*, to apply a veto. Moreover, Company and paupers alike were protected from miscreant acts of the official establishment of the House: each officer was responsible for the behavior of his fellows—every one would watch every one, the possibility of which having been ensured by the obligation that "all official acts" be exercised "in the *common room*; viz., the central lodge." It was a social system in which, as in the larger Benthamite society, private solidarity to the exclusion of public visibility was impossible, and Bentham had clear expectations as to how it would operate—"The plea of self-preservation will thus afford a shield against the imputation of officiousness and ill-nature."[14]

Other measures protected interested members of the public. Regulations of the Company's constitution and reserved Parliamentary power guarded against stockjobbing, speculating with company capital, creation of monopolies, and the recurrence of such sorry affairs as the "South Sea Bubble" (the popular name for speculation in the South Sea Company, which collapsed disastrously in 1720, ruining many stockholders). The arrangements Bentham suggested for payment of dividends are of special interest. None could be paid until accounts were published, and published in an easily comprehensible form: "according to a pre-established form: *i.e.* digested under pre-adjusted heads."[15] Company officials would be met with public visibility and hence inspectability at every turn; accounts, like laws, were worse than useless unless they were both knowable and known: the publication of digested accounts was an extension of Bentham's earlier plan for the publication of a "Digest of the Laws."[16]

The payment of dividends had yet another feature, for the "Disposal of the growing Receipts" (as Bentham optimistically put it) was to be made according to a list of preferential categories which, as usual, would galvanize the link between interest and duty. Significantly enough, maintenance of the pauper community was only third in priority in the disposition of Company receipts—"rent dividends" and "bond dividends" ranked first and second—indicating the approximate status of the poor themselves in Bentham's hierarchy of values. Last on the list came the "Profit Dividend" payable to the Company and parishes (for reduction of the rates).[17]

This version of the inelegantly but accurately phrased "interest and duty conjunction prescribing principle" is strikingly reminiscent of a proposal of which Bentham had read many years earlier, a proposal which may well have been the origin of the principle itself. If so, we might pause to muse on the irony of the history of ideas, for the author of the earlier proposal was none other than Edmund Burke.

Early in 1780, Burke presented to Parliament a scheme published as *A Plan for the . . . Oeconomical Reformation of the Civil and Other Establishments*,[18] which evidently attracted some interest, since it went through at least three editions in one year. One of its most attentive readers was Bentham: his copy, preserved at the British Museum, is heavily annotated and underscored in his own and another's hand. (The second hand may well have been that of one of his readers.) In the course of his discussion Burke invented an ingenious way to insure the judicious handling of public monies: nine categories of those paid by the Exchequer were established, the lower categories receiving nothing until the higher were paid. In the lowest class were the salaries and pensions of the First Lord of Treasury himself, the Chancellor of the Exchequer, and other commissioners of the treasury.[19] The rationale Burke offered for this clever piece of thrift insurance strikes a certain note of *déjà vu* among those familiar with Bentham's work: "I know of no mode of preserving the effectual execution of any duty," Burke wrote, "but to make it the direct interest of the execution officer that it shall be faithfully performed."[20] This passage in Bentham's edition is underlined, and the probability that he marked it himself or else had it marked is obviously of a high order; and Burke's language—"interest" and "duty"—makes it somewhat less than wild speculation that here indeed was the germ for Bentham's famous principle.

The National Charity Company was Bentham's Welfare State, the ultimate safe haven from the contingencies of nature and the indifferent fluctuations of the market. The Company took it as its obligation to receive and maintain *every* sick or able-bodied pauper child or adult who applied for relief and was prepared to work for it.[21] That was its primary function, but secondary functions, or, as Bentham called them, "collateral uses," were of almost equal importance. These—in *Pauper Management Improved* seventeen were listed—were designed to envelop the entire range of affairs of the *independent* poor, and to inculcate into them the cardinal Benthamite virtues of industry, thrift, and prudent regard for the future. Thus, poor-Panopticons doubled as pawnbrokerages, "frugality banks," "frugality inns" and "conveyance houses," lying-in hospitals, and as schools teaching a variety of subjects relevant to the great task of ensuring that one did not become an unwilling inmate of a poor-Panopticon.

Yet another "collateral use" is closer to our theme: these "Houses of Industry" were to become omnibus dispensers of 'social security,' in the American sense. They sold insurance. The idea of insurance—Bentham's era has been called the "Age of Insurance"—was close to his heart: modern insurance involves using the laws of chance to defeat chance ravages. Now there was, of course, no small incidence of insuring taking place among the working class of eighteenth-century England. That was the formal *raison d'être* of Friendly Societies. (Occasionally, even in the seventeenth century, private employers provided sickness, accident, and other insurance schemes.)[22] But, as Bentham learned from Eden,[23] Friendly Societies were but too prone to failure and dissolution, were too much a part of the dark and evanescent netherworld of contingency to be a bulwark against it. Members quarreled, some funds were dissipated, others embezzled: the insurance of the Friendly Society could be a will-o'-the-wisp. And, as Bentham emphatically pointed out, no insurance plan can be adequate without the requisite data: long footnotes in *Pauper Management Improved* were devoted to the subject, especially to the lack of reliable "mortality tables" (actuarial tables) and to the requirements of funds for old-age, sickness, and life ("Widow-Provision") insurance.[24] Moreover, Bentham considered the Friendly Societies of his day singularly unfit to inculcate into the poor the great moral teaching of regular saving—the blessings attendant upon frugality. If only the poor could be taught to postpone gratification! Friendly Societies, meeting as they did in public houses, were not exactly what he had in mind: ". . . choosing a tippling-house for a school of frugality, would be like choosing a brothel for a school of continence."[25]

One great method for entangling the tentacles of the Company in the fabric of the lives of the independent poor was the creation of a unitary national holding company for existing Friendly Societies. This company's superior services as insurance broker would, Bentham hoped, wean the lower orders from its competitors. Personal saving was a good thing, and the Company's banking facilities, dealing in the most minute sums, would promote it; but in this case individualism was decidedly inferior to collective association and cooperation. Bentham contrasted the utilitarian merits of "self-insurance"—his term for individual saving—for adversity or retirement with "insurance by contract." In this case as in others, he argued, the latter form maximized happiness: " . . . the distribution of good and evil being in this way more equable:—for though what there is of personal suffering in the case is incapable of being distributed, yet its concomitant, the pecuniary burden *is* distributed by this means; and, by being distributed the pressure of it upon the whole is lessened. . . ."[26] Bentham did not dispute that, for all their faults, Friendly Societies had rendered valuable services of relief in the cause of happiness; what now bothered him, given their instability, was the possibility of false expectations of their future benefits:

> What regards relief under sickness is unmixed good:—thousands and tens of thousands must have been preserved by it from death, misery, and pensioned idleness.—But, of what concerns provision against future contingencies, the result is in the clouds. It is in vain to inquire into remote effects, when the state of existing causes is wrapt in darkness. Who can say to what extravagancies overweaning hope may not have soared, while unlettered minds have been left to wander in the field of calculation without a guide?[27]

The reference to unlettered minds wandering without a guide is suggestive of the sometimes avuncular, sometimes arrogant, and more than sometimes condescending paternalism that characterized Bentham's attitude toward the poor. The association of paternalism with the Welfare State is usually made derogatorily by critics of one or the other (or both). Neither is intended here. I do not mean to imply that every paternalistic policy is unjustifiable or even undesirable. What else but a paternalistic policy forbids us from sampling the joys of heroin? The problem with Bentham is different: his overweening paternalism is partly responsible for the repressiveness (as we will see later) of poor-Panopticon and for the attempt to control its inmates totally. And if the truth were known, we would soon suspect that it wasn't only the indigent that Bentham wanted to control, but *us* too—*all* of us. That is, we might suspect that Panopticon was a version of Benthamite society writ small. After all, in his original Panopticon tracts published in 1791 he asked this question: "What would you say, if by the gradual adoption and diversified application of this single principle,"—the central inspection principle of Panopticon—"you should see *a new scene of things spread itself over the face of civilized society?*"[28] However, it would require many pages to confirm or allay this suspicion, and we shall have to leave the matter unsettled.

"No one," Bentham wrote, "ought to be left destitute of proper guardianship necessary to prevent his hurting" himself or others.[29] Among this group were minors; and included in the class of minors were the poor. They could not be trusted, particularly with money: "The comparative weakness of their faculties, moral and intellectual, the result of the want of education, assimilates their condition in this particular to that of minors. The money of the poor man, like that of the school boy, *burns* . . . in his pocket."[30] The poor, he said, "are a sort of grown children."[31] In this demeaned status, the poor in need of relief, whether or not they were beggars, were in no position to be choosers. Exceptions excepted, their only alternative was to starve or to accept relief "upon terms which it is thought fit to be offered," that is, under confinement. (If they *were* beggars, even the choice of starvation without confinement was removed.) And, as if to underline the inferiority of the indigent, Bentham revived the all-but-defunct practice of badging them: "*Soldiers* wear *uniforms*, why not paupers?—those who save the country, why not those who are saved by it?"[32] The answer is that soldiers wear uniforms in order not to kill members of their own army and also because the laws of war demand it. Furthermore, soldiers are not required to wear uniforms as humiliating stigmata but rather, as a rule, regard them as badges of honor.

One consequence of the poor's childlike state was that someone had quite literally to keep an eye on them; they could not be entrusted to themselves. We have already seen how Bentham assumed that as a matter of course Pitt's "cow-money clause" would be transformed into a "gin-money clause" by the ungovernable, rapacious appetite of the poor for deleterious tippling. This inability to control desire, so characteristic of children, was one part of the rationale for eliminating outdoor relief. An even more important reason was that getting rid of home relief was a step without which it would be inconceivable to make the "charity" business profitable. It was a step, moreover, which Gertrude Himmelfarb has rightly called "the truly radical innovation of Bentham's plan." It is not quite so clear, however, that he intended the "total abolition of outdoor relief, in any form and for any purpose."[33] Usually this seems to be exactly what he was proposing, as the following passage suggests: ". . . to this economy, . . . it seems an indispensable condition, that the system of out allowances should not be so much as preserved in any instance. . . ."[34] There is nothing to contradict this statement in *Pauper Management Improved*. Nevertheless, at two points in his manuscripts he did approve of home relief. Agricultural workers and manufacturers who were ill and who earned less than a specified minimum (Bentham suggested ten shillings a week) might be relieved at home, though in the case of chronic illness indoor relief would be at the option of the authorities.[35] A second category, the poorest of the aged, might also escape the rigors of Panopticon and be relieved at home. "It appears proper," he wrote, "to confine this home provision to old age" for reasons of expense.[36] But not all the aged would be so provided for: workers should be divided into two classes, those whose wage allowed a surplus over subsistence to buy superannuation annuities, and those whose wage did not. The former could go straight to the poorhouse; such was their punishment for lack of prudence and foresight. But for the latter class, Bentham was willing to budge from his otherwise immovable stand against outdoor relief, "provided the period of commencement were a late one, suppose 65 years of age, without any very heavy national expence." (A moment later sixty-five years of age was revised to "not earlier than 70.") In this instance, he would tolerate a compromise between opposing considerations of justice and Utilitarianism:

> On these terms a composition it should seem might be made between the demands of indulgent humanity and those of rigid justice: humanity which requires that every individual shall be made happy: justice which requires that of two members of the community, if possible equally innocent and equally deserving . . . , one shall not be compelled to part with the fruits of his own labour without necessity for the benefit of another.[37]

Whether these cracks in the locked vault of public funds should be considered part of Bentham's 'final position' is anybody's guess, and in any case, the underlying tenor of his thinking on the poor is hardly altered by them.

For the apex of the Company Bentham set his hopes of procuring the services of the most renowned contemporary administrator of the poor, the idol of the progressive reading public, his sometime correspondent and visitor, Count Rumford. Now, Bentham had scant regard for Rumford's ideas about the poor, although one would never guess it from the praise the former American received at his hands in the *Annals of Agriculture* articles, where he said that Rumford's "essays relative to the Poor, are entitled to a distinguished place. . . ."[38] This was, however, just another bit of Benthamite diplomacy, or rather hypocrisy, since his real feelings were that, agreeing with Wilberforce, there was "not much in it."[39] On the other hand, Bentham did respect Rumford's undoubted probity and administrative abilities; and besides, his illustrious name would be a political asset, a living advertisement lending credence to the substance of the plan as well as substance to credence in lending money to the Company. The Count might be off in Bavaria, but Bentham believed that the "call of Britain" would bring him 'home.'[40]

Aside from Count Rumford, there were two others available to heed the "call of Britain" to serve the Company, two others for whom Bentham had a high regard. This happy fact should be "regarded surely as a circumstance of no ordinary felicity" since they were the "two men in the world the best qualified for attracting public confidence." These two were (who else?) the brothers Bentham.[41]

2. Farming the Poor

Since Bentham's plan called for "farming out" the entire pauper population of England and Wales, he was anxious to refute the criticism of those who believed that, as he put it, "farming out [the] poor is—everything that is abominable."[42] Humane Englishmen were quite aware of the abuses that sometimes resulted from private contracting. For example, Bentham's friend Romilly was scandalized by the sight of poor London children sent off to Lancashire mills "in carts like so many Negro slaves."[43]

Oddly enough, Bentham set out to defend the practice of farming out the poor, not as it would be practiced in the idyllic setting of the Panopticons of the National Charity Company, but in reality, as it was currently practiced. Stranger still was the character of his argument. He claimed that critics based their objections not on good evidence but rather had been misled by the "hobgoblin" drawn up by Dr. Richard Burn in describing the "Farmer of the Poor."[44] The "hobgoblin" took the place of rational argument: "Led away by prejudice, the result of passion—though a passion of the most laudable and purest kind—men talk, on this as on so many other subjects, as sheep walk."[45]

What, then, were the facts? What indeed? Having gone to immense pains to accumulate empirical evidence on the state of the Poor Law, Bentham cast to the winds any effort to survey the known facts and instead relied almost entirely on *a priori* reasoning. First he argued the force of public opinion operated as an effective check against possible abuse by contractors. Sensitive men, he said, would be roused by jealousy and suspicion "by the spectacle of an arrangement in appearance so unpromising to the comfort of the persons who are subject of it."[46] These suspicions afforded a security "of the strongest kind" against abuse. He continued:

> I do really take it for an indisputable truth, and a truth that is one of the corner stones of political science—the more strictly we are watched, the better we behave. Management on the interested plan, acts as a stimulant on the superintending eye: management on the uninterested plan, as a relaxant. The Farmer of the Poor will always be watched. . . . All superintending ears are open to hear complaints against him: and therefore all interested tongues are upon the watch to find matter for such complaints.[47]

The contractor's court was the "Court of the public eye" which controlled him "without troubling the King's Bench or the Old Bailey."

Next, Bentham said that abuse was most unlikely because under the contract system the connection between the employer's interest and his duty was "as strong as possible." It was nonsensical to suppose that the "farmer of the poor" would either work or starve his wards into ill health or death, for then he would get no work from them and consequently no profit.[48] And in any case there were always the magistrates to correct any complaints of maltreatment, just as they so often overturned harsh decisions of the Overseers.

What of the charge that the farmed-out poor were little better than the slaves of their masters? Bentham had little respect for such arguments; human dignity figured scarcely at all in his scale of values. What mattered was that the poor were *bound* (so he thought) to be treated better at the hands of a contractor who had a monetary interest in their physical well-being than at those of an Overseer who had none. "Call them cattle—suppose them treated on no better footing than cattle. I farm them. So long as I continue to farm them, they are at any rate *my* cattle." Who would look after them better, the owner "to whose share the loss by their death falls" or "the prentice, or fine gentlemen, or fine gentlemen's footman, who has them of me, and whips and spurs them on terms which ease him of the loss?"[49] The answer was obvious.

Upon such reasoning, Bentham declared that the existing contract "mode of management" had been "proved" a good one.[50] The only piece of empirical evidence he cited was a visit he had made "not many years ago" to two poor-relief establishments (of what variety we are not told).[51] One was under contract, the other was not, but both seemed to him well managed. (He had, in fact, been shown them by a friend[52] precisely *because* they were well managed.) But the contract system seemed to be the better of the two, contrary, evidently, to what his friend had led him to expect. From this one instance, he made a daring logical leap:

> How to reconcile then, what I *saw* with what I *read*?—the inconsistency is apparent, but not real. My friend had taken his theory from theory. The general horror had been imbibed from general horror: and the particular example on the other side did not seem sufficient to countervail the general voice. What was taken for granted was the general rule: what was visible passed for no more than an exception.[53]

But in fact it was Bentham who took his "theory from theory"; he did not consider that what was visible to him (that is, his sole visit to a contract establishment, admittedly chosen for its "good management") could indeed be an exception. Instead he used this single incident to bolster an argument that was framed chiefly on *a priori* grounds. His reasoning was logical and forcibly expressed, but it was quite wrong.

"Opinions as to the advisability of farming the Poor," remarks a distinguished student of the subject, "varied according to whether the writer in question had regard to the theoretical advantages to be derived from it, or to the practical results which ensued."[54] For there is ample evidence of widespread abuses of the poor under contractors. The practice of contracting for children has already been mentioned, although, with no evidence to the contrary, it is perfectly possible that Bentham did not consider this an abuse: he certainly had nothing in principle against putting even three-year-olds to work.

By many accounts, the scene of contract workhouses was often one of unmitigated wretchedness. With the work of the poor so universally unprofitable, the only chance of profit lay in minimizing the cost of food, clothing, etc. Interest and Duty did not coincide. Gross overcrowding, filthiness, and ill health were commonplaces. In one instance several years after a contract began, most of the poor had died or escaped. Overseers inspecting the site found only eight paupers remaining "and those mostly children who bore evident marks of injury from disease and hunger; one of the elopers was said to have perished under a haystack."[55] This was no "hobgoblin" cribbed from Richard Burn, and there is no reason to doubt the judgment of Dorothy Marshall that where "the contract system of managing the poor was in vogue, the results appear to have been disastrous for the poor."[56] It was simply not true that the watchfulness of the "public eye" was sufficient to deter abuses. Vigilance hardly even existed. Bentham might have known (since he was so fond of the phrase) that everybody's business was nobody's business. Justices (who had the right to authorize the contract) did occasionally intervene on behalf of mistreated paupers, but this did not amount to an effective system of inspection. One must conclude that, since it suited Bentham's interest to paint the contract system in glowing colors, he contented himself with arguments about what he believed ought to be true without bothering to find out what was true. Bentham the rationalist had triumphed over Bentham the empiricist.

3. Old Objections, New Replies

The difficulties surrounding the issue of farming the poor were one high hurdle Bentham had to clear, but there was yet a higher one. This obstacle lay in objections made nearly a century before—by Daniel Defoe—to a project quite similar to the one now receiving so ardent a defense. To review this difficulty we need to turn the clock back to the last decade of the seventeenth century.

In the year 1695, a Bristol merchant, John Cary, published a scheme (John Locke, as the Webbs remark, thought his pamphlet "the best discourse I have ever read upon that subject")[57] to eliminate beggary, equalize the rates among the parishes of his city, and (no small matter) reduce the cost of poor relief. For this he proposed a single Poor Law Authority for the entire city. This new body would build and operate a workhouse or hospital responsible for caring for the old and feeble and setting the able-bodied to work. (In 1782 this plan found an echo in Thomas Gilbert's proposals for incorporating parishes for the sake of erecting a common workhouse.)[58]

Two years later, John Locke's *Report* for the Board of Trade on the "Relief and Employment of the Poor" attacked many of the same problems dealt with by Cary's pamphlet. The cost of poor relief was a "growing burden," but the cause proceeded neither from lack of provisions nor from the want of employment for the poor ("God has blessed these times with plenty not less than the former") but from the "relaxation of discipline and corruption of morals." As a remedial policy Locke suggested a general roundup (as we will see, Bentham, like Count Rumford in Munich, urged his own variation on the roundup theme) of all males aged fifteen to forty-nine found in Maritime counties begging without a pass: they were to be kept at hard labor in port until "some of His Majesty's ships . . . give an opportunity of putting them on board, where they shall serve three years under strict discipline."[59] Older and disabled beggars and those over fourteen found illicitly begging in inland counties were to be consigned to Houses of Correction for a like period. But Locke thought the House of Correction too good for the indigent seeking relief on the rates. They were too commodious, too lacking in discipline to satisfy the celebrated author of *An Essay Concerning Human Understanding*. Instead he favored a form of what became the eighteenth-century practice of "contracting for the whole poor": a master would be paid a *per diem* allowance for each able-bodied male, from whom he could attempt to profit by extracting maximum labor. The same treatment would be given women and children beggars, except that the children would be "soundly whipped."[60] For idle and able-bodied men not seeking relief, Locke had something different in store; they were to be employed "out of doors" by local employers who would be obliged to hire them, but at less than the usual rate—it was a sort of early "labor rate" system, which, as the Webbs remark, was reinvented in the early nineteenth century.[61]

This left only the less-than-able-bodied to be accounted for. Locke was sure that at least some of the expense for their maintenance could be recouped, and to that end he divined a system of "working schools," one in every parish, eking out from their members (who included children) what produce they could. After all, Locke calculated, if a hundred thousand otherwise barren paupers could be made to earn but a penny a day, "this would gain to England £130,000 per annum."[62] (We will see how similar a thought later struck Bentham.)

Locke's ideas fell on fertile ground among his audience. Plans were made to form a joint-stock company that would employ the poor, so that hereafter they would not only earn their keep but also make a profit for the company's investors. In 1698 a Parliamentary bill for such a company was unsuccessful; but by 1704 four bills were pending, one of which, as the Webbs put it, "introduced by the great capitalist *entrepreneur* of the day, Sir Humphrey Mackworth, met with almost universal acceptance, and in the following session actually passed, with great applause, through all its stages in the House of Commons."[63]

It was this bill that was killed by the toxic arguments of Daniel Defoe in *Giving Alms no Charity*—the title continued, *And Employing the Poor*

a Grievance to the Nation. We saw earlier how Defoe defended his proposition that ample work was available to the poor who would but seek it, for
otherwise why weren't the armed forces overrun with new recruits?[64] But
Defoe made a further argument, a poison more deadly by far to a would-
be company like Mackworth's, and if to Mackworth's, why not to Bentham's? In a word, Defoe predicted that "public" local manufactories
would ruin private competitors. And not only that, for the industrious and
deserving poor would be thrown out of work in the bargain:

> I think therefore, with submission, to erect Manufactories in every
> Town to transpose the Manufactures from the settled places into pri-
> vate Parishes and Corporations, ... must be ruinous to the Manufac-
> turers themselves, will turn thousands of Families out of their Employ-
> ments, and take the Bread out of the Mouths of diligent and industrious
> Families to feed Vagrants, Thieves and Beggars, who ought much rather
> to be compell'd, by Legal Methods, to seek that Work which it is plain
> is to be had; and thus this Act will instead of settling and relieving the
> Poor, encrease their Number, and starve the best of them.[65]

This potent argument had not been lost or forgotten by the time Bentham set pen to paper, for anybody could read it in Eden's *State of the
Poor*, and everybody was reading Eden. Bentham himself could hardly
have missed the point during his careful study of these meticulous and
copious researches,[66] and to some extent he answered it directly in *Pauper
Management Improved*, since indemnification was promised for the losses
of existing poor contractors.[67] Although this provision hardly met the
brunt of Defoe's objection, it did attempt to neutralize one obvious group
of potential enemies to the Company. More to the point was another promise—that precautions would be taken against applying the Company's capital to possible monopoly-creating ventures, "pouring into any particular
channel of production so large a proportion of capital and stock of hands
as to overstock the market, and by a *temporary* underselling ruin individual competitors."[68] Later on in the same work, he again sought to reassure
private employers by showing why laborers would not flock to the Company in preference to these employers—which should (to put it mildly) have
gone without saying, given the nature of what he wanted to spring on the
unsuspecting poor of "South Britain"; but, no doubt for safety's sake, he
said it anyway. The Company's paupers would be paid less than on the
outside, and they would lose their liberty. He might have added that they
would also *eat* worse and *live* worse, pauper comforts or no pauper com-

forts: Bentham's "pauper comforts" were not, to understate the case considerably, nearly so comfortable as he made them out to be. The Company's employment, he told his readers, "is but a make-shift—a [last] resort.—*Free* employment is the primary and preferable object: . . . preferable as to individual employers, because profit on their part goes along with it. . . ."[69]

This genuflection in the direction of private profit raises two related questions. First, for whose benefit was the plan primarily intended—for the paupers themselves or for others? Second, was Bentham's desire to placate private employers responsible for the very nature of his proposed reforms: might it, as one critic has suggested, have "contributed to the unique character and focus of the plan?"[70]

The answer to the first question is that more than a little doubt can be cast on the notion that Bentham saw the indigent as the foremost beneficiaries of the Company's creation. That beggars cannot be so considered there can be no doubt at all. "After all," Bentham wrote in a manuscript deliberately withheld from publication, "in proposing compulsion in this instance it is not for the benefit of the individuals to be subjected to it, that I propose it."[71] And the fact is, of course, that, however much it might be disguised or evaded, the interest of the indigent in care and comfort was potentially in direct conflict with the Company's interest in profit. The purpose of the rules for managing "Working Hands," for example, was described this way: "*Motives: End* view,—the extraction of labour to as great a value as may be" consistent with health, religion, and "customary relaxation."[72] In his remarks on "pauper comforts," Bentham said that economy is "but the *means*" to "true charity,"[73] but the entire system gave the lie to this remark. In the description of pauper education, for instance, he admitted that the pauper's benefit was not all he had in mind. The end of education is no different than the end of life, that is, wellbeing: "The wellbeing here in question is, partly that of the individual to be educated, partly that of the parties at whose expense, and by whose care, he is to be educated—viz. the proposed Company."[74] In his unpublished writings, Bentham identified the group which would chiefly benefit from the plan and which ought, therefore, to bear the brunt of initial finance. "It is for the reliable class of inhabitants,"—the ratepayers—"whose relief the system has in view: theirs is to be the principal benefit, theirs ought accordingly to be the burthen."[75] Those who risked their money in the new venture risked it "with an eye to their own profit."[76] Furthermore, in seeking the principal beneficiary of the system, we might recall the utilitarian consequences cited earlier for the "reliable classes" of a profitable National Charity Company:

> But in proportion as a saving is made in the amount of the Poor Rates, so much money is left free in the hands of the rateable inhabitants to be spent in the gratification of their own desires of all kinds, instead of taken from them to be spent in the satisfactions of the necessary desires of other people: viz: the indigent poor. . . . [77]

Finally, if the poor's benefit were Bentham's first consideration, why imprison them at all? Certainly, once he had the poor in his grasp, he was going to reform them; but even though moral reform was an essential part of life in poor-Panopticons, profit for the "reliable classes" and not reform of the unreliable stood in the forefront of the rationale for setting them up in the first place: it was the real reason for abolishing home provision. Relief at home was inferior "considered in respect of the very capacity of being made so far subservient to the purpose of economy as to afford a profit."[78] And again, "Under the Home-Provision System, all chance of deriving a profit from the head of any employment being plainly out of the question, no attempt to give birth to any such profit is made."[79]

In Bentham's defense, it should be said that his desire to protect the poor from a variety of abuses was quite genuine: witness his pamphlets *Truth versus Ashurst* and *A Protest Against Law Taxes*, both of which were composed only a few years before the birth of the National Charity Company. In the tracts on Poor Law reform he was careful to show how the poor were to be protected. For one thing, the venerated old English tradition of whipping many classes of paupers was for the most part to be done away with.[80] And Panopticon paupers had the right to register their complaints against Company officials (as well as fellow inmates) in a book provided for the purpose; the book would be regularly scrutinized by inspectors.[81] Nor was verbal abuse to be tolerated. "No term of abuse or vulgar reproach," Bentham wrote, "such a rascal, villain, dog, fool, Blockhead, etc. etc. to be used by any officer in speaking of much less in speaking to any pauper."[82] The end to the official oppressions that so often characterized the eighteenth-century workhouse was one of the "comforts" to which the paupers could look forward.[83]

On the other hand, whenever the interests, desires, or comforts of the poor conflicted with the Company's paramount purpose—profit—those interests, desires, and comforts were consistently sacrificed. The only limiting condition was paupers' health. Sleep would be cut to a minimum to enhance working hours, and the food would be so coarse and undesirable that Bentham actually listed as a pauper "comfort" the prospect of its improvement.[84] Palatable food might have provided the poor with a real comfort, but palatable food would cost more money; and when Bentham heard the words "increased costs," he reached for his gun. Consider, for example, another pauper "comfort," the possibility of living outside Panopticon, beyond the everlasting gaze of the representatives of the "reliable classes." A few categories of trusted inmates would be allowed to live in "outlying cottages" on the House grounds. *There* was a real comfort. But here again the question of profit was the deciding factor, for there would be no "outlying cottages" without "an assurance of a correspondent number of inhabitants, so circumstanced, as that they can be made to do as much work in value, *out* of the main building as *in* it."[85] It appears, therefore, that any argument that the poor were intended as the primary beneficiaries of Bentham's system collapses under the weight of demonstrable evidence.

The other question, whether the desire to conciliate private employers contributed in any essential respect to the character of the plan, is more complex. More than likely it did not. Bentham was not a socialist; he had no wish to intervene in free-market competition. He had adhered to Adam Smith from the first dawn of *The Wealth of Nations* (1776). He did criticize the great man, but his criticisms were never radical or sweeping; he merely dotted this "i" or crossed that "t." Smith was wrong, Bentham believed, in his condemnation of usury, and so Bentham wrote his *Defence of Usury* (1787); but it was written as a series of letters to Smith himself in the manner of a reproving disciple and not like a son hell-bent on patricide. When shortly before his death the old man gave his blessing to the book, Bentham was thrilled.[86] It therefore seems unnecessary to avail oneself of the conciliation of private interests to account for the fundamental nature of the plan, especially its separation from the market economy, though such conciliation did figure in its defense and in some of its details.

Another point is more far-reaching. If direct interference in the market economy was unwarranted, one implication was that the economy of the National Charity Company would have to be, so to speak, 'outside' it. There was a further reason for the isolation of the Company from the market economy. The poor were the frail leaves that shook and fell with every wind of economic change. One purpose of poor relief was to shield the propertyless from personal catastrophe amid the vicissitudes of the market. To accomplish this, the vehicle of their succor, the Company, would itself have to be insulated from economic instability. For the poor, the Company was to be the limiting condition of their economic insecurity. Leaving aside the question of profitability, the primordial exigency of carving out from market society a sector freed of its suzerainty was the single most important determinant of Bentham's plan. In his hands the Welfare State is an economy within an economy.

4. The Functions of the Pauper State

It was also a state within a state. So much is implied in the initial discussion in *Pauper Management Improved* of "political arrangements": the arrangements are very much like a constitution. The same idea is implied in the description of the Company's provinces as an internal colony. "*Colonize at home*," Bentham wrote, "—is an advise I have seen somewhere given in print. To adopt the plan in question would really be—to *colonize at home*."[87] Internal colonies, he argued, have a number of advantages over foreign ones, which have the unpleasant propensity of setting up for themselves and siding with enemies. (His readers did not have to be students of Thucydides to need reminding of *that*.) The internal colonies he had in mind would "exist for ever in a state of natural and unavoidable and unregretted dependence"—rather like South African "homelands" (except for the "unregretted dependence"), an island chain, an archipelago, spread out across England and Wales. More than that, the internal colony, instead of spending the lives and treasure of the mother country, created lives and treasure for its benefit.[88] In fact to Bentham the very life of a well-disciplined worker was *itself* a treasure: it *created wealth*. That is why he called apprentices "living treasures." How fitting it is to analogize the childlike status of the poor in this Welfare State to a colony–mother country relationship!

That the National Charity Company was a state within a state is further suggested by a remark that Bentham made about idleness under its aegis. It was, he said, "treason in this little commonwealth."[89] Bentham's attentive reader Dumont caught the drift of things as well. In the course of his "Memoire et observations sur l'administration des pauvres, d'après un ouvrage de Bentham,"[90] he makes the following observation: "Il est difficile de se faire une juste idée de toutes les resources que presente l'inspection centrale pour maintenir dans *ce petit état* les regles. . . ."[91] And if this is not evidence enough, we have Bentham's explicit words. "Saving the supreme authority of the country," he said in an unpublished manuscript, "the establishment is itself a state. *Imperium in imperio*, which *sub imperio* does no harm."[92]

This state within a state had a number of subterranean functions. One of them was that this particular poor reform self-consciously tried to divide paupers amongst themselves in order to rule them. To Bentham the lower orders were a dangerous and unruly mob to be dealt with cautiously; "To whose lot so ever it may fall to be the harbinger of forced economy in this perilous time, it concerns him to be well armed. . . ." If a respected minister were in the vanguard, "a body of Dragoon" had better be close behind; "the multitude," he said, is "nothing-taught," "all-knowing," and "never-reflecting." He sarcastically added that it was by the wisdom of the "always patient multitude" that "everything ought to be ordered"; the "politics of the day" was merely another way of saying "the state of political warfare."[93]

It is instructive to compare this hostile and suspicious frame of mind with the attitude of the young Bentham twenty years earlier during another revolutionary crisis. Then it was a matter of conciliating the people, not manipulating them. Here is Bentham in November of 1776 pleading his case for the establishment of a government newspaper:

> It would probably have a good effect to communicate through this channel such anecdotes respecting his Majesty as would . . . make his Majesty's personal character better known [than] it is at present: anecdotes respecting the manner in which he spends his time, his attention to business, his unremitting industry, his extensive knowledge [and] his domestic felicity. . . . Nothing could contribute more powerfully to conciliate by degrees the affections of the people, and dissipate those prejudices against his Majesty's conduct which have been instilled with such malignant industry.[94]

In the "perilous times" of 1796, the earlier policy of candor and conciliation was hardly dreamt of, much less advocated. Placed in its stead was the devious stratagem of divide and rule. Existing divisions in the ranks of the lower classes could be exploited and others created; and all the while the upper classes had better join in a common front. One means lay in adopting a unitary system for dealing with the poor. The system of unity and the system of divided authority reminded Bentham of "the parable of the Faggots—divided, they become a prey to the lawless classes who break and destroy the discipline of them one by one: united they would have mastered the adversary without difficulty, [in] spite of his utmost efforts."[95]

Another method of increasing control over the poor involved gradually undermining their own independent associations, the Friendly Societies, and replacing their influence with the guiding hand of the National Charity Company's "frugality banks." Friendly Societies were nothing but "the multitudinous and unbridled concourse of rough and uncultivated minds," and they were far too democratic: "democracy is no more of the essence of frugality, than it is of prudence, tranquility, or science."[96] Such popular institutions were dangerous; they were breeding grounds for plots and discontents. Bentham listed several of their "collateral mischiefs" "from all which, by the management of the proposed Company, the business would be cleared." Besides their drunkenness, dissipation, disagreements, and quarrels, they were prone to "[c]ombinations for sinister purposes . . . such as a rise of wages, (always in favour of occupations already overpaid,) or diminution of working hours." A further "inconvenience" more relevant to our theme was the propensity in Friendly Societies to combinations "for sinister purposes of a *public* nature—the raging malady of the times."[97]

Subverting the Friendly Societies was one aspect of Bentham's strategy; co-opting them was another. Their members were not down and out; they were self-maintaining poor, quite capable of political resistance. The dregs of the lowest classes were not to be feared—"From the paupers themselves much is not to be apprehended in the way of violence." "Debility," he went on, "is among the essential [characteristics] of the vast majority of the class."[98] But what was to be feared was the "force of sympathy" of the independent poor. To co-opt them Bentham hit on the scheme of inducing the Friendly Societies to help finance the National Charity Company. Gaining "so large and powerful [a] part of the people on the side of the Company" was an object "neither hopeless nor useless"; the only group capable of thwarting the entire project would be efficiently and effectively disharmed.[99]

The success of the scheme would create an artificial division among the poor, but there were in Bentham's opinion already existing natural divisions waiting to be exploited. Divide the poor, and you become their master: "Neither to the burthensome Poor nor to such part of the self-maintaining Poor as appear particularly exposed to the danger of falling into that class," he argued, "are the numbers of the Friendly Societies bound by any particular tie of sympathy." They could be detached from the pauper class because the natural effect of their situation in the community "would rather be to look down with an air of superiority upon other individuals of the labouring class"; and their natural disposition vis-à-vis these inferiors was "to exercise authority over them rather than join with them in opposition to authority."[100] Bentham justified his policy of divide and conquer as nothing more than honorable prudence. "Disunion" for the purpose of exercising violence was "profligacy"; but "division for the purpose of averting violence is prudence. In a policy which has no other object than the preservation of good order, good economy, peace and justice there is no place either for secrecy or for shame."[101] This implied, obviously, that Bentham suspected some of his readers might find a place both for secrecy and for shame: neither was unwarranted.

Bentham felt reasonably confident that the stratagem just outlined would be effective, but he admitted that he was not completely sure. One thing bothered him: the havoc that contingency can wreak on the most carefully contrived plans. In this case, the element of chance stemmed from the unreliability of emotion, especially the emotions of the lower classes. Even though the "natural leaning" of the independent poor ("this powerful class") would be on the side of the proposed plan, both interest and affection "may be overpowered by sudden storms of passion excited by prejudice." "Every thing," he said, "is caprice as in cards. . . ." Nevertheless, there was hope in this political game of chance as in any other—". . . there [is] the favoured prospect of success from the industry of a skilled player."[102]

Bentham invented one final means for subduing the poor—subduing them gently, imperceptibly, without their even becoming aware of it. In a word, this means was "peoples' capitalism." The term was not Bentham's, but he did develop the idea behind it a century and a half before it was re-invented by American Business. At the heart of this notion lies the desire to secure the loyalty of the relatively poor by inducing the feeling among them that they partake of certain benefits, when in reality these benefits are virtually nonexistent. With revolutionary ideas in the air, securing the loyalty of the lower classes was no matter for complacency. "The state of the present times," Bentham urged, "suggests the policy of giving to the lower classes a more palpable interest in the existence of government itself."[103] To accomplish this, he hit on the device of selling small shares in the new Company among the independent poor. In *Pauper Management Improved*, he explained why shares in the Company should be sold as cheaply as £5 or £10, though for most of the poor this would be a very considerable sum. Frugality among the poor would be encouraged, and satisfaction in participating in a "work of beneficience" would be diffused more extensively than if shares were more expensive. More importantly, "*content*" would be promoted "by giving, to the frugal among the self-maintaining poor, an interest in the economical maintenance and due employment of the burthensome poor." Nor was that all, for content would promote "*national quiet*" "by giving to some of the classes most disposed to turbulence, an interest in the prosperity of the proposed company, and of the government under which it acts. . . ."[104] One marvels at the ingenuity of the scheme: the poor would not be bought-off on the cheap; on the contrary, *they would buy their own loyalty themselves.*

The same argument reappeared a few years later in Bentham's "Abstract . . . of a Tract Intituled Circulating Annuities"(1800).[105] The annuities, a sort of paper money, would be sold in very small denominations so that the means would be available to "the least opulent and most numerous class of individuals (Friendly Societies included)—in a word, to the great bulk of the community—the means of placing out *small hoards*, however minute." One collateral advantage was the creation "on the part of the *lower* orders . . . [of] a fresh and more palpable interest in the support of that government, on the tranquility of which . . . their property will depend."[106] Indeed, Bentham set aside a separate chapter to discuss the "Constitutional Advantages" of his proposition. He pointed out that one of the effects of the existence of the national debt in its early stages "was the security it afforded to the old established constitution, by engaging the *purses* and the *affections* of the moneyed *interest* in the service and support of the new-established government." The advantage of converting that debt into circulating annuities would be "the securing to the constitution and government now grown into one, the support of what may be called the *little moneyed* interest by the same powerful tie."[107] As in 1797, it was a question of securing the political loyalty of the poor, for they might otherwise succumb to the potentially fatal political disease of revolutionary inflammation. "The body *politic*," he warned his readers, "not less than the body *natural* is subject to constitutional diseases." Tyranny may once have been the greatest danger, but now anarchy was the foremost peril: ". . . the danger *now is* from the great multitude: in respect of the disposition to unruliness which has been, and continues to be, propagated, with but too much success, among the lower orders—among those (let it never be out of mind) of whom is composed the vast majority of the people."[108] Moreover, the benefit of securing loyalty need not be confined to Great Britain. Certainly no harm would be done if this plan were extended to the lazy, drunken, turbulent Irish.[109] In fact, there was no reason not to extend it to the entire Empire: "From the Zemindar to the Ryot," that is, from the landowner to the landless tenant-farming peasant, "every Hindoo, every Mussulman who possessed *this* money . . . might thus, and without impeachment of probity be converted into a pensioner of the British government." Here was an exciting prospect, since, Bentham concluded, for "a premium equal to the interest the paper yields, he would be underwriting—perpetually underwriting—to the amount of the principal, the security of the Empire."[110]

The means to divide the poor in order to rule them which we have been discussing have so far all involved detaching the sympathies of the independent poor from the dependent poor. But Bentham's proposals also included a way in which the dependent poor, ensconced in poor-Panopticons, might be used against such of the lower orders as remained free, should the latter group fall prey to the seductive ideas wafting their way across the English Channel (or to some momentary passion). To this end, those pauper "apprentices" fit for military duty could be formed into a domestic militia available "as an eligible and universally present *succedaneum* to the less popular assistance of the regular force, against casual tumults, the result of *sudden* and *partial* discontents." This "collateral benefit" ("of a most important nature") could be gained "without effort—without disbursement—without expense to anybody"; and there was the added advantage that once the pauper children had graduated from these Panopticon "schools of industry" and diffused themselves into the general population, they would "form an ample fund of disciplined force, ever ready in the hour of exigency." Nor was such free service an unjust burden even when it was "irksome" and "the dangers ever so serious," since the apprentices were "indebted to public charity, all of them for maintenance, and education, many of them for life itself" and might therefore "literally be termed the *foster-children of the country*."[111]

This latter argument is very strange. The pauper children were the backbone of Bentham's claim that the Company could turn a profit: they themselves would receive only a small portion of the value of their labor. They would pay dearly for this so-called "charity"; and anyway, their entitlement to maintenance as paupers was a matter of legal right, part of their birthright as Englishmen, the exercise of which had hitherto created no greater legal obligation than if the Poor Laws had never been enacted. Furthermore, if the obligation to serve in a 'home guard' continued after release from the Company—Bentham is not precise on this point, but his language ("ever ready in the hour of exigency") suggests that it would continue—then these "foster-children of the country" would be placed in the position of never being allowed to grow up; they could never achieve the status of the ordinary citizen.

Finally, one striking aspect of the militia proposal is Bentham's openness in describing how the pauper's physical separation from the self-maintaining poor could be used to advantage. Here 'divide and rule' was quite literal. The powerlessness of the indigent could be used to inhibit the exchange of dangerous ideas among them and to prevent the creation of associations considered imprudent or subversive by Company and government: "Sequestered from the world at large," Bentham wrote in *Pauper Management Improved,*

> the intercourse, as between house and house, written as well as personal, being altogether at the Company's command, (that is, through the Company at the command of Government . . .) no existing body of military force could be equally proof against seductions and combinations.[112]

Thus divided amongst themselves, the poor—the "vast majority" of English men and women—would find successful revolt well-nigh impossible.

6

The National Charity Company: Social Control in an Alternative Economy

The poor appeared to Jeremy Bentham in various guises. They appeared as children to be led and reared, and, once they were reformed, as apostolic messengers, as bearers of the "good news" of Utilitarian salvation; they appeared as a dangerous political force to be assuaged and pacified, as mouths to be fed, as bodies to be "mustered," and as wild, migratory animals to be corralled and tamed. But before all else, Bentham saw them as economic beings, not in their capacity as consumers, but in their capacity as *producers*; and as we turn to a discussion of the National Charity Company as an economy within an economy, this primary *persona* should be borne in mind. For if he usually considered mankind as sentient beings, as capable of pleasure and pain, when he thought of poverty, or rather of indigence, he placed its victims in a special category.

As he described the indigent in *Pauper Management Improved*, they were "that part of the national live stock which has no feathers to it and walks with two legs."[1] Because they walked upon two feet, two hands were free for useful labor. To Bentham the hands of the pauper were less the extensions of his body than his body was the extension of his hands. "People" produce and consume; hands only produce. Thus the categories of his "Table of Cases Calling for Relief" were classes of "hands." There were insane hands, imperfect hands, feeble hands, ruptured ("tender") hands, as well as out-of-place hands, stigmatized hands, lazy hands, unchaste hands, and so on.[2] He did not use the term "hands" either casually or unconsciously. On the contrary, he was at pains to tell his readers not only that he had quite deliberately *chosen* the word to characterize the poor but also *why* he had chosen it. A special "observation" was attached to the first use of "hands" in the "Table of Cases" and preceded by a "Nota Bene": "The word Hands is chosen as bearing reference to *Employment*, serving thereby to point the attention to the consideration of the *Employments*, to which the persons thus characterized may respectively be competent or incompetent."[3] The emphasis is Bentham's.

1. An Alternative Economy

There is a variety of evidence in both published and unpublished sources to show that Bentham intended these "hands" to make a separate economy of their own. An economy independent of the fluctuations of the market could alone guarantee the stability of the National Charity Company. Surely the well-being of the Company ought never to depend on anything so contingent as *fashion*. The failure of industries, he pointed out, was often the failure of the fashion to which they are indebted for their several employments;[4] consequently he stipulated that one rule for choosing an employment for the Company's poor should be "that it include no business dependent on fashion in respect of the demand for the produce."[5] Thus, producing items for export was banned since they would be "in most instances dependent on fashion" as well as on the whims of foreign governments, the state of navigation, and so on.[6] And home markets could be just as fickle: "In many articles purchase is so much governed by fancy, that many an article may be unfit for sale" by flaws which do not in the least determine its value in use.[7] Contingency would be eliminated within the domain of the Company by strict adherence to the crucial distinction between market value and use value. "In the world at large," he wrote, "fashion and caprice bear sovereign sway: here their authority is utterly disclaimed. Whatever use can be drawn from any article will certainly be drawn from it." If value in use was the only value depended upon, "the value in exchange would be a matter of indifference."[8] Security from the market could then be complete—"The value of the employment which the Company furnishes consists in its *certainty*. . . . Uncertainty is the essence of all free employment—of all employment offered by individuals."[9]

To secure the economic moorings of the Company against the hazards of the market, Bentham invented a principle which he described as "another of my sheet anchors": the "principle of self-supply."[10] By filling its every need through its own production, the pauper economy effectively shielded itself from the unknown fortunes of the business cycle; for unlike exchange value, use value was incapable "of being destroyed or reduced by glut, competition, stagnation, change of fashion, war or other causes."[11] What "self-supply" meant was that the market (that is, the demand for goods) could be known in advance and more or less kept under control: "self-supply," Bentham said, "secures a market, and a market which for articles of any other destination might be precarious."[12] Or again: "Under the principle of self-supply neither *market*, i.e. *demand*, nor capacity of production are exposed to failure."[13] Moreover, with so large an interlocking pauper economy, the advantages of the division of labor could be exploited to the hilt; each "House of Industry" might be occupied exclusively with some particular branch of production. (Obviously the current system of what Bentham called "divided authority" made this impossible.)[14]

A relatively unregulated market economy, furthermore, gave rise to a related set of difficulties which made a separate, completely controlled economy even more attractive. The worst of these was the unemployment created by depressions in the business cycle and by less general causes. Bentham invented special categories for those who found themselves without employment through no fault of their own. "Stagnation hands" could be found in every quarter, and in his *Table of Cases Calling for Relief*, he listed every conceivable variety. Some idleness, like that of gardeners during a prolonged frost, or of disbanded soldiers after the conclusion of a war, had little direct connection with market forces; but other unemployment did. One class of "casual stagnation hands," as Bentham called them, were manufacturing laborers thrown out of work "in the event of a general stagnation of the Manufacture."[15]

Bentham was among the first European writers to have shown more or less systematically, if not quite intentionally, that the benefits of the release of market forces from medieval restrictions—the abatement of the seventeenth-century flood of royally granted monopolies, the spread of non-guild industries, the opening of foreign markets and the creation of more truly national markets—were not quite everything writers like Adam Smith made them out to be, that is, were not so unalloyed with suffering and mischief as generally advertised. In fact, his manuscripts reveal him to be keenly aware of the dangers inherent in an unregulated industrializing market economy: "In comparison with the mass of indigence that may be generated by stagnation in the line of manufacture," he wrote, "that which can take place in the line of husbandry with the occupations bordering on it, is very inconsiderable." A worker of the "manufacturing class," he continued,

> at least of the class occupied in those sedentary branches of manufacture which alone present themselves in idea upon the mention of the word, is a very helpless animal. When the period of stagnation arrives, it finds in him an unarmed unresisting victim. No fund of unemployment opens to receive him. He drops through mere weakness into the yawning gulph of Out-allowance, or Poor-House idleness.[16]

This description is not far removed from Karl Marx's portrait of the fall of proletarian man from membership in the universal class, the class of the elect, into the abysmal limbo of the "lumpen proletariat." In any case, the possibility of economic "stagnation" was a critical reason why a separate pauper economy insulated from market forces was to Bentham's mind a pressing necessity. Independent local poorhouses could never fulfill the needs of these "helpless animals" in times of real crises—only a *single national system* could be adequate to the task.[17]

Nor ought the policy of that system to be the one now universally adopted by the modern Welfare State, cash payments to the unemployed. Bentham considered it, and, predictably, rejected it. He admitted that if there ought to be a "superannuation fund," it seemed to follow that there ought to be a "stagnation fund" available to all employed persons; but "whether the [benefits] would outweigh the prejudical consequences may appear problematical."[18] Once again, Bentham meditated on the virtues of busyness and on the pitfalls awaiting vacant minds and idle fingers: "Vacancy is a dangerous companion to affluence. Vacancy calls in drunkenness." So long as the unemployed did not starve, "[w]hile hands are unemployed, pockets are better empty perhaps than full. . . . But the permanent fund of employment provided by the company solves this as well as so many other difficulties. . . ."[19] In place of "vacancy," a secure alternate economy could respond by "filling up all the gaps liable to take place in regard to supply of employment by want of indoor employment for bad weather and by want of employment . . . in the intervals between job and job."[20]

If Bentham was unwilling to adopt wholesale the now current policy of unemployment insurance, he nevertheless did travel some distance in its direction. Since industrial stagnation could be such an enormous burden, a restricted "Stagnation Fund" should be created, stocked with funds subtracted weekly from the wages of "manufacturers in general"—the workmen only, not the owners—or at least of those "manufacturers" with weekly incomes above a certain level.[21] Were such funds found unnecessary within a specified time, they would automatically be converted into government-sold "superannuation annuities"; or, if the stagnation funds were needed, the money would go to the Company, and the worker would go to one of its pauper Panopticons, where he would receive not a jot more in benefits than if he had never paid anything, and where his uniform badged him as a public burden. In either case, the money would be gone for the present: the "Stagnation Fund" had the neat effect of skimming off what Bentham called "excess wages."[22] To prevent cheating, payment in kind would be taxed as cash; to forestall idleness and drunkenness, "the stoppage to be made not only upon the daily pay for the days actually employ'd in work but upon what would have been the week's pay supposing every day to be employ'd in work."[23] Sick days were expected, but penalties would be exacted for false certification. Bentham knew full well what these lazy tricksters would be up to!

If periodic depressions were one evil of an industrializing market economy, mechanization, if not exactly an evil, nevertheless led to the same result—unemployment. Now, Bentham was anything but an opponent of mechanization; after all, he was well aware that it was a formidable progenitor of wealth, the most desirable social commodity except for security (wealth was also a great contributor to security) and subsistence. However, the distress produced by mechanization among the displaced was so severe in Bentham's view "as to constitute no inconsiderable drawback upon the advantage." The rumblings of the Luddites (the machine-smashing rioters who flourished between 1811 and 1816) were already in the air: Bentham spoke of the "asperity of opposition flowing from this source," and of "the clamour, the threats, the opposition in every [quarter] produced by the apprehension of a calamity that falls with so severe a pressure upon so large a part of the population." What was required of an alternative economy was not simply secure employment once workmen had been dispossessed of their livelihood by machines, but active retraining in skills in demand for future re-entry onto the market. Otherwise, the "superseded hands" might sink into the "degrading list of pensioned idlers" (idleness was "that deadliest of all enemies to happiness and innocence"), "or into the uncomfortable as well as degrading idleness of an ordinary Poor-House."[24]

Bentham believed that the "superseded hands" would not be the only beneficiaries of industrial re-education; he thought it would help cement "an alliance between wealth and ingenuity." If new inventions threw men out of work, the "unconcerned classes"—the more wealthy and educated— by reason of humanity to those who would suffer and by fear of personal attack from frenzied and desperate nascent proletarians, might decline to invent or to introduce labor-saving devices. If industrial progress were going to be maximized, the upper classes would have to be weaned from their paternalistic concern for the fortunes of their inferiors: employment and re-education by the National Charity Company would soften the plea for humanity, or else weaken its course and give encouragement to the "species of ingenuity in question—improvements tending to the reduction of the quantity of labour employ'd in productive industry."[25] By this, of course, he did not intend a fillip to idleness but rather a spur to mechanization, that is, to economic growth.

The alternative economy of the National Charity Company was premised upon two notions suggested by the "principle of self-supply" and by the need for its stability—notions which served to distinguish it sharply from the market-governed society that surrounded it. One of them was that competition among separate "Houses of Industry" was utterly pernicious and ought to be replaced by a system of cooperation: that was one reason why a single company was preferable to multiple establishments. Bentham's description of economic competition was not unlike Hobbes' portrait of men without the state—it was struggle, it was a form of *fighting*. Even if assistance between independent poorhouses could be expected, "hostility is perhaps as much so"; plans would be different, opinions jarring, "interests continually at variance, or what is to this purpose the same thing, liable to appear so." Each would inevitably deal in the same commodities as the other: "Hence should the goodness of the Economy and the quantum of productive industry rise in them to the wished for height, a *struggle of all against all*: and of all against individual dealers" would eventuate.[26] "Fighting one another" (an alternative word was "struggling"), independent poorhouses would "go on spinning and weaving against one other and the neighbourhood, till spinning and weaving have lost their value."[27]

And so far as they succeeded in producing the goods, "they would be ruined by competition."[28]

Precisely because laissez-faire competition prevailed in the economy at large, its horrors could not be endured in this scept'red isle, this other Eden, demi-paradise, the National Charity Company. Implicitly contradicting Adam Smith, Bentham argued that "progression and all-comprehensive improvement" would follow from "homogeneous constituent parts" directed by a centralized "superintending eye"—the obverse of the model of perfect competition.[29] In short, the order of the day was centralized economic planning. Accordingly, he directed that

> . . . the distribution of the whole mass of employment among the component parts of the collective strength of the system of Industry Houses be performed by *one general authority* extending over the whole system, that is extending in this behalf over the whole kingdom, the choices not being left in this instance . . . to the choice of the local authority of the district.[30]

Having taken command of supply and demand within the pauper economy, a national management could "adjust them to one another with undeviating accuracy";[31] indeed it might be "bound by law" to avoid gluts and deficiencies.[32]

Having repudiated the discordant medley of eighteenth-century Poor Law practices, Bentham proceeded to adhere to the most 'progressive' features of contemporary economic life. The factory system would be substituted for the traditional "putting out" system; an "ample scale principle" would be followed, as would a "whole-sale purchase principle";[33] and the laborer, being a consumer of his own product, would find his work less onerous—"self-advantage will help to sweeten it."[34]

Bentham listed nearly a score of rules to govern what work was to be undertaken by the Company's charges. Some had purely internal reference, and others were directed to the pauper economy's relations with the larger society—we will see in a moment how the two existed in a kind of symbiotic harmony with each other. Three kinds of economic planning can be detected. First there was the internal logistical planning of the work: how many would do what, and where would they do it? Next came the delicate question of what products would be offered for external sale. The pauper economy was, as we have said, meant to be sufficient unto itself for its own needs, but that did not preclude it from producing for the world at large: without a money income, from whence would the Company derive its profits? (True, it was to receive the proceeds from the poor rates, but one must recall that Bentham promised to eliminate them, making the poor pay, and more than pay, their own way). Finally, there was a third sort of planning. This was intended to gear "the industrial education" of the paupers to the needs of the external labor market, and it is here that the symbiosis of the two economies is most evident.

Bentham insisted that planning the work to be undertaken by the Company was an essential aspect of his proposal. "I have elsewhere expatiated on the improvidence of any interference on the part of the legislature in the . . . choice of employment for the hands meant to set to work." He was thinking of his original Panopticon tracts; but the present case was altogether different: "My present proposition is that it would be improvident in the legislature to abstain from such interference." The two positions were not inconsistent, he said, since in the first he was thinking of a single Panopticon, while in the latter it was a question of a "system of establishments covering the whole kingdom."[35]

The degree of control which Bentham sought over the internal arrangements of the Company's work would rival that of many a socialist planner of the last century and a half. There was, for example, the question of the geographical allocation of labor. As we saw before, Adam Smith had excoriated the Act of Settlement for inhibiting the mobility of labor. Bentham remedied this with the flick of a pen, for the Company would simply transfer by administrative order "the transferable part of the stock" to wherever "provision is cheap, or the demand for labour in general, or for a particular species of labour is high."[36] There was also the problem that, if relatively immobile productive capital were to be invested in, it would have to be known with some precision that a certain number of workers would be available in one place for a certain time. Here Bentham suggested dividing the "stock of hands" into those who came and went with relative frequency, those who would stay for longer periods, and the more or less permanent, or "standing stock." Fortunately, the Company was blessed with a prized storehouse of long-term labor—children and youth.[37]

There would, furthermore, have to be criteria for the kinds of employment undertaken (omitting, for the moment, employment which might affect the external market economy). It was obvious, that is, that exclusively outdoor work would be inappropriate; the weather might be inclement,[38] and some would be unsuited to it. Again, unwholesome work ought to be excluded: work was obligatory, and "an obligation to exercise an unwholesome employment in any such way as to bring an habitual ill health is a condemnation to torture and slow death."[39] Nor should work be chosen which would be dependent on a "system" of machinery which might be destroyed or damaged or rendered temporarily unworkable by "awkwardness, negligence, or malice on the part of the workmen." (Malice, it seems, could creep into this "Utopia.") Finally, any employment would be unsatisfactory which required a special skill "or other personal qualification" on the part of the managers.[40]

Secondly, there was the intricate problem of planning that portion of the Company's production that would be sold on the open market. We have already seen that Bentham was anxious, the better to avoid their hostility to the proposed Company, to reinsure private entrepreneurs against the possibility of the Company seeking monopoly power or otherwise misusing its position; and we have also seen how he trembled at the thought of producing anything whose exchange value lived or died at the whim of anything so chameleon-like as fashion.[41]

Bentham therefore adopted as general rules that production which involved appreciable injury to third parties or which involved hazardousness of any kind would be unfit for the National Charity Company. High-profit industries fell under the first stricture, as did those with high wages. An influx of supply into a high-profit industry reduced the price and hence diminished the profit of those whom he alternatively called "managers" and "master manufacturers."[42] It would be highly improper for government (in this case, "government" was the Company) so to enter the market: the effect would be nothing else but a "partial and very oppressive tax"—partial in extent and oppressive in amount. Private competition was another matter; that is what every trader bargains for when he enters the market (". . . nor has John Stiles any more reason to complain of John Nokes on the score of competition, than John Nokes has of John Stiles").[43] Similarly forbidden were articles whose production was likely to increase unemployment or lower wages among independent laborers.[44]

There were other planning considerations as well. Productivity requiring secrecy entailed contingencies that were best avoided, for it is a hazardous market which might disappear as soon as rival producers are introduced into the mysteries. The same prophylactic measure applied with equal force to production which might become mechanized (and therefore require large transfusions of public capital to maintain economic health), to products for which there was "extraordinary hazard" in finding markets or in maintaining the products in a condition fit for sale, and to articles whose fabri-

cation involved great skill.[45] Furthermore, it was a matter of simple prudence that even if all these conditions were met, and even if every class of
pauper could aid in proposed production, no "one species of employment"
should "occupy the whole strength of the system of Industry Houses":
what if the market failed?[46]

The final species of economic planning in which Bentham found himself
engaged is perhaps most important, for one sees in it how the controlled
pauper economy, which we have characterized as a predominantly but not
entirely separate entity, sought to come to the aid of market forces, to involve itself in the market's difficulties. That is, it attempted to push the
external market economy towards the Smithian model of perfect competition, all the while maintaining the pose of non-intervention. Like Franklin
Roosevelt, Bentham tried to make capitalism *work*.

Bentham proposed to embark upon the business of training workers: he
would process and package them, and send them out to the market for sale.
But in what trade should they be trained? As usual, several rules were drawn
up, but difficulties inevitably presented themselves. There were, he said, but
two directly influencing causes by which the price of labor ("the source of
all commodities") can be changed, namely, supply and demand. Increase
the supply of labor, and the price drops. If the Company planned unwisely,
in other words, it would injure the very souls (or rather "hands") it attempted to benefit. He mentioned one alleviating "counter cause," the introduction of fresh capital into the industry now glutted with labor. "But
if no such new stock of capital accompanies the sudden accession to the
stock of proffered labour, then the reduction in the sum total of the wages
of labour is inevitable."[47] Consequently, training should be avoided in occupations which appeared to be "surcharged already," where the rate of
wages "comes under the head of barely living wages, still less if it comes
under the head of less than living wages." On the other hand, where wages
are far in excess of subsistence, in Bentham's view (as we know) an increment in labor yields no legitimate grievance; and where the market is relatively even in wages, then, clearly, the proper policy is an evenhanded disbursement of new labor.[48]

How Bentham proposed to predict future markets for the training of
apprentices is anyone's guess; the truth seems to be that he never specifically thought of the matter. Nevertheless, one of his more striking suggestions was geared to easing the difficulties arising from a changing labor
market. Thus, the "employment mixing principle" dictated that no one be
possessed of one skill only; at least two trades, perhaps more, would be

taught so that the pauper could adjust to "every fluctuation which the demand in relation to the produce of labour seems likely to experience."[49] An instance was illustrated in Bentham's scheme to make the Company the foremost defense contractor in the land. In wartime, when labor was scarce and ships were sorely needed, the Company, having educated part of its force in the art of shipbuilding, would be prepared to sell vessels to the government (at a high profit); but when peace broke out, and disbanded soldiers flooded the labor market, the Company's workers would revert to peacetime trades.[50] But—and here was the rub—they would forever retain their shipbuilding skills and could be called upon during future exigencies. Nobody else, he pointed out triumphantly, could afford to inculcate "two or three distinct and unconnected trades"; only the public "may take this liberty with its own children" who were indebted to it for maintenance, for education, and even for life itself. A force of workers with multiple skills, he said, "is an advantage altogether peculiar to the proposed plan:— and surely it is no light one."[51] Small wonder that Bentham repeatedly referred to his plan as a "*system* of employment."[52]

Working hand-in-hand with these symbiotic arrangements between the planned and the unplanned economies was a novel device: a public employment bureau in the guise of a newspaper. Bentham spoke of an "immense mass of private distress and public loss" of "vast and unmeasurable" proportions which was ascribable beyond doubt "to no other cause, than want of an adequate channel of intelligence: a cheap and accessible channel of appropriate intelligence" by which employer and laborer could find each other.[53] Deliverance was an "Employment Gazette" consisting of detailed advertisements of those available for hire, Company inmates and independent laborers alike. It would be distributed (or, as Bentham put it, "promulgated") through parishes, being sent to the parish clerk. (In this regard the struggle with contingency was again apparent; the parish clerk was "the only species of public officer whose abode is permanent, and his residence constant and certain.")[54] If the demand was sufficient, there would even be regional editions; and in addition, a "system" of "Employment-Register and Intelligence-Offices" spread at equal distances across the country would supplement its operation.[55] The "Gazette" would also be an aid in controlling the more unruly elements of the lower orders: an "escape list" might be included in the intelligence reported—a list not merely of escapees from the Company's Panopticons, but of *all* escapes, whether from the army and navy, from prisons, from guardians (such as children on the wing from foundling hospitals) or from masters (as in the case of apprentices).[56] As for the advertisements themselves, Bentham drew on his *desiderata* in legal reform; they would, on both sides, "be thrown into settled *forms*; in the framing of which, amplitude of matter and conciseness of expression would be the main objects in view."[57]

The rationale for this enterprise is especially noteworthy. Bentham was at pains to argue that he was attempting no interference in the economic laws so painstakingly set forth by Adam Smith. Now, it was not as if he were unalterably opposed to government interference in the market place, if warranted by exceptional circumstances. In fact, not many years later he proposed setting a legal maximum price for grain.[58] But on this occasion prudence or perhaps hesitation dictated a more anodyne statement of policy. "It is only in some such indirect and remote, in some such gentle and uncoercive way, that government can occupy itself, to any good effect, either in raising, sinking, or steadying prices. . . ." The newspaper and public employment bureaux were confined to indirect means; that is, they did not operate through the "creation of inducements, but by bringing into *notice* inducements which spring of themselves from other sources."[59]

Nevertheless, true as this may have been, it was also true that Company planning in general and the "Employment Gazette" in particular were intended to have very definite effects in the market place. We have already mentioned how the choices of occupations in which to train Company inmates were meant to affect the price of labor in the economy at large. The newspaper was to accomplish the same and more; not only would wages be stabilized and more or less equalized (domestic servants were singled out as being among the "overpaid" classes),[60] but "combinations" by masters or workers to lower or raise wages could be combated as well. Moreover, there was the additional benefit that, in so far as "excessive" wages raised costs, the price of commodities would be reduced or kept from rising.[61] In what must have been one of the first uses of the term, Bentham identified the beneficiaries of this last effect as the "class of *consumers* (that is, everybody)." Only to the "over-paid" would the resulting fall in wages "from a certain point of view" be disadvantageous ("to their immediate feelings it cannot but be galling"); but this view was in fact superficial, since a high wage was not to the interest of uneducated laborers unable to amuse themselves this side of an ale-house. They drank it up and ruined themselves.[62]

Finally, the facilities of the "Industry Houses" interlocked with the advertising newspaper to form a single system whose purpose was to increase the mobility of labor for the unregulated market. *System* is the word, for it is the one which Bentham uses over and over again. Its import lay in this, that (in Bentham's work) it conveys the idea of knitting together what would otherwise be disparate and unrelated. This is a theme to which we will return presently. Here, Bentham described how the "universally extensive system of intelligence with regard to employment, and the system of cheap-conveyance" which the Company provided as it threw open the doors of Panopticon in its role as "Poor-man's Inn" would "co-operate with each other"; the single laborer might be a "self-conveying animal," but an entire family was in practice immobile.[63] Once again, in aiding labor mobility, the separate, controlled, and planned economy found within the walls of the National Charity Company came to the aid of the marketplace.

2. E Pluribus Unum: The Maximization of Labor

Interlarded amongst the many hundreds of pages of Bentham's writings on the Poor Law and its reform was a series of remarks which, taken together amounts to an obsession, an obsession with the maximization of labor—the utilization of every conceivable scintilla of labor power available. In *Pauper Management Improved*, he had written that economy was only of secondary importance compared to charity ("Charity is the *end*; economy but the *means*");[64] but the statement was thoroughly disingenuous: the search for saving every farthing that might be saved and for gathering together every fragment of labor took on a life and purpose of its own. Poor-Panopticon was a sort of social cesspool out of which Bentham would distill a socially useful brew; the "fragments of ability" which when separate were worthless assumed value when united under his direction.

Here at length are his own words: one of his reforms was "gathering together the fragments of ability with regard to labour, in all its degrees, wherever they are to be found";[65] ". . . this stock of refuse labour [is] composed thus of fragments of ability";[66] "In the situation in question employment may be afforded to every fragment of ability, however minute"; ". . . employment might be found, even in agriculture . . . for almost every species of *refuse* labour"; "Largeness of scale of management, thence faculty of finding suitable employment of ability, however circumstanced";[67] "Gathering up the fragments of ability that nothing be lost is an advantage peculiar to establishments constituted upon so large a scale, because it is only in such establishments that such *fractions* can be made up into *integers* . . ."; ". . . collecting all those fragments of . . . ability with regard to profitable labour which otherwise would be, and hitherto in this country for the most part have been, thrown away"; "... collecting of the stock of useful labour which their remaining abilities enable them to yield ...";[68] "For health, for amusement, for preservation from mischief, as well as for profit, let care be taken not to leave in the instance of any individual what ever the smallest fragment of ability unemploy'd";[69] and, finally, to complete this repetitious cycle where it began, "gathering together the fragments of ability with regard to labour, wherever they are to be found."[70]

Added to this obsession with gathering "fragments" of labor was a similar fetish-like concern with exploiting them to the hilt: "... not a particle of time," Bentham wrote, "shall remain necessarily unemploy'd";[71] and therefore he laid down as one of his rules of management the "all employing principle." "Not one in a hundred," he said in the *Annals of Agriculture*, "is absolutely incapable of all employment. Not the motion of a finger—not a step—not a wink—not a whisper—but might be turned to account in the way of profit in a system of such a magnitude."[72] No contrivance was too petty, too absurd, or even too obvious to be overlooked in the search for means to maximize labor. Thus, even pocket money for inmates (presumably for the transient members, "the coming and going stock," for only they could leave the House, and then only on Sundays) could be justified if more labor could be *"extracted"* in return.[73] Hence, too, part of the rationale for having "infirmary huts" on the Company's grounds: *"Saving,* (to the Company,) of *pretended* sickness, and convalescence purposely *protracted.*—Profit by the work."[74] Again, here is Bentham arguing against out-allowances: "Every penny thus bestowed upon an individual from whom ... recompense might have been *extracted,* is so much more bounty money given for idleness. ..."[75] Moreover, special devices were dreamt up to aid in the holy quest. In one instance, he advocated a system which can justly be characterized as Stakonovite: one management principle was the "Peculiar premium, prize giving or competition exciting principle" whose advantages were that, first, by "paying one or a few victors, you get the result of the extra-exertions of the whole multitude of competitors"; and secondly, such competitions combined well with the piece-rate principle which he so enthusiastically endorsed.[76] Or, descending to the absurd, consider the following means of utilizing the labor capacity of the old and feeble or otherwise incapacitated, for the care of infants:

> ... in regard to exercise, ... whether the motion be of the vibrating kind as in a cradle, or of the up and down kind as in the mother's arms

when dancing the child, the attendance of a single individual incapable of almost any other kind of exertion, might (with or without the aid of machinery, either by generating the motion as well as regulating it, or by simply regulating a motion produced by more frugal sources of mechanical power) suffice for a very considerable number of children at once. [77]

With his exuberance for the mechanization of child-rearing, it is a pity that Bentham never heard of the Skinner box.

Besides the old and feeble, where did Bentham believe "fragments of ability" lay awaiting the hand which would gather them for productive use? One category we have already mentioned: children. Bentham argued that much of their capacity would lie fallow unless the coercive hand of government rescued their potential from oblivion. "Children," he wrote, "could not by any private hand be collected from the tenacious however improper possessors of these living treasures, from those who were either in law or in fact in the possession of them, howsoever ill qualified to maintain [them]." [78] It was true that one private charity "collected" (Bentham's word) "young vagabonds of the male sex" and sent them off to sea, but this excluded an entire sex! Granted that girls were able to exchange relief for honest labor, but this left out the unwilling who were "precisely those of whom it is most to be wished that they could be *made to turn their hands to honest labour.*" Similarly, children of convicts were "collected" (again Bentham's term) by another charity (this time including girls); but he believed that their labor merely took work from the hands of the independent poor and was therefore inefficient. [79] On all counts, the Company was superior.

Other categories could be profitably gathered together as well, for the insane, the deaf and dumb, and idiots were all possessed of untapped ability. "I see no reason to despair," Bentham wrote of the insane, "but that the labour that might be *collected* even from an establishment of this sort might be sufficient to defray the annual part of the expence." [80] As for the deaf and dumb, if they were "[c]ollected from all parts of the kingdom and nurtured in a suitable establishment . . . they might in a pecuniary sense be worth to the state from £18,000 to £40,000 or £50,000 a year. . . ." [81]

Added to the mania for collecting every species of labor was a similar drive to save—save labor, save time, save goods, in short, save everything that plays the minutest role in the search for increased efficiency and profit. Take, for instance, the bookkeeping system in each of the Company's houses. Every article to be accounted for should be allocated a separate book since that would save the writing the name of that article as many times as it would occur in a general book.[82] There was also the matter of saving on sheets for bedding—"Stretching the undersheet on hooks, pins, or buttons, will save the quantity usually added for tucking in"; in fact, the bedstages themselves could serve as tables, and the partitions between the beds could be turned horizontally to serve as work tables.[83] Less trivial was the extension of the division of labor (the "Labour-division principle"): time could be saved in "passing from employment to employment, and from place to place." And there was the additional attraction that with each operation simplified "the better the chance it has of being brought within the competence of the different classes of *confined-ability* hands"— the poor who were maimed, the halt and the blind.[84] Instances of this passion for saving run amok could be multiplied virtually endlessly.

Two further examples, however, cannot be ignored. The first had reference to what Bentham described as the advantages of "saving refuse of all kinds on a large scale."[85] The advantages were considerable enough to warrant a distinct management principle—the "Refuse-employing or Save-all principle." On so large a scale as the National Charity Company, there would be, he said, "no species of refuse but has its value: all animal—all vegetable substances—if good for nothing else, are valuable as manure."[86] Taken on its own there is nothing especially unusual about this; but combine it with an incessant striving for orderliness, neatness, discipline, monetary frugality, and saving in every form, and what emerges is a portrait of an excessively disciplined and fetishistically parsimonious social order too obvious to be denied. Here is Bentham, in a passage from his manuscripts entitled "Manure," explaining how various forms of waste would be utilized in poor-Panopticons: at the close of each week, straw from inmates' beds would be spread on "Soil troughs" (latrines); these troughs "with the straw in them" were to be "slid under the seats in the Houses of Office (one for each sex) there to receive the ordure of the next week," after which the next stop would be the compost heap.[87] Thus nothing would be wasted at one end of the alimentary canal, and Bentham sought to secure the same result at the other. Therefore nothing—*nothing*—would be wasted in the kitchen: "Waste water," soapsuds, and vegetable skins all would be utilized—the latter as feed for hogs or rabbits, the former we know not how.[88] Bentham hoped that the use of such refuse would become a national habit.[89]

The other source of frugality to be practiced within the Company's premises that deserves mention concerns the paupers' diet. Bentham took great umbrage at the liberality of the diet often provided at existing poor-houses: why should the dependent poor eat better than the independent poor? The consumption of meat was particularly scandalous, for according to Eden the independent poor ate meat scarcely once a week, while seventy-seven poorhouses he (Eden) examined averaged four days a week.[90] Bentham sought to reverse the situation. In his manuscripts he sometimes called the appropriate management principle the "Neighbour's Fare" principle, but the term did not convey his meaning. Food was to be of the "coarsest and cheapest kind,"[91] by which he meant that paupers' food should not be "neighbour's fare" but *worse* than "neighbour's fare" if possible—care being taken to maintain adequate nourishment. More accurately phrased, it was called the "Suitable-fare" principle.[92] Here was the idea of "less eligibility" at work.

Such were the general principles with respect to diet, but Bentham added important qualifications. As always, he was careful to avoid flying headlong into the face of established expectations: concessions would have to be made for those poorhouse dwellers used to less Spartan fare than he intended to offer. (Private charity might make up the added cost.) The diet for this class might be coarsened (less meat, worse meat, no bread), but only gradually—"time should be allowed to the class in question to accommodate themselves to their new situation."[93] Nevertheless, one ubiquitously present item in the diets of all classes of the poor would be strictly eliminated, expectations or no expectations—alcoholic drink of every kind. ("Small beer," a weaker version of ordinary beer, was a standard part of the eighteenth-century poorhouse diet.) "Fermented liquor" he announced, "is a drink not natural to the human frame." It was not nourishing—Hogarth's "Beer Street" was, after all, only a comparison to "Gin Lane"—it produced vice and misery, and anyway, "[n]o line can be drawn between the use and the abuse.—Some constitutions are kept in a perpetual state of intoxication by small beer."[94] In the case of alcoholics he was surely correct.

Children, on the other hand, having been in some cases born and in any case bred in captivity, had no expectations: past experience could hardly be a source of the pain of privation in either the quantity or quality of food, and the quest for saving could proceed full throttle. Health and strength alone would determine the limits to frugality. "Health being the mere *negation* of *disease*, if there be no disease in any instance . . . the *smallest* allowance is preferable as being the *least expensive*."[95] While this seemed to be involved in no overt contradiction, Bentham had in fact impaled himself on the horns of a dilemma—which would take precedence, the avoidance of hunger and malnutrition or minimum expenditure? This was no trivial question, for he had calculated diet to be two-thirds of the cost of paupers' maintenance. In the case of children, the greatest amount of food he would consider dispensing was all that they wanted, the clear implication being that they would receive less. They would not be famished, but they would not be satisfied either; the negative formula just cited from *Pauper Management Inproved* (the "smallest allowance" in the absence of disease) seems also to imply the same conclusion. But on the other hand, when Bentham in the same work tries to persuade his readers that the plan offered great "comforts" to the poor themselves, he lays it down that the "system of management" in allotting differing amounts of food to children of different ages should "lean to the safe side, that is to the superabundant side"[96] —a flat contradiction of the assertion that the *"smallest allowance is preferable as being the least expensive."* Given the fury, the tenacity of his impulse for "saving," for frugality, and hence profit for the Company at the expense of those unfortunates within its clutches, it can hardly be surprising that he got himself into such difficulties. Indeed, he was obliged to fight back his own guilt. In one breath he said of the "neighbour's-fare" principle, "Wide waft it, ye winds—God speed it among the throng"; but in the next he spoke rather differently:

> I am fighting some of my best and most respected friends—I know it but too well—I cast myself on their forgiveness—Will this obtain it?—I am fighting myself likewise.
> What has been said of Dr Johnson on the subject of infidelity may not be inapplicable to myself on the ground of false humanity. The stronger my propensity to yield to it, the more strenuous my efforts to subdue it.[97]

When the Welfare State seeks a profit, decent food can be devalued as "false humanity."

Bentham did not restrict his efforts to maximize saving to the management of poor-Panopticons. Using them as a vehicle, he sought to radiate their influence to the hinterlands of the independent poor. It was not incidental that the section "Frugality assisted" occupied well over ten percent of the material published in the *Annals*.[98] We saw previously how to some extent he wished the Company's establishments to replace Friendly Societies as insurers. This was even more true of the intended network of "Frugality Banks." The inadequacy of banking facilities for the poor (as distinctly opposed to the rich, for whom there was no such inadequacy) in his opinion was a principal cause of the paucity of regular saving among the lower classes: there scarcely existed the physical means for safe custody— Friendly Societies and strong boxes were both unequal to the task. Also unequal to the task were pocket and purse. In *Pauper Management Improved*, he described one "Difficulty of Hoarding" as the difficulty of "opposing a never-yielding resistance to the temptations afforded by the instruments of sensual enjoyment, where the means of purchasing them are constantly at hand";[99] and in his manuscripts he said much the same thing:

> The difficulty of resisting the incitement to expence, afforded by the sensible presence of money, is a difficulty which comparing man with man in an adult state, will be found to press with peculiar force against the Poor. The comparative weakness of their faculties, moral and intellectual, the result of the want of education, assimilates their condition in this particular to that of *minors*.[100]

This was a far cry from what he had written a decade before in his *Defence of Usury*, where the poor were portrayed as more mature than merely irresponsible children: he argued that the indigent man compared to ordinary men "knows what is his interest as well as they do, and is as well disposed and able to pursue it as they are."[101] But the assumptions of this argument ill suited his present purpose.

Bereft of the means of saving, furthermore, the poor man was all the more at the mercy of contingency; he was apt to fail "in his endeavours against the dangers of the caprice of fortune, and the improbity of man." To oppose this state of affairs, Bentham banged the drum loud for prudence: prudence is that regard for the future which denies present gratification. For the poor, saving was "placing in security the pittance which prudence would enable them to snatch from appetite";[102] the "ingenuity of appetite" was ever ready to oppose "the voice of prudence, but more especially of that melancholy sort of prudence which has fear of pain rather than hope of pleasure for its prompter"; a "Frugality Bank" would "serve as a shield to prudence against the assaults of prodigality in the shape of present pleasure."[103]

Bentham was convinced that if only they *would*, the poor *could* lay away substantial savings. The obstacle lay partially in the stubbornness of customary expenditure, for custom and necessity were by no means the same. He was convinced that the usual spending of single men both before and after marriage and of families allowed for considerable retrenchment.

Using out-of-date data supplied by David Davies, he calculated that a single male could subsiste on less than £4 a year, or 17 percent of his wages.[104] This ignored the current soaring food prices, but Bentham insisted that the poor switch their diets to potatoes and oatmeal. It also ignored the fact that he himself had existed for years before his father's death on £103 a year, or more than four times the laborer's wage, all the while complaining of penury; but he probably would have objected to this comparison on the grounds of class expectation.

Bentham contrived an ingenious scheme to encourage poor single males to embark on habits of thrift. Savings at the Company's banks could be converted to a "marriage fund," a sort of informal eighteenth-century version of Christmas Club, and the "publicity inherent to all transactions to which the Company is a party, will of course, . . . give a correspondent publicity to these exertions of individual virtue." A maiden with many suitors might withhold her hand "till the degree of attachment thus demonstrated has risen to a certain pitch."[105] Overcome by love, the young man would succumb to thrift. "Frugality, being thus brought forward by desire, as it were in a hot-bed in the spring of life, will maintain itself without difficulty in the maturer seasons."[106]

This droll vignette of life and manners in a prospective Utilitarian society has more serious overtones. It is one illustration of how Bentham intended gradually to instill Utilitarian values—in this case, the postponement through saving of present material gratification—among the independent poor. They could use the saving facilities or not, as they pleased, but in either case "the Company, with its *all-comprehensive* and *omnipresent* Bank, would never cease to hold out to them a sure and inexhaustible resource."[107] However, if they failed to clutch its outstretched hand, in the event of adversity, whether or not of their own doing, they would share a common fate from which there would be no escape: all would be marched off to Panopticon. Between the carrot of security and the stick of involuntary servitude, Bentham might, or so he hoped, draw them within his grasp. As for the glories and pleasure of saving let Bentham speak for himself:

In this new case [saving in a bank] it is not only pleasure that lays the first stone: but fresh pleasure is stamped upon every succeeding one. Each period of payment brings a man so much the nearer to the enjoyment, and every addition to the *quantum* of payment brings the enjoyment so much nearer to the man: the satisfaction, instead of wearing off by repetition, is brightened by it. . . . Not a penny of what he has advanced is ever sunk in any case: it . . . is all of it for ever at his command, ready at any time for the purchase of any suddenly proffered benefit, or for his protection against any extraordinary misfortune.[108]

3. The Last Roundup: A Silent Revolution

At one point in the voluminous arguments in support of his reforms, Bentham attempted (however vainly) to soothe the qualms of those who might view his policies as inflicting upon the poor the severe punishment of confinement and banishment. In reply, he suggested that the critical question to be asked in this case was "how the obligation" to reside in a House of Industry "comes to be imposed: with a man's consent, or without it?" How could one speak of hardship "when the obligation is never imposed but with consent, and as a condition annexed to a favour by which a man is saved from perishing by the labour and at the expence of another?"[109]

The argument was at best replete with difficulties. The idea of consent, to be anything other than a mockery, necessarily implies a voluntary act, and it is more than a little silly to suppose that a pauper "consented" to enter Panopticon when the only alternative was starvation. And how could relief be called a "favour" when giving it was a longstanding legal obligation? If relief was a "favour" under the Poor Law, then duty and charity are indistinguishable. As for the last part of the argument, we already know that the poor would pay and more than pay for their keep: so much for salvation "at the labour and at the expence of another."

Part of the argument, however, was more carefully drawn up. Was the obligation, he asked, "without cause or in the way of a condition annexed to the grant of a benefit?" If there was no consent *and* no benefit, "it may afford a ground for regret at least, if not for censure. . . ." (One wonders what *would* be a ground for censure!) The obligation imposed in the latter case would be unjust "if without delinquency or beyond delinquency, or if a tax which is unjust, if without necessity, or beyond a man's ability of endurance."[110] Leaving aside the obvious case of criminal liability, this formula flung open the door for the justification of policies which imposed *de facto* obligations without consent.

This open door policy was almost certainly intended to lay a foundation for the treatment to be meted out to the 'marginal' members of society— to beggars and prostitutes, to convicts and orphans, in fact to every variety of unsettled, unknown, and unpredictable figure who hovered in that limbo which lay beyond the fringes of respectability: they were all to be the subjects of a general roundup, and there were no sophisms about "consent" to justify it. Rather, Bentham resurrected the arguments from the 1782 *Essay on Indirect Legislation* discussed earlier.[111] Most important was the demand that the Company be delegated the authority to commit to its prison-factories what marginal men, women, and children that it would, and to commit them without trial. Involuntary incarceration was simply redefined; it was not *intended* to be and therefore *was* not a punishment: no punishment, no crime; no crime, no trial; no trial, no established Judge. Justices of the Peace, the traditional protectors of the poor from overzealous Overseers, would conveniently be left out of the proceedings—they would only cause "complication and delay, and might render the execution of the law less steady."[112] "Less steady" seemed to mean that some might slip through the Company's hands.

The Company's proposed coercive powers were to be general and sweeping. They were defined as powers for "*apprehending* all persons, able-bodied or otherwise, having neither visible nor assignable property, nor honest and sufficient means of livlihood, and detaining and employing them" until they were hired by a "responsible person."[113] Those tried and acquitted, those untried for lack of evidence (these formed a category of "suspect" hands), were all on the purge list. So were unsupervised children of various descriptions, unwed mothers, their consorts, "loose women" (who formed a category distinct from prostitutes), procurers, "female brothel keepers,"[114] and so on: the list was as endless as human vice, misery, and unmoneyed eccentricity. Even (to Bentham's mind, *especially*) convicts who had completed their sentences could not escape the dragnet. And by now it is easy to guess Bentham's reply to the charge that no one ought to be punished twice for the same offense—"Answer—Accordingly, no one is here punished. In the provision here made there is nothing that can with propriety be termed a punishment."[115]

Two classes of prospective inmates, beggars and prostitutes, deserve special attention. With respect to prostitutes, it may come as some surprise that in Bentham's estimation they did not lie at the very apex of this mountainous human dunghill excreted from the body politic. Rather, he had a special place in his heart for the practitioners of the world's oldest profession: prostitutes, he said, were "*that unfortunate and persecuted tribe.*"[116] As early as the *Essay on Indirect Legislation* he had advocated eliminating legal penalties for prostitution, and by 1797 he had not repented. He had, however, despaired of the wisdom of public advocacy, and none of the following discussion reached the readers of *Pauper Management Improved*. *Legalized* prostitution, he professed, was an idea "not to be endured"; but on the other hand, like Cato the Censor and St. Augustine before him, he would not supress it altogether even if he could, lest the cure be worse than the disease: "When there is no prostitution there is said to be no chastity." Nevertheless, even if it could be proved that a "repeal of all coercive laws" against the practice would reduce the number of prostitutes by as much as three-quarters and "the sufferings attendant on that unhappy state reduced on the same proportion," he doubted the public would approve. "Yet," he added ironically, "dram drinking is tolerated and protected. There is nothing obscene in dram drinking; it is only poisonous, nothing worse." By contrast, his description of the prostitute was more benign by far: "Permanent connections are suitable to some situations in life: transient, to others. This the legislator sees, because every man sees, but thinks it not decent to acknowledge."[117]

Still, prostitutes, those black sheep who strayed so far from respectability, were included in the roundup of the "national live-stock that walk on two legs" and consigned to the House of Industry "under the general provision consigning to that place all persons not having a visible means of livelyhood or in other words not capable of giving a good account of themselves."[118] Or, in other words, they were vagrants. Some, he thought, would surrender voluntarily—the repentant, the old, the diseased, and those who lacked custom. Lack of public toleration for repealing criminal penalties was only one reason for collecting the rest; all except the terminally ill could pay for their keep, but the old and repentant would probably become permanent residents and "as such it will be a valuable addition to the strength of the house."[119] Permanent members were more likely to be *profitable* members.

As for beggars, Bentham had no sympathy whatever, and he proposed a relentless campaign to rid the streets of their terrible visage once and for all. In his estimation begging was a scourge without a single saving grace, not even to the beggar himself. Beggars exposed passersby to the pain of sympathy and to the pain of disgust;[120] they facilitated crime by removing shame, "one of the chief safeguards to honesty" and by offering a *persona* to real criminals. They were also a discouragement to industry, for they insulted the industrious "child of industry" by "holding him out as a dupe, who toils and torments himself to earn a maintenance inferior to what is to be earned by canting and grimace";[121] and every moment spent begging was so much time lost to work which the beggar might be compelled to perform.[122] Finally, the happiness of beggars themselves would be maximized by their moral reformation. For every prosperous beggar, many more were deep in the quicksand of immiseration, powerless to extricate themselves. Beggars continue begging, Bentham argued, as some needlessly endure toothache, "not because the tooth-ack is pleasant, but because the resolution to get rid of it is not to be found"; and, like aching teeth, habits in general, but especially the habit of sloth, could not be discarded without a "pang." "But the pang [having been] endured, in the one instance as in the other, comfort may be the result."[123] And "pangs" there would be: removal to the Company's employ would fall "heavy and severe" on the mendicant; there were many who for at least a time "would, unquestionably, be no inconsiderable sufferers by the proposed change."[124]

"Beggars, therefore," Bentham wrote in his manuscripts, "must be compelled to come in or beggars they will remain."[125] "Compel them to come in"—the reference is unmistakably to the parable in *Luke* in which the "poor and the maimed, and the halt and blind" were brought to a feast (the rich begged off, as it were, making excuses); there still being room, a servant was sent to the highways and the hedges to "compell them to come in, that my house may be filled."[126] The feast, by analogy, was the feast of salvation: the poor and the maimed and the blind having entered, Bentham too had his House to be filled up, salvation to be dished up, so the beggars in the highways would be rounded up.

He did it this way. The beggar caught in the act could be apprehended by *anyone* and delivered either to a constable or directly to the nearest of the Company's establishments, "with or without his consent." Bentham provides for no administrative or legal procedure or appeal—no trial, no *habeas corpus*—once the "accused" was handed over. He tells us that this power already exists in the case of felons and "seems in little danger of being abused" since in presenting the beggar, one must also present himself.[127] Bentham gives no further rationale to assure us that no abuse would result (leaving aside the question of whether the whole proceeding was not itself an abuse); the civil liberties of accused beggars were not issues which much concerned him: the point was to ensnare them without allowing the hideous legal jungle of English rules of evidence and procedure to impede the catch. In fact, there was every reason to fear abuse. Felons were tried; but beggars would receive no trial, and therefore would have no chance to defend themselves. And besides, apprehenders of felons did not necessarily merit rewards, but a pound or ten shillings awaited whoever delivered a beggar to the Company: who would protect the poor and helpless from false accusation?

Once in the hands of the Company, the beggar was obliged to work; even if he had money, he could not buy his freedom.[128] Release would come upon fulfillment of two conditions: when he worked off his bill, his "self-liberation account," and when a ratepayer offered him employ. The bill included many items. There was the reward, the costs of conveyance (if any), food, clothing, medicine, and other such miscellanies, in addition to his share of the joint expense for the House during his sojourn, the Company's profit, and finally the cost of life insurance, lest he die before the account was settled.[129] Once out of the House of Industry, the chastened and, with luck, rehabilitated former beggar would be placed on probation for a year. If he left his master's service, he returned on the same day to the House or faced charges of escape (publicized in the Employment Gazette) with quadruple the original reward to be paid off in sweat when caught; and a relapse, or supposed relapse, into familiar habits brought a double reward, a second quadruple, and so on, as Bentham liked to say, *toties quoties*.[130] One can imagine how lucrative the ensuing lottery could have been—how many times might *this* beggar have fallen prey to recidivism?

Those suspected of begging or worse ("unavowed employment hands") were treated somewhat differently. Called before the Company's representative, the suspect was examined in accordance with Bentham's well-known system of procedure (the parent-child method): "Have you or have you not, any honest source of livelihood?—If you have, produce it:—if you do not produce it, it is because you cannot: if you cannot, it is because you have none:—if you have none, then—in that Industry House you will find it." "Such is the language," Bentham continued, "to the use of which no valid objection presents itself that I can see."[131]

However, Bentham did divine that others, those unduly sensitive to matters of the rights of "freeborn Englishmen," might see what he did not. In particular, they might see a certain unwarranted loss of liberty, the institution of an inquisition, and the willful violation of the right against self-incrimination. He set out to counter the attacks of glib tongues and to assuage the fears of the fainthearted. The terms "liberty" and "inquisitive," he argued, are "capable of being made up into a phrase that is in possession of being accepted in lieu of argument." Inquiries which are not liked are termed inquisitions: "with the sound of the word inquisition are associated the ideas of Spanish or Portuguese Priests, with racks and other instruments of torture in their train" to extract false confessions or true statements of harmless acts. Granted that the lazy would object to such inquiries as those he proposed; they had been but too successful "in this enlightened country" in making their aversions known: "We *will* the end, but as to the means by which alone the end can be obtained, there is not one of them all that we can endure."[132] Critics would simply have to take their medicine. As for self-incrimination, the question did not exist, for redefinition won yet another battle:

> For the present it is sufficient to observe, that in proposing the abolition of the crime, I abolish the incongruity of employing and even employing . . . to no use, this unpopular expedient of exacting self-incriminative evidence: no punishment being inflicted, no crime [implied], the result of the enquiry will not admitt of being entitled incriminative.[133]

Post hoc, ergo, propter hoc. Did he really expect any but the most gullible to believe this?

Bentham had still other weapons in his armory to parry the blows of potential antagonists fearful for the Rights of Englishmen. He granted that his plan entailed an infringement of liberty: but what of it? Liberty necessarily is circumscribed in direct proportion to the increase of security; the liberty which his plan would in fact destroy was the liberty of doing mischief.[134] Restraints upon liberty were "inconveniences": "To these inconveniences correspond so many objections against Industry Houses: but so are they against government, not against corrupt and tyrannical government only, but against government on the best and purest form of it. . . ." And not only against government, but against society itself—"against every condition of life you can name."[135] It was foolish to denounce the deprivation of beggars' liberty as punishment; it was no more punishment "than sending a boy to school."[136] Anyway, the "inconvenience" to the poor was not the only inconvenience to be considered, for it was "equally the lot of perhaps an equal number of the superior classes who are maintained at their own expence."[137]

The need to sacrifice liberty to security outside the "House of Industry" was mirrored in its internal government. Inmates, for example, would not be free to come and go as they pleased: that to Bentham was one of the worst failings of the current system. The pauper "may quit the house today, and by his absence derange the whole . . . manufacturing operation." If he left unreformed, he might well be imprisoned or whipped, but "whipping will not pay anything towards the expence of the House." Even if by chance he were reformed, he and his new employer would be the better for it, "but it will not pay the house for the machinery and tools which had been appropriated for his use."[138] Thus did profitability fundamentally dictate the shape of Bentham's reforms.

Liberty was also sacrificed in the day-to-day life of the House. Violation of rules would inexorably result in punishment. Infractions would be entered in a "punishment-book" and the infliction of penalties strictly controlled to prevent the exercise of arbitrary power. But Bentham fully expected there to be no punishment. It is important to see why, for here, in what might be a microcosm of Benthamite society, we may gain an insight into his hopes and strategies for the government of society at large. "I speak of punishment," he wrote in *Pauper Management Improved*, "because punishment is, in the existing order of things, a thing of course. Here, however, how can punishment gain admittance?—for from what occasion can it arise? No cessation of inspection, no transgression;—no transgression, no punishment."[139] (Bentham's original book on Panopticon, after all, was entitled *Panopticon or The Inspection House*.) He justified the rigors of this regime in a very odd (not to say dishonest) way, for he claimed that, so far from destroying liberty, his system actually enlarged it:

> If security against everything that savours of tyranny be liberty, liberty in the instance of this hitherto luckless class of human beings, can scarcely ever have yet existed in anything near so perfect a shape.

But liberty had another meaning, namely, *"lawless power"*: in that sense, he confessed, "there will not only be little liberty, but in plain truth there will be none."[140] By this logic, an entire society could be detained in Panopticon without losing any liberty worthy of the name.

As further justification, Bentham compared his plan with the treatment given the poor by the Vagrancy Act. Again he revived the arguments from *Indirect Legislation*, already discussed.[141] Placed beside his own proposals, existing law could not bear scrutiny. "Let us confront them then—and the result will be—on the one side . . . , efficiency without injustice—on the other, flagrant injustices coupled with perfect impotence."[142] Current law was unknowable by the very persons it sought to regulate; it was prolix and vague and even subjected the honest to punishment.[143] Its would-be replacement was a perfect foil; it maximized benefits while minimizing inconvenience:

In the texture of this provision I have endeavoured to do as much as could be done for the security of the community, and at the same time as much as could be done for the alleviation of whatever unpleasant effect is necessary to be produced in the situation of the individual.[144]

The poor, Bentham suggested, had consistently been the victims of never-ending changes in fashions of poor relief; they were "perpetual" but "always disastrous revolutions" inevitably heaping suffering on already suffering humanity. The vast national roundup of marginal men, women, and children which he urged on his readers was itself another revolution in the affairs of the poor, but it had a saving virtue: "One revolution the proposed system (it must be confessed) supposes and proposes and this too an universal one. But it is meant to be . . . a *final* one; and it ensures the community against annual, besides contingent ones."[145] But this revolution would differ fundamentally from the one proceeding in France. It was to be no raucous affair: if Bentham's strategy was effective, there would be no riotous mobs, no emptied prisons, no severed heads; rather this "final" revolution would be a silent one.

4. Riding Herd: The Will to Control

In a moral point of view, the formation of the people into little combinations and fraternities is of the greatest importance. It concentrates the eyes of all upon each individual; and renders good conduct a thing of infinitely more value to him, as it renders bad conduct for men detrimental. . . . In this manner, without difficulty, and without care, is exercised one of the most vigilant & effectual of all censorships; the most salutory of all inspections.[146]

This passage, found among Bentham's papers, was almost certainly not written by him; but it nevertheless neatly sums up two ideas without which his social theory would be unrecognizable. The first is the desirability of strict and pervasive social control—not that lazy, haphazard, and unrationalized variety of his own day which exasperated him so much, but something with teeth, something efficient, something that really did control instead of merely playing at it. The second idea was the means: the human eye, the inspecting eye, that censorial visionary instrument which revised desire when desire was translated into action.

Bentham's blueprint for dealing with the poor is replete with the means of such control. The management of poor-Panopticons was in need of control nearly as much as the poor themselves. "Management," he wrote, "which can hope to elude observation, may be, and often is, extremely bad." But management which "is sure to be looked at—and generally looked at—and constantly looked at can scarcely fail of being as good as the managing hands know how to make it."[147] Management required precisely what management had hitherto lacked—"strict discipline, steady constant and close inspection. . . ."[148]

The pauper inmates received the same treatment, only more of it. Every circumstance by which they could be influenced would be, he told his readers in *Pauper Management Improved*, "remarked and inventoried, nothing left to chance, caprice, or unguided discretion, everything being surveyed and set down in dimension, number, weight, and measure."[149] Again, as he put it in his manuscripts, "Whatever is done amiss is seen by everybody and each one knows that the others see it."[150] The disorders of contemporary poorhouses would be impossible; clamors, indelicacies, indecencies, or any kind of vice would be most unlikely when there was not "so much as a look or a gesture of any . . . that is not subjected at one and the same time to the eye of . . . the management, as well as of as many inspectors, permanent or occasional."[151] The result would be tranquility (one of the many pauper comforts) and "constant cleanliness and tidiness" (another one).[152] The neatness, the "patterned" character of the Houses was a theme Bentham was fond of repeating and once more underlines the seemingly compulsive and decidedly excessive orderliness of the plan.

"Inspection," Bentham argued, is a "perfect and general instrument of good order."[153] And the essence of inspection was sight. When he criticized John Howard's proposed villages for the poor, he confessed at being mystified how "a body can be present in two thousand houses at a time"— as if Howard had thought of omnipresent control—and drew an analogy between a poorhouse and a clock: "That 2,000 persons—that twice or thrice the number should form a piece of clock work, is what I can easily conceive: but in conceiving the clock put together, I take for granted all along, though scarce conscious of the assumption, that it has the Inspection-Architecture principle for the main spring."[154] To Bentham the law must have eyes to espy its transgressors, and the law's eyes are men's eyes; "Houses of Industry" were considered "as continually exposed to the superintending scrutiny of the eye of government, spurred and controlled by the eye of the world at large."[155] The rule of chance, of contingency abandoned hope when it entered there; "determinateness, fixity, and consistency" as well as "steadiness" best described its intended regime.[156] However, it is not true that *none* of the poor would *ever* be allowed an instant's privacy, for screens would be placed "in certain places, at certain hours—in behalf of certain persons" (obviously not everyone) "for comfort or for decency." This only *seemed* like a dangerous concession ("no prejudice can result in either respect"), since removing the screen was "left to the option of the party in whose instance inspection may at some periods be either necessary or of use."[157] Bentham evidently found the customary privacy accompanying the natural functions especially worrisome, since he made mention of it in a long note on toilet facilities in his Panopticon Letters of 1791. There he spoke of the same sort of screen just described, but he resolved the difficulty in a slightly different way: while the screen "answers the purpose of decency" for the inmate, it "might be so adjusted as to prevent his concealing from the eye of the inspector any forbidden enterprise."[158] Thus the crisis of privacy passes from us.

There were other ways to control the poor even when they left the House. Escapees' descriptions would include identification marks,[159] the French *signalements* which had captured Bentham's attention when he penned the *Essay on Indirect Legislation*; all the better if the fugitive was a native-born citizen, as it were, of the "petit état," for then the "birthmark" which had been indelibly etched upon him as an infant would facilitate his capture: "The use of a name is to distinguish a man. But this function it performs imperfectly—since a name, like a garment, may be put on or off at pleasure." And, he implied, objections to such "birth marks" would be rather silly, for when natural, they "have been treasured up as gifts of fortune."[160] Should not artifice improve upon fickle nature? What joy computerized files of fingerprints would have brought him! The English, of course, would object, because the English were forever objecting to such novelties: "No animal but a sheep [is] so sheepish as an Englishman. None has such a horror of anything that seems out of the way. None so blind a propensity to imitation, to infer reason from practice, instead of keeping practice by the rule of reason." Here he cited what seems to be his favorite passage from Bacon, "Let Reason be fruitful and Custom barren"; in England custom forever spread the land with its pilgrims—"Reason seems doomed to perpetual sterility."[161] That Englishmen might be hostile to unnatural "birth marks" from a healthy commonsense suspicion that, once in the hands of the state, they might prove prejudicial to civil liberty, was a notion that Bentham could not bear.

For the same reason, Englishmen were also suspicious (and to this day still are) of that latter-day version of the Doomday Book, the Census. Bentham was not. When he could quantify, he quantified. As he had numbered the clauses in Pitt's Poor Bill, he would number the advertisements in the "Employment Gazette," and number had other uses as well. The vegetative resources of the Company's premises would not be left at the mercy of "careless, malicious, or predatory tenants," for the Company would keep a "perpetual count of it, tree by tree"; after thinning, "the place of each remaining plant might be marked, and the plant denominated by a number."[162]

A Census, then, might keep track of the self-ambulatory forms of life; a "universal register," as he called it, would "give the plan, even as against habitual depredation, its utmost degree of efficiency." Such a register, he noted in *Pauper Management Improved*, would merely be a comprehensive extension of Morton Pitt's proposed census (a census in fact began in 1800) and would not be unlike registers such as the *London Directory* and others already extant. That his own register would be an instrument of *control* he lets slip in a backhand way; King Alfred's law of *"decennary aggregation"* (the Frankpledge system in which each member of a group of ten was responsible for the actions of every other) was "an infinitely harsher measure" whose "roughness fitted the roughness of the times."[163] Objections to his own far milder institution were ludicrous. A law having less to do with unwarranted infringement of liberty could not be found; and in any case, it was fantastic to believe (as we saw before) "that there had been, or ever could be, such a thing as a law, which was not, or would not be, some how or other against liberty!" And, to clinch the point, he continued, *"Counting,* the first operation of *American Independence.*"[164]

The most potent tool for control in poor-Panopticon was, of course, central inspection itself. To some degree it functioned as a sort of solitary confinement, cutting off every inmate from every other.[165] Beyond that there was the device of "separation and aggregation," an important facet of the operation of Panopticon prison. The primary function of separation lay in its capacity to insulate more completely than even central inspection the morally diseased from those not yet infected with the viruses of corrupted and cantankerous spirit (training in the House would serve as inoculation for the first class, as cure for the second). High on the list in this exercise in preventive medicine was prevention of the fouling of the air with coarse language. One reason to separate "indigenous hands" from the extraneous was that "in virtue of the association of ideas, the habit of immoral language has no inconsiderable influence on practice."[166] Even among the "corrupt" inmates such language would be made anathema, for control might otherwise be precarious: "No profaneness, no indecency, no malefactors cant, nothing of that sort of language that marks abhorrence of controul, proclaims and solicits outrage and rebellion would here be endured. . . ." Denunciation by fellow inmates could be expected since revenge was impossible and attention by authority assured. "Resistance being plainly hopeless," he wrote, "the most refractory spirits would presumably subside into the channel marked for them by the regime [?] of the House."[167]

"Suspected" classes, that is, those against whom no wrongdoing could be proved, were to be specially insulated from the entire pauper community, particularly from children over six. Suspects ought to be placed "under the guardianship and controul of some of the elder members of the [pauper] community" who would be given a special title and would "continue intermixt [?] with them day and night."[168] Bentham believed that the infirm, whether from age or otherwise, were particularly suited to the task, being beyond corruption—whether this was corruption in general or one species of corruption Bentham did not say, although the phrase "day and night" perhaps suggests an answer.[169] This was one instance in which separation and aggregation worked hand in hand to achieve the desired result; the control of children was another. The old served to "moderate any occasional impetuosity, violence, or passion" of the young. Bentham compared the effect of the mixture to military discipline: "It renders the younger temperate and orderly in their conduct, under the authority and example of the older; and it enables the whole to subsist, like soldiers in a mess, with more economy and advantage."[170]

Together with the inability to leave at will (and the compulsion by which many arrived in the first place), this *modus operandi* is strongly suggestive of prison procedure, especially *Bentham's* prison procedure, where control is at a premium.[171] Several further points confirm the impression, if it is not obvious enough already. For one thing, the "uncorruptible" members of Panopticon pauperdom were to be induced to become what amounts to prison guards. Power, "the ultimate aphrodisiac," according to someone who ought to know, was the magic brew which would seduce those selected: ". . . authority has charms for every human breast. From the humble station of a charity-fed Pauper, a man will find himself raised to the respectable situation of a guardian of morals and a depository of power."[172] At a distance from central inspection, perhaps obedience could be evaded; but if the "chief of empire" were a few feet away, control would be utterly unavoidable: "the aged Guardian has but to raise his voice or make a signal, and instantly and without so much as a change of place the official body hears the complaint and gives redress in consequence."[173]

Also reminiscent of prison was the double fence surrounding the premises—the space between its rings filled with a timber plantation. Bentham called it a belt, a "sequestration belt." The term is significant, for it suggests that sequestering the inmates—removing the world from them rather than them from a world improved by their removal—was the primary object. It is not accidental that in his manuscripts the prevention of the "inconvenient intrusion of strangers" was the first of its purposes he listed and that in *Pauper Management Improved* it was the *only* reason given.[174] The stranger! What havoc might he play upon an antiseptic Utilitarian monastery? What sabotage might be dealt to expectations so carefully cultivated—what seeds of unrequited desire cast among the well-pruned rows of flowering youth? What was strange could not be calculated, could not be "measured, counted, and weighted": in Benthamite society the stranger represents contingency itself. There was also the danger of his smuggling in Pandora's Bottle—liquor.[175] Needless to say, the "sequestration belt" was also intended to remove the inmates from the world, to prevent escape. In fact, Panopticon poorhouse was like a Utilitarian fortress—it came complete with a set of movable "Watchhouses."[176]

The will to control also explains an often puzzling aspect of Bentham's writings, namely his penchant, like Philip II of Spain, who "loved to decide details,"[177] for providing a plethora of minutiae on any subject, not infrequently (also like Philip) to a ludicrous degree. Instances of this habit abound in his writings on the poor. There were, for example, his arguments for exclusive provision of relief within Panopticon. One was the certainty, not simply (as we have seen) that relief would not be converted into "slow poison," but also that it would be administered "*in the precise shape* in which you mean it should be administrated." Food or fuel, clothing or medicine, housing or education: *you* choose. "You may say grain or potatoes, wheat or rye—beef, veal, or mutton—surloin fillet, or saddle" —or no meat at all—"you may choose the colour as well as the stuff of each man's cloaths—you may see each man's mess served out to him—and each man's coat fitted to his back."[178] Wasn't it marvelous that *you* controlled every decision and the poor man none? And dense forests of detail flourished among the descriptions of the fixtures of each House. In a large-scale system "the minutest atom by dint of repetition and extension, swells with importance."[179] Thus partitions between beds were to be six feet high, the walls eight feet, leaving two feet for light to enter—"Yet a moderate gloom is congenial to the occupation of the day."[180] In the *Annals*, a host of minutiae on the means of ventilation were presented for the reader's inspection.[181] The point is that the delineation of detail is a form of vicarious control. Like the architect of its constitution, the architect of Panopticon is a legislator: the *Constitutional Code* is a monument to Bentham's belief that the legislator, to be successful, is under heavy obligation to legislate in detail; if he does not, his care makes no sense whatever.

Finally, one more instrument of control reveals all over again Bentham's supreme insensitivity to the plight of the poor. This was his proposed resurrection of the moribund practice of badging recipients of public relief. In this case, badging took the form of distinctive dress, a uniform (which may or may not have been less onerous to the poor than wearing the letter "P", as the practice had been). All inmates were to be uniformed, not just permanent residents; and if deterrence of those without the House was one of its functions, control of those within was another. The utility of uniforms was "for order, distinction, and for recognition, as well as for tidiness."[182] "Distinction" here referred to the would-be policy of using distinctions in dress as forms of punishment (as well as reward); "recognition" presumably meant that the pauper could more easily be distinguished from afar from visitors or authorities and, as with prison uniforms, detection of escapees would be facilitated.

Bentham's defense of badging was similar to his defense of imprisonment without trial: he simply denied that it was in any way problematic. Just as imprisonment was no punishment, badging was no degradation. "The expedient of a Badge," he wrote, "has experienced violent condemnation: it is a degradation of the human character; it is stamping infamy with misfortune; it is confounding innocence with guilt." Nothing of the sort. To degrade a man is to place him in a lower class than he is, in fact, in. But badging changes no man's class: "The Badge marks the class in which it finds him: and then it leaves him." It might mark him as being in the lowest class, but he *is* in the lowest class; were he marked as a felon, then infamy would indeed be stamped upon misfortune. The badge, however, was not a mark of infamy: "The Mark . . . of a pauper does not certify him to be a delinquent in any shape. What it does certify is that he is

Poor: and so he is; that he is a burthen upon others: and so he is."[183] Bentham conveniently forgot that this "burthen on others" would be earning a profit for his keepers.

Details of his own reforms also slipped Bentham's mind when he defended the deterrent effect of badging. Paupers, he said, were ninety-five percent of the time "idlers," "hangers-on": what good purpose, he asked, could it answer "that the condition of the idler should be exhibited as upon a level with that of the man of industry—the condition of a hanger-on, upon a level with the condition of those on whom he hangs"? The good of showing the "real" situation he did see; it consisted of making the "condition of the man of industry in appearance more eligible than that of the man of no industry."[184] But such arguments ignored the composition of Bentham's pauper population, as a glance at his "Table of Cases Calling for Relief" will show. How could badging deter the victims of industrial stagnation, sickness, or old age? And what of those impoverished by any of the other innocent causes which he presents—causes such as war, fire, earthquake, shipwreck, and "bankruptcy, or failure, without a man's own fault"? Evidently it mattered not that the many would pay the price for the sinful sloth of the few:

> Rank is relative: you can not raise one of two contiguous ranks, but you depress the other: you cannot depress the one but you raise the other. Poverty you have on both sides: poverty you have at any rate. How do you like it best?—with or without industry—take your choice.[185]

Bentham had taken his choice. He liked it best with industry, and he liked industry very much. He liked it very much indeed.

7

The Making of Utilitarian Man

1. Secularized Asceticism: The Ethic of Disciplined Work

Idleness has not enjoyed a good press for a long time, and when it did, there was no press. Although today idleness is occasionally praised, its celebrants are self-consciously heretical or whistle in the dark. Twentieth-century men have something called "leisure," which is generally praised; but leisure (as everybody knows) is for *doing* something. Idleness is doing nothing. Not since the Middle Ages has idleness, at least the idleness of religious mendicants (but sometimes secular beggars as well), been tolerated and even glorified. The Reformation, however, gave idleness a bad name: Luther branded the demands of beggars blackmail, and Calvin condemned the Roman practice of wholesale almsgiving as corrupt, citing Paul's "if any would not work, neither should he eat."[1] In England the attitude of the Puritans that idleness is sinful had by the eighteenth century thoroughly insinuated itself into the mental baggage of the literate public.[2]

Bentham represents the secularized form of Protestant abhorrence for idleness and praise of methodical work. For him idleness is an uncertain calm awaiting some inevitably ensuing tempestuous evil. Idleness was "that deadliest of all enemies to happiness and innocence";[3] when "coupled with indigence" it was "pregnant with unhappiness to the idle, and danger to others."[4] Thus, "superfluities" from the public purse for indigents with a history of past prosperity were condemned not only as contravention of justice and economy but of "good morals" as well, for they opened the door to the encouragement of idleness;[5] one principle in the management of Panopticon poorhouse was the "no idle hand principle."[6]

The trouble with idleness, as we have seen before, is that it leaves the mind devoid of content. The void, however, is but temporary: "Nature, corporeal nature, was conceived in former days to entertain an abhorrence for vacuity. That incorporeal nature does, is beyond dispute. . . ." Just as surely as the mental void has nothing innocent to occupy it, "so surely it will be filled up by mischief" of either a dishonest or an imprudent variety. It followed that "every pleasure free from mischief is valuable . . . , not only on its own account, but by rivalry to mischief: as a candidate for the possession of the human breast in opposition to mischief." And since the worst of these mischiefs, their "parent and ally," was drunkenness, he coined this variation of his notorious epigram that the children's game pushpin is as good as poetry: "Pushpin is morality in as far as it keeps out drunkenness."[7] What he was saying, obviously, was that even such a trivial and otherwise useless activity as pushpin was valuable if it prevented positive evil. It should be noticed that this is something less than a full-hearted embrace of the virtues of pushpin as opposed, say, to chess or Bach (both of which he preferred immeasurably).

"Manners and morals were regulated," writes Tawney of John Knox, "because it is through the *minutiae* of conduct that the enemy of mankind finds his way to the soul. . . . Regulation meant legislation, and, still more, administration. The word in which both were summarized was Discipline."[8] The passage is striking, for it applies in every detail (if "self" is substituted for "soul") to Bentham's program for the indigent. What he called "the uninterrupted and unfluctuating discipline of the House"[9] was not simply discipline for the sake of maintaining "good order," however desirable good order might be.[10] Discipline had *moral content*; it was the whip that drove the unrighteous along the road to moral salvation (and prevented the spread of "moral infection"):[11] Bentham tells us quite explicitly that one purpose of inspection architecture for the poor was morality insofar as it depended on discipline.[12] The essence of moral life for the poor was unremitting work.

We saw earlier how tenaciously Bentham tried to gather every fragment of the ability to labor and to extract a maximum from it; here there is a somewhat different point to be made. Forcing paupers to labor, aside from the prevention of mischief, had three principal justifications, viz., justice, economy, and regard for "the lasting welfare of the individual himself": "The habit of industry is a source of plenty and happiness. The habit of idleness in one who has property is a source of uneasiness, and in one who has no property, of indigence and wretchedness."[13] "The habit of industry" (like the "habit of obedience")[14] was of overwhelming import; and it behooved any plan of poor relief to inculcate, through the association of ideas, the connection between work and subsistence. That is why money from "prosperous" beggars was unacceptable in payment for their accounts; and that is also why Bentham insisted on rendering "the connection between relief and labour inseparable" according to the rule that "Nothing ought to be given for nothing, where labour can be had for it."[15]

For Bentham, work has a value quite apart from its external consequence, the work product. Its internal consequences were a good in themselves as a buttress to good moral character. He would therefore require work from paupers *"though it were unprofitable."* One reason was the familiar injunction to avoid idleness; the other was "to keep up the habit of exertion."[16] The process of working (without respect to its product) was so critical a value that Bentham was at times willing to give it precedence over justice to producers as an argument for the adoption of his plan. Thus the very first reason why home relief should be scotched was that "the tendency to slacken industry is *of itself* a price too great to pay for an advantage of so refined a nature as the avoidance of that sentimental hardship."[17] If this seems unduly insensitive to those who preferred home to Panopticon, consider the greater generosity of feeling toward the infirm —"Relief for infirmity without work, [is] better than no relief, but [is] otherwise bad." The first two of the reasons for this were economic—the "loss of value" and the encouragement of "voluntary infirmity"—but it is the third that interests us: "humanity—withholding occupation,"[18] that is, leaving the infirm idling at home ran counter to humane policy. Under this fanatic of the work ethic, even the sick would be required to labor: one advantage of transfering sick-relief from a hospital "on the common plan" to the infirmary of a Company establishment was that "habits of *industry* [will be] maintained without relaxation."[19]

All of this underlines how the work ethic permeated every aspect of everyday life in a Benthamite workhouse. "In the choice of occupations," he wrote in the *Annals*, ". . . productive labour ought to take the lead: and that to such a degree that no part of the time allowed by religion to be employed in productive labour, ought to be employed in any occupation directed exclusively to any other object"—eating, sleeping, washing, and worshiping excepted. In the case of children's education, productive labor took the lead with a vengeance: every object of education other than productive work was to be accomplished *before* the capacity to work emerged, and the commencement of instruction should not come as custom dictated but rather as physical capacity allowed.[20] This implied that full-time academic, sedentary learning would be complete as soon as a child was able to work productively, which to Bentham meant the age of four.

The work ethic in Bentham, moreover, is self-consciously individualistic. In allotting tasks, he advocated what he called the "separate-work" or "performance-distinguishing" principle, according to which, wherever possible, tasks would be separated and gang work avoided. Even when gang work was necessary, the principle would be applied to the extent that the gang's size could be diminished; and in some cases, a novel twist might be applied: "N.B. If the gang be not large, by shifting the hands from gang to gang in the same work, the share contributed by each to the result of the joint-work, may be obtained separate."[21] There were even schemes to measure *precisely* how much work was performed; one method was to find how many revolutions of a wheel it required to grind a certain amount of grain.[22]

The moral purpose of this individualist work ethic was the personal and social identification of the person with his work. Or, as Bentham put it, *"that every one may be known by his works and with reference to his works."*[23] Even more interesting was his self-conscious attempt to harness religious sensibility, redirecting it toward fulfillment of a thoroughly secular purpose, arising from a completely Utilitarian premise, viz., methodical productive work as a moral ideal. Thus, one of the "Advantages resulting from the application of the Separate work principle" took a religious turn: "What a man's fruits are must be known, or the instruction 'By their fruits ye shall know them' must remain without fruit." (An alternative version read, "What a man's works *are* must first be known, ere a man either be punished or be 'rewarded according to his works'.")[24] Such utterly disingenous passages had the obvious intent of appealing to the religious sensibilities of a Protestant audience. For Bentham, the justification for work could derive from he cared not where, from sanctions natural, divine, or human: "Work or starve, such is the law of nature; work or starve, such is the law of God. . . . Where is the house, public or private which can exist without it?"[25]

What all this is highly reminiscent of is the idea of worldly asceticism so brilliantly analyzed by Max Weber. Worldly asceticism is work in a "calling" ("a man's sustained activity under the division of labour") which abjures the frivolous use of time and wealth. Seventeenth-century Puritan attitudes inveighed against irregular work which bred idleness, impulsive enjoyment, and the irrational uses of wealth and counseled restraint of consumption, especially of luxuries.[26] We have seen all of this in Bentham's view of poverty. Irregular work led to drunkenness; impulsive enjoyment ("merry making"[27] was a synonymous euphemism) was the irrational use of wealth. Consumption should be curtailed to save for marriage, unemployment, and old age.

Richard Baxter, the Puritan minister whom Weber considers paradigmatic, condemned excessive sleep and praised intense work: "Labour hard in your callings"; "see that you have a calling which will find you employment for all the time which God's immediate service spareth."[28] Bentham, as we will see in a moment, likewise denounced excessive sleep, and Baxter's injunction to labor during *"all the time"* unrequired by service to God is mirrored almost exactly in Bentham's dictum cited earlier that "no part of the time allowed by religion to be employed in productive labour ought to be employed in any other occupation directed exclusively to any other object." Bentham's view, however, involved a fundamental difference from Baxter's, for Bentham begrudged religion much of the time forbidden to employment. It also infuriated him that the amusements of the Public House were allowed on Sunday but more serious enterprises were not. It may be argued that for Bentham, once the religious justification for methodical labor dropped away to reveal a purely secular guise, the activity of working became very nearly what it was for the ascetic practitioners of the "spirit of capitalism"—an end in itself.

Asceticism crept into nearly every aspect of life under the unceasing gaze of the National Charity Company. As if the strict discipline of work were not enough, there was the virtual absence of amusement. This is shown well enough by Bentham's attempts to convince his audience that the reverse was true, that the pauper community would indeed get their chance to be entertained. One entry in the list of "Pauper Comforts" was "Entertainment of various kinds, a day in the week." Various kinds there may have been; entertainments they were not. The day for "entertainment" was, needless to say, Sunday, and it consisted of "psalmody and other suitable music," "concourse drawn by the music, physico-theological lectures, and other exhibitions."[29] In other words, the poor's sole amusements were to be religious music, sermons, and scientific lectures. The English lower classes had a long and rich tradition of merrymaking centered around the Public House—a tradition that Bentham mocks and mocks knowingly with his sketch of Panopticon's Sunday "entertainment": Saturday night at the King's Arms was never like this.

A similar policy was applied to the young. Their "amusement" was to be strictly utilitarian; no part of their time, he argued, "ought to be directed exclusively to the single purpose of comfort," amusement being a "modification of comfort." Amusement could be "infused, in the largest possible dose which economy admits of, into every particle of the mass of the occupations by which time is filled," but it should never be the "sole end in view"; for the result of such training is likely to be the sacrifice of comfort itself. *"Profit,"* whether immediately through the accomplishment of useful labor or indirectly through the attainment of dexterity and skill, was to form part of the child's every activity. Play ('pure' play, that is; the kind devoid of redeeming social value), obviously, would be outlawed. Bentham defended this view by arguing that, whatever prejudiced adults might think, productive properties in a child's activity do not necessarily diminish its amusement in the child's own eyes. He took the case of a doll's house as an example. Both the duration and the intensity of the child's amusement could be far better provided for by giving him a hand in the making of it than by its ready-made presentation.[30] Whether or not he was correct, Bentham might have informed his readers at this point that children would not be employed in making their own doll's house, but set to work for the profit of a very different sort of House.

2. Sex and Asceticism in a Benthamite Society

Asceticism was further visited upon the poor in the form of the repression of all but the most rigidly conventional sexual behavior. Conjugal pleasures were permitted to the conjugally attached, but every other manifestation of sexuality was strictly taboo and enforced to the hilt. The aggregation-separation and inspection principles were admirably suited for this work, and Bentham set out to wring from them every ounce of control of the "venereal appetite" that his imagination could devise. Accordingly, there was to be an "unchaste ward" in a detached building, where the unchaste (all of whom were women—the category consisted of prostitutes, unwed mothers, "loose women," female brothel-keepers, and "procuresses") could be separated from "those of a susceptible age, of their own sex, as well as of the other."[31] And, of course, the sexes would be divided beyond a certain age—for the prevention "of unsatisfiable desire." This latter arrangement formed the basis of an additional "comfort" for female inmates, the "security against seduction, and its attendant miseries." As in "well regulated" families, the opportunity for "conversation with the other sex" would come only "in a safe manner and at safe times." Thanks to the "uninterrupted presence of the governess and her subordinates" and "guardian elders of the proper sex," female virtue would actually be safer than in the "best regulated, even the highest families."[32]

On the other hand, this "comfort" took on rather a different character when Bentham so chose. Poor-Panopticon might function as an "asylum" for the wife of a tyrannical husband; but she would have had to be seriously mistreated indeed to exchange "matrimonial comforts," home, and family for "celibacy under inspection—in company of her own sex only, and not of her own choice."[33] The regime of the House was like that of a "well-regulated convent," only better, for in convents celibacy was by no means assured, while in Panopticon no jealous husband need fear conjugal infidelity. The same benefit accrued to unemployed domestics; the utility of the regimen of the House "would be a preservation of chastity and of reputation of chastity: so of the habit of industry and regular obedience, in both sexes."[34] The only members of the pauper state who would be allowed (as a special reward) the "extra comfort" of living apart from the ubiquitous eye of authority in an "outlying cottage" were those thought safe from the weaknesses of the flesh—"An aged married couple,—a pair of sisters—an aunt and a niece."[35]

Over and over Bentham gave assurance that the prophylactic measures against unsanctioned sexual expression would be effective. More than once he compared the lives of independent "manufacturers" with the monastic existence of those under the Company's discipline. For example, the demand for medical attention would be greatly diminished compared with independent manufacturers "almost all of them engaged in . . . sedentary [occupations], many in poisonous ones, and all of them by their habits of promiscuous intercourse exposed to the seduction of the unhealthy vices."[36] In the independent "manufactory" such licentiousness might be curbed during working hours, "but it can not be so ordered during free hours." In poor-Panopticon, by contrast, the regulation of social intercourse was never in question: "it may be ordained that between certain ages individuals of different sexes shall not be within sight or even so much as hearing of each other, except at certain hours and under actual inspection." More than this, it could be ordained that "youth even of the same sex should not exist either in sleeping or even working hours but under the inspection of a superintending eye."[37]

This last comment suggested that when it came to public discussion without benefit of pseudonym, Bentham made a strategic retreat (or rather *volte-face*) from the position of toleration for sexual "non-conformity" that he had defended before and would defend again. There would be no "irregularities of the impure class,"[38] and there would be no toleration for the 'public school thing': "In those schools, uncleanness in the scriptural sense is constantly to be [found], and the habitual absence of the master's eye renders it impossible to prevent or check it." In Panopticon things would be different—"not an individual being for two moments together out of sight and all promiscuous intercourse with the world without doors cut off, there is not a moment at which it could find entrance."[39]

Now, having said all this, having shown Bentham to be so repressive in his public (and publicly intended) statements on sexual matters, we have now to do our own *volte-face* and beat a retreat on this one-sided view of sexual repression in Panopticon. For in fact Bentham quite publicly, in the pages of the *Annals of Agriculture*, made a determined stand, even an impassioned plea, for the maximization of conventional sexual pleasure of the young. This plea was not made on behalf of all inmates of these "Houses of Industry"; nor does it rescind or contradict anything we have said of his asceticism. Nevertheless, the argument he did make cannot be ignored.

At the end of *Pauper Management Improved*, Bentham presented a list of "comforts" which attempted to show that, with the adoption of his plan, benefits would accrue to pauper "apprentices" otherwise unavailable not only to them, but even to the children of the upper classes. One was that marriage would be allowed at the "earliest period compatible with health." Evidently he suspected that the idea of early marriage might be objectionable since he added a long footnote to buttress it, most of which was devoted to a straight-forward Utilitarian defense of sexual pleasure for youth.[40]

"The maximum of clear happiness," he began, "is the object, and the sole object, of every rational plan of conduct, public or private." The maximum enjoyment yields the maximum of happiness; all else being equal, enjoyment is maximized when its duration is longest, and duration is longest with the earliest commencement. In this case, the dangers to be considered were physical and moral; physical, if too early a commencement of sexual activity injured health; and moral, if from a premature state of power and independence, intellectual faculties had not attained a growth commensurate to that state. If neither of these applied—and here was the crux of the argument—then "every portion of time, which . . . might have passed in the social state, and yet is suffered to pass away in celibacy, is so much lost to happiness."

This loss, he believed, had hitherto gone quite unnoticed. The upper classes had actually been victimized by prolonged celibacy more than their inferiors, but even among the lower orders "the number of years thus lost, must, upon any calculation, or rather without any calculation, leave a blank much to be regretted in the book of life." If in private life consideration of the moral and intellectual maturity necessary for both self-government and the government of "the little family empire" might justify the delay of marriage, it had no place where the government of youth was so amply provided.[41] "Nature shows the commencement of the ability," he wrote; "—nature shows the commencement of the desire.—How long must the ability continue useless? How long must the desire be a source of vexation, instead of enjoyment?—Questions, surely, not uninteresting—surely, not undeserving of solution!"

The "solution" would come by experimenting with pauper apprentices under the controlled conditions of Panopticon; but meanwhile, there was *prima facie* evidence that youthful marriage was not inappropriate. Bentham cited Sir George Staunton as authority that the Chinese married early, were for the most part sober, were less exposed to the temptations of debauchery, and lived lives "more regular and uniform." Then, too, there were the French: "In France,—when France was France,—among the first families in the nation, and in others" marriage came as early as health and economy permitted. Sixteen was not early, nor fourteen uncommon: "What under the French monarchy, was the best privilege of the Prince, is in our Utopia, the universal lot of the whole community." And, he added, it was to the pauper economy, which endowed "infant man" with "an indubitable and universal value" that this "gentlest of all revolutions" was indebted:

> Turn now to the palace, and behold what a fund it affords for pity, when confronted with our industry-house. Princes unmatched or late matched, or unprosperously matched, or incongruously matched—Princesses . . . all ripe, but all too high, for happiness.[42]

We have, then, a somewhat confusing assortment of passages and sentiments on the encouragement and repression of sexuality. That Bentham would present himself in public as the arch-foe and implacable critic of the same "sexual eccentricities" that he defended in private (writing for the drawer or for pseudonymous publication) is quite understandable in both senses: it is intelligible and it is excusable. One whiff to the reading public that he would countenance committing what a long Christian tradition following a longer Jewish tradition called "the abominable crime against nature," and he could abandon all hope for the approval of either Panopticon poorhouse or Panopticon prison. Prudence is a virtue which does not beggar the practice of hypocrisy. Nobody but *nobody* who was anybody in the eighteenth century supported the legalization of homosexual practices —not Montesquieu, not Voltaire, and *certainly* not that arch-rebel, Jean-Jacques Rousseau. Furthermore, thanks to the horror stories of moral turpitude aboard the hulks (the prison ships in the Thames and elsewhere), the English public was sensitive to the issue. Bentham had already dealt with it in *Panopticon*, and there is no reason to expect him to have remade his public face in 1797. And this same public sensitivity to sexual 'misconduct' goes far to explain why he took such pains to assure the strict regulation of sexual behavior of every variety.

But why did Bentham publicly air a scheme for the maximization of sexual pleasure when he had just dotted the social landscape with the most stringent measures of sexual repression, perhaps far more stringent and explicit than necessary to assuage the fears of an audience apprehensive of venereal 'disorder'? Why indeed? Two possible explanations suggest themselves which are not mutually exclusive. The first possibility is simple enough; it is that Bentham was trying to show that an institutional system that might seem to more conventional minds a horror of total control was *not* so bad after all. That is why the long and contrived list of "Pauper Comforts" published in the *Annals of Agriculture* was devised in the first place: to placate the conscience of the morally unsure. Add *this* "comfort" and the justification of the plan was that much easier—the prince and the pauper exchanged places in the hierarchy of happiness.

The second explanation is, if anything, more obvious: it is, quite simply, that Bentham was being honest, that he did sincerely wish to maximize happiness (who can doubt it?), and that he believed that the sexual pleasure (and the avoidance of vexatious desire) which early marriage provided was an effective means to that end. If he were sincere in private advocacy of "nonconformist" emancipation, why not sincere in public advocacy of "conformist" emancipation? It is evident that he thought such advocacy safe enough—he did it. And there is yet another reason to take him at his word. The advocacy of the emancipation of others may well have provided vicarious relief from his own "vexatious desire": when he spoke of the pains of celibacy, he spoke from experience.

3. Living Treasure: Exploiting and Educating the Young

Source of profit, hope of years to come, youth was at the heart of this system of national "charity." As sources of productive labor, they were "living treasures" that would yield rich dividends to their temporary owners; as raw, unmolded clay, the stuff that Bentham's dreams were made of, they were the receivers and bearers of Utilitarian values, destined to be the models that all the world would gaze upon and imitate.

It was, therefore, no trivial matter to maximize the production of such a rich resource; like the other "fragments of ability," the young would be gathered together from whatever source, by whatever means. That was the purpose of Bentham's list of "measures for augmenting the stock of Apprentices." Pregnant women, "indigent or not indigent," would be admitted for birth on the condition that the child be ceded to the Company: according to Bentham, everyone would gain—mother, father, child, Company, and the state itself. Children could also be had simply by requisitioning them as a condition for the relief of any pauper with more than two children "within the age of perfect self-maintenance," age ten, twelve, or perhaps fourteen. Or if the pauper had but one or two, one child might be pledged as collateral for loans.[43] Still other "apprentices" would be gathered from the families of the confined, suspected, or released from prison; and in the case of men about to go to trial, their children might or might not be taken before the trial itself: Bentham was undecided.[44] The children would go in any case; if the verdict was guilty, they would probably go as offspring of prisoners; or if innocent from lack of evidence, they would go as offspring of the suspected. Moreover, children of the blind and even blind children who required relief would be apprenticed to the Company. Of this latter category, Bentham admitted that of course parents or relatives of such blind children would find it "more pleasant" to be provided for at home, but "this indulgence would be in contradiction to our fundamental principles."[45] And if children were themselves found begging, it went without saying that they could be rightly collected; but in this case their "self-liberation account" would not open until they passed their twenty-first year, and the Company would reap the profits of the intervening time.[46] Finally, there was one further source of "living treasures": anyone had the right to board a child at these "schools of industry" for a fee. If the fee went unpaid, the child was to be forfeited until twenty-one, and the Company would have snared yet another prize.[47]

Considered as productive resources, the powers of children were to Bentham virtually untapped and of inestimable value. Economically as well as morally, they were "of the very essence" of the plan.[48] "In the early stages of the period of non-age," he told the readers of the *Annals*, "a large proportion of the natural value, or capacity of yielding a clear profit, is lost, by lying unemployed. . . ." And in the later stages of minority, over-consuming youth dissipated its produce by the habitual purchase of luxuries. No wonder that "the pecuniary value of a child . . . should generally be regarded as *negative*, in this country": giving children a positive value was a problem whose solution would be "an inexhaustible source of wealth, population, and happiness, to the state."[49] This positive value began at the age of four: "Upon a general view then," Bentham wrote,

> ten years, ten pretious years, may be looked upon in the existing state of things as the waste period of human life, the period lost to industry. Ten years, in which except the reaping of that stock of amusement which might be reaped in no less plenty from the field of rational education, ten pretious years in which nothing is done! nothing for industry! nothing for improvement, corporal or mental, moral or intellectual![50]

The cultivation of the "waste expanse" of "juvenile time" was "another vast mine of national wealth remaining . . . unwrought"; "rational" education would substitute "garden culture" for "barrenness or weeds." This was one more application of the Baconian vision of the conquest of nature. "The parentage of Plutus' Wealth"—Plutus was the blind Greek god of wealth—"is no secret. He is the child of Earth by Labour. . . . He has Earth for his Mother, and Labour for his Father, and Adam Smith for his head Geneologist."[51] Labor, then, was the essence of Benthamite education for pauper youth—"the time [during] . . . which productive labour is interdicted by religion will suffice for all other objects."[52]

In his discussion of the education of the pauper child, Bentham was at pains to insist (lest there be doubts to the contrary) that the young under his care would in every respect be better off than if left with their natural parents. "Home education," he argued, "is in fact . . . the same thing as no education at all"; the parents of poor children had neither the time nor the knowledge, and frequently not the moral disposition required for the purpose, while in the Industry House "every one is [found] in perfection."

Even if the child were sent to day school, the result was not much different; he then had two masters to obey, "a task which divine concurrs with
human wisdom in pronouncing an impossible one." Regulated instruction
governed the day, "rough ignorance" the night.[53] Anyway, sending children
to day school wasted an invaluable commodity, *time*—time wasted traveling, time wasted due to bad weather, time wasted tarrying after school.[54]
He did not emphasize the fact that not a little of the education in his own
scheme consisted of pauper children teaching each other.

Pauper children were better off with the Company for other reasons as
well. With school in one place and home in another, that foremost principle
of mental activity, the association of ideas, would see to it that school was
associated with pain and home with pleasure.[55] More important, outside
of the walls of poor-Panopticon, chance and caprice stood at the ready to
take up their role as foils to rational human planning. Thanks to caprice,
the child might often not even be sent to school: "The affections, the
caprices, the little interests of the day would be perpetually productive of
the desires of keeping the child at home."[56] Shielded from caprice by the
strict control of Benthamite management, the child received benefits unavailable to those unfortunates beyond its doors. Thus the supposed disadvantage of the "want of natural parental affection on the part of the
Guardians" was really advantageous, since "the disposition of their Guardians . . . is uniform—exempt from the anger incident to fondness and
from the anger and caprice that without fondness is formed . . . among uncultivated minds."[57] The same theme was addressed in the *Annals of Agriculture*. Goodness of child care was enhanced by attention being "uniform, systematical, governed by principle:—not exposed to be relaxed by
casual want of affection; or to be misguided by ignorance, prejudice, or
caprice."[58] In unpublished material, the point was expanded:

> This disadvantage [the lack of natural parents], simple as it is, vast as it
> is, is not without its compensations. . . . The affection of the parent,
> especially in rude and uncultivated bosoms is wont to be clouded by
> caprice: the deportment of the comparatively indifferent, but select
> and cultivated mind of the appointed Father, may not unreasonably be
> expected to stand clear of such inequalities. Natural Fathers are of all
> tempers: negligent as well as careful; rough and brutal as well as tender
> and affectionate. The appointed Father is . . . of but one temper: and
> that temper selected for the purpose. The government of the natural
> Father is severed [?] from observation, exposed to no suspicion, and
> practically speaking, without appeal. . . . The management of the ap-

pointed Father is laid open purposely and studiously and as much as possible to observation, subject to account and to appeal, yet happily as well as unavoidably exposed to suspicion notwithstanding.[59]

We might add parenthetically that part of the impetus to protect the young from mistreatment had its origin in Bentham's own experience, in particular his experience at Westminster School, where he was on one occasion robbed and in general made miserable; and he was quick to make favorable comparison between the bullying of the weak and poor in Public Schools and the absence of arbitrary oppressions among his own pauper apprentices.[60]

For Bentham, the education of the poor was a subject all too often overlooked in favor of exclusive attention to the training of the "superior classes." This was because education, rather than being viewed (as Bentham did) as the means to happiness, was seen instead as the tool of ambition: "A treatise on education is like a treatise on the art of war: if all were equally masters of it, it would be of no use." Hence writers on education thought of no children but the rich, for "the end in view in the education of gentlemen is distinction: in distinction, in superiority consists the essence of this class."[61] But because the poor were more numerous and because their need was by far the greater, theirs was the "most important branch of education." Perhaps we can sniff out some of the flavor of this education in one of Bentham's epigrammatic comments—"Education is government in miniature and necessarily monarchial."[62]

It was in the young that Bentham placed his hopes for a more Utilitarian future; they were the *tabulae rasae* on which this would-be Moses might etch the commandments to work and save. Much of the adult poor was "dross," though "the cost of refining it being so amply paid for need not be grudged." But children were purity itself: "they possess the Ore as it comes out of the hands of nature: upon that the profit is great, and altogether at their command."[63] Infused with "inbred habits of systematic frugality"[64] which guaranteed their future happiness, these fruits of the legislator's labor once ripened to maturity would become models for the independent poor to emulate. "The benefit to the country will not end with the apprenticeship," Bentham wrote; the "stock thus poured into the community at large will be [predisposed] to habits of frugality, and will inculcate it by example." And again: "All will not preserve their habits of frugality and sobriety—But some will, many probably will."[65] Their value, in fact, would be of the very highest, for one's value "is in the direct ratio of what he produces, and in the inverse ratio of what he consumes," and the value of these "hands" would be "augmented at both ends."[66]

Because the young were blank sheets awaiting the author of the Book of Life (the legislator) to write upon them, no fears should linger that what might seem a life of harsh privation and toil would be painful: they had no expectations. Such was Bentham's argument, and he repeated it mercilessly. The pauper child's diet, for instance, would occasion "no sense of privation: none of the pains attendant on the emotions of regret, discontent, or envy on that score." And no one need fear ill health because of excessive energy—"quantity of food not stimulating enough to invite excess."[67] Nor would less than the usual amount of sleep be a hardship; "the quantity allowed ought to be, the least that can be made sufficient for health and strength." Anyway, Bentham thought, sleep is not life but "the cessation of life: laying a-bed without sleep, is a habit productive of relaxation, and thence pernicious to bodily health: and in as far as it is idleness, pernicious to moral health."[68] To objections to any of this, Bentham had his stock answer at the ready. "In regard to mere absence of pleasure, hardship or no hardship depends upon experience or no experience."[69]

Hardship or no hardship, there was an obvious objection to 'educating' the apprentices to the aggrandizement of the National Charity Company, for they would not receive "the produce of their own labour—they will not have their earnings to themselves."[70] Logically, Bentham ought to have confronted squarely the issue of justice. How could he condone depriving youth of the fruits of its labor merely for the profit of shareholders? But this 'merely' was no 'merely' to Bentham, and in the event, he shilly-shallied around the question and never answered it. He spoke to the far less germane problem of what would motivate them to work without profit or with little reward; and if he responded at all to the charge of injustice, his answer seems to have been that if the "public" were bestowing great benefits on the young by caring for them, why should the public go unrewarded? Once again, however, relief in English law was long established as a *right* of the poor, a right stoutly defended by Bentham against the onslaught of abolitionists; and besides, it was not a matter of public but of *private* profit in this case. Even if forcing the poor to pay their own way could be defended, extracting a profit is something else altogether. In the end, Bentham's answer to the objection he posed for himself was that independent laboring youth were not better off for the extra consumption their earnings brought, "but to the whole of it and in every respect the worse." The crux of the matter was this: "Every penny spent before marriage over and above what the individual can afford to expend upon his own personal consumption after marriage is a penny laid up in the formation of a fund of privations and regrets"—precisely the privations from which the Company's youth were exempt. ("The Company's guardianship saves [them] from this . . . period of penury and retrenchment . . . .")[71] So far as the produce of labor was concerned "the greater the quantity extracted from them during their minority (so it be without prejudice to health) and the greater the degree of skill and dexterity which they have been made to acquire in the exertion of it," the better their condition would be when they left. He continued: "Labour, so long as it is neither by its immediate nor in its remote effects prejudicial to health, *can never be too severe*."[72] A further argument, that in proportion "as their habit of privation has been strict during minority" the greater the faculty of enjoyment from "superfluities" would be upon independence, was rather dubious: wasn't Bentham's point that, on account of their "education," apprentices would not, in fact, consume superfluities?[73]

The end of education for Bentham is well-being, and the state of well-being is one of happiness. But if pauper education is training for the life of labor, and if labor is pain, how could the life of toil be justified in Utilitarian terms? Bentham responded that in the first place pleasure is "inseparably connected with the gratification of a variety of natural appetites" which if left ungratified would result in pain, for example, hunger, thirst, sleep, repose, and so on. Now, Bentham saw the removal of the pain of the appetite through gratification as itself a pleasure, and so was the contemplation of the future removal of the pain: "the state of him whose thoughts are occupied with the conception of a pleasure of that or any other kind considered as future is a present pleasure."[74] And since these appetites recur so regularly, and since so much of one's existence is occupied in their gratification,

> no life which is exempt from pain, can, in the instance of those classes whom the necessity and habit of labour secures against *ennui*, fail of possessing its share of pleasure, and that too, a share little if at all short of the utmost quantity of which a person of the temper and disposition of mind possessed by the person in question, would in any situation have been susceptible.

Once the cup of the gratification of these appetites was full, "the means of pleasure may change the quality but can add nothing to the quantity of pleasure."[75]

We have, then, the remarkable description of the good life of the poor, the life of pleasure and therefore of happiness, as the successive gratification of the most basic animal appetites. The pauper child knew little of other pleasures, or rather, Bentham would see to it that he knew little else. Labor was the linchpin; it was justified as the guarantor of these present and future pleasures. To clinch the argument, he repeated his familiar rationale for the denial of other pleasures. There was "a great difference between the non-administration and the refusal of a supply of any instrument or opportunity of enjoyment," between the mere absence of an instrument of enjoyment and the disappointment and frustration created by the denial of "a desire already formed": in the case of the pauper child bred by the Company to the life of toil, there could be no hardship.[76]

There was one more proof of the future happiness of apprentices educated to labor and frugality. Once absolute necessities were provided for, "comparative happiness as between man and man depends, even as far as his wealth is concerned, not in the absolute quantum of wealth through the period of his life, but the proportion of wealth at a more advanced period in comparison with the quantum possessed at a more early period." In other words, it depended upon "the rate of affluence being in a state of encrease, or at least not on the decline."[77] This was a view, with the exception of the last phrase, very much like Hobbes' well-known declaration that "felicity of this life consisteth not in the repose of a mind satisfied" but is rather a "continual progress of the desire, from one object to the other."[78] For Bentham, whatever one's income is at one time, however small it may be, "every accession it receives excites in his bosom the sensation of affluence," and every diminution generates a sense of privation and penury. Thus a prince, who enjoys more happiness with £30,000 a year than the peasant with £20, is actually less happy when his income drops by a third than the peasant whose income climbs to £30. A similar spurt of happiness awaited the youth of Panopticon:

In this article, so far as depends upon pecuniary circumstances, wants and means both taken into the account, he is during his apprenticeship, at any rate not worse off than his fellows without doors: and at the expiration of his apprenticeship, at his entrance into the world at large, he is much better. The habit of living upon a little, is a source of affluence and such a source as no external accident can dry up.[79]

Finally, we come to that curriculum of subjects to be studied by pauper children during the one day's hiatus from productive labor required by religion. Like so many other activities in life, Bentham saw the exercise of the mind, at least during an extended period, as "a continued sacrifice of the present to the future."[80] He set himself the task of pruning from the tree of knowledge those branches which were not worth the sacrifice of the poor. Education had for its object imparting a knowledge of what gives pleasure and pain—knowledge of oneself, others, animals, and inert matter as sources of enjoyment. "A man may be said to have an interest in an object if it is a source of pleasure or pain, or security against pain." This formula was a guide not only to what ought to be included but also to what ought to be excised from curricula. First on the list of excludables were those dead languages, Latin and Greek, as well as every other foreign language. (Bentham knew full well from his own experience the 'useless' pain of imbibing them.)

Banned also as useless to the lower orders were higher mathematics ("all high and difficult branches"), grammar ("even English"), and astronomy (except, in the case of sailors, "so much of the practical part as is necessary to navigation"). That poetry and oratory would be proscribed goes without saying: oratory was an unnecessary skill for those born to political quiescence; and poetry was worse than useless since it positively misinformed. Logic was on this index, as were geography (excepting "so much as is attained by looking at a map") and history. All of these were undesirable *absolutely*.[81]

The exclusion of history, and to a lesser degree geography, is significant for its political overtones, for they were the overtones of political quietism as an injunction which pervaded pauper education. Geography was left in the dark night of obscurity because it was subservient "to history, to foreign politics, or to foreign commerce"; knowledge of one's own country can be learned as it is needed, without formal lessons. The exclusion of history is hardly surprising; it is as Benthamite as the rejection of custom for Reason. History for Bentham, as for the Enlightenment generally, was largely a catalogue of error and human folly. It was also a fund of examples for the oratory of political men: what was implied by the rejection of the study of history by the poor was that they would be kept as far as possible from political action. Since Bentham seldom spoke of history at any length, it is worthwhile to allow him to speak here at some length:

> History, meaning general history, can have but two objects, amusement and instruction. In the way of amusement, the universally agreeable and most morally useful fictions, fictions avowed fictions, bear the palm from the mixture of real and pretended truths called histories. In the

way of instruction history is of use . . . to nobody but to politicians. The realities of the transactions of political men is of no use to any man but him who is or wishes to be their fellow. The tendancy in general is to familiarize the corruptions and the affections of men with blood and carnage, to dress out in gaudy and attractive colours the most destructive vices and to annex the idea of honour to injustice and murder upon a large scale.[82]

Law was to be still another unstudied subject—not as being undesirable ("for what could be more desirable?") but as being "in the present state of it, unattainable."[83] Bentham's attack on the chaotic state of the law was compulsive: throughout his life, regardless what he was discussing, an attack on the common law was never far off. The only wonder was that on this occasion he did not launch yet another diatribe against the common law's foremost defender, William Blackstone.[84] He did, however, launch a missile at another favorite target, Natural Law. "Natural law," he said, "is neither more nor less than what positive law ought to be." This comment should be set beside his famous aphorism that Natural Law is "nonsense on stilts." "Positive law," he went on, "as it stands in this country, not to speak of others, is essentially incapable of being taught. A thing that does not exist, cannot be produced."[85] It was the old story of the 1770's—who could know what the law was? Legal mythology had it that judges 'found' it in each case, but Bentham knew better. Only a *code* could furnish those "standing laws" that John Locke had so emphatically said are prerequisite for political freedom and which Bentham had pointed to so often as a *sine qua non* of security from misrule. As for customary, "judge made" law, it was incapable of accurate determination; that is, "no statement whatever of the rules of Common Law can be other than a false one: and the more determinate it is the falser and more unfaithful."[86]

Having said all this, Bentham did want certain legal lessons inculcated into the minds of all pauper children. "Instructions" were to be delivered to the young which would dispose them to "peace and quietness," to "be contented with their lot." Two propositions in particular were to be "inculcated": that their circumstances ("conditions they are doomed to") are as good as any, "i.e. as favorable to happiness as any other"; and that no show, on their part, "of their collective force would have any tendency to improve it."[87] The pauper was to be informed that his government "such as it is and whatever it be, is better than any other to the formation of which he can have any chance of contributing, were he even to quit [his] occupation" and devote his whole attention "to the accomplishment of the supposed improvement." Even though instruction in law in general and constitutional law in particular might seem "full of absurdity and extravagance," there was really nothing to worrry about, since "the system of instruction is understood to mean neither more nor less than a sermon and that a short one," on the text " 'to be quiet and mind your own business'."[88] How could William Pitt feel uneasy reading this? Quite obviously it was written by no democrat.

If all of this was *off* the list, what was *on*? Besides the rudiments of reading and writing, scientific subjects were on, especially chemistry, the science with which Bentham had been so preoccupied during the days after he left Oxford when he performed chemical experiments in his rooms in Lincoln's Inn. Chemistry, he said, is the "hand maid of frugality." Too many knew Greek, too few chemistry.[89] Naval Science was another safe and useful tool too much left unstudied by those attending University—Samuel Bentham, who was a naval architect, no doubt had told him that. "The moral feelings and elevation of mind that characterise the gentleman," Jeremy wrote, are "beyond dispute: but in point of appropriate information scarcely to be distinguished from their subordinates."[90] In less polite words, the upper classes were ignorant: miseducated at Oxbridge, they lacked the knowledge that Bentham believed should be pushed to the forefront—knowledge that promoted economic growth, that created the only "wealth of nations" worthy of the name. This implied, however, that if Bentham's curriculum were to instruct the poor, they would possess knowledge the rich knew nothing of: such proposals were dangerous. How far could this education go? He found it prudent to suppress the following implicit threat to the upper class monopoly of knowledge that counts: "To have gone on and spoken of . . .Ornithology, Ichthyology, Entomology would have been too alarming—what? make paupers men of science?— qualify Pauper-boys for the *Royal Society*, and Pauper girls for the *Blue-Stocking Club*? Yes verily."[91] On closer look, however, this is only a rhapsodic flight of Benthamite fancy, since Sundays and only Sundays were available for any other education than the "education" of productive labor, and the qualifications for admission to the Royal Society required a rather greater depth of learning than could be acquired in the time left unoccupied by divine service and, in the case of boys, militia drill.

A final item in the pauper child's education occupied Bentham's attention to a far greater extent than the reputation of his Utilitarianism would lead one to expect. Although it would be an extravagance to think of Bentham as a music lover, he did enjoy chamber music, and he considered the

National Charity Company as a potential "musical seminary" which might develop what otherwise would be a wasted national resource—the musical talent of the poor. It would be too much, however, to expect Bentham to consider the enjoyment of music for its own sake as opposed to its economic and moral utility. He regarded music as a commodity like everything else, and he intended to bring it "to that market where the commodity will find its highest value." That market would be found among the wealthy, where music contributes to "the augmentation of innocent at least, however light and unprofitable pleasure, on the part of the superior classes."[92]

But the function of music as a consumable commodity was not, to his mind, its greatest importance, for there was a moral significance as well. Over and over Bentham stressed the value "of musical skill [from] a moral [point of] view, as supplying a fund of amusement constantly at command —and as filling up the vacuity of thought that might otherwise be filled up with drunkenness or other mischief."[93] Music had a special quality, for like drunkenness, it had the capacity for "furnishing sensation for every moment," but unlike it, music was all innocence "pure from [all] danger: and in much greater perfection."[94] The more occupied one's mind with music, and "with the sentiments with which music is . . . accompanied," the less exposed it was "to the temptation of engaging in . . . pernicious enterprizes."[95] Music was "favourable to *moral health*, by filling up vacancies in the mind, and thereby blocking up the entrance of vitious ideas and desires," for the mind was "that field in which if [a] man sow not wheat, the devil will sow tares."[96]

Such were the neutral properties of music, but there were also more positive features which a skillful government might exploit. Musical notes "bear for the most part a natural resemblance to the notes expressive of the social affections, of the affections which are so many modifications of benevolence: complaint, entreating, soothing, condolence, congratulation, co-exultation and the like."[97] Vocal music, it was true, could be a vehicle for mischief, but properly engrained into youth, it was "an anchor with which everything that is . . . to be taught and never to be forgotten may be riveted into the tender mind"; it was the "perfect form" for inculcation of the "perception of every duty"; and it was "the most effective as well as the gentlest instruments of the empire that . . . ought to be acquired by a good government over the affections of the people."[98] Music could thus be fashioned into one more tool of social control; it was a form of "indirect" or "transcendental" legislation all the more powerful because of its subtlety:

> Vulgar legislation drags men to its purpose in chains, from which, thanks to the bungling of the grim gribber man at the anvil who forges them, . . . the captives break loose in crowds: transcendental legislation leads men by silken threads, entwined round their affections, and makes them its own for ever.[99]

Music could even be made subservient to *"productive industry* by giving regularity and quickness to the motions of the workman, and in works performed in concert, by . . . enabling to keep time—at any rate by cheering him during the work." Finally, musical education would aid in the spread of Utilitarian values after the "emancipation" of the apprentices; it would act as a "most valuable *bond of union"*; and by way of example it would spread among the members of the independent poor.[100]

In summary, youth had two primary functions in Bentham's reform plan. First of all, they were the guarantors of the National Charity Company's profitability. Mobilized and assembled from diverse sources, youth were the one stable component of profitable labor in the entire system: without their involuntary attendance and compulsory unpaid labor, the claim that the Company could turn a profit collapsed. Bentham therefore had a compelling interest in the argument that pauper youth were better off if reared in an institutional setting devoid of both the usual childhood freedoms and parental love than they were if reared amongst their families. This led to a rather misleading description of pauper youth's education. In fact, little of the scientific and other education then available could be imparted to youth on the one day each week allotted to the task, and little could be learned in the first few years of life, that brief whisper of existence before the commencement of full-time labor during which Bentham allowed the whole of a child's time to be given over to schooling. Benthamite education of any real depth was reserved for the "Middling" Classes who were to attend his "Chrestomathic" schools.[101]

Their second function was as foot soldiers in a surreptitious guerrilla war which he hoped to wage against the entrenched mores of an unutilitarian society. Bentham knew that the re-creation of the habits of half a lifetime or more among older paupers would be a chancy business at best, but the fresh unmolded clay of young minds was something else again: he fully expected that a great many of his wards would retain the habits of productive activity, frugality, and sobriety. But if this system of education—and the pauper kingdom as a whole—were to meet with success, it would need to be founded on sound management principles, and it is to this subject that we now turn.

4. Bentham and Management

"Pauper Management Improved": the word management in Bentham's title deserves special emphasis. "In this system of 'pauper management'," writes Gertrude Himmelfarb, "Bentham's primary concern was with 'management'; the 'pauper' occupied a secondary, adjectival position."[102] The remark is apt. The institution of a system of management was an embodiment of his desire for the rationalization of society; all else lay before it. Management, properly conceived, spelled an end to arbitrary decisions and actions, the end of the rule of chance whim or emotion, of the merely contingent. As routine, as uniformity, rationalized management controls the world it touches and for Bentham makes it knowable "In ordinary economical concerns, the whole system of management is single and insulated"; but in his own "unprecedented multitude of establishments," management would be required to be "conducted upon a plan in most points exactly the same."[103] Even the territory for each of the National Charity Company's five hundred (initially two hundred fifty) establishments was to be precisely uniform; all of England would be divided into squares of the same area—"Average distance accordingly between house and house 10 2/3 miles: viz. the side of the square, of which four contiguous houses occupy the angles"; and the distance between the remotest part of the industry-house district and the House itself was calculated "upon the supposition of an exact equality of distribution, 7 1/2 miles: being the semi-diameter of a circle circumscribing that square."[104] Thus do the niceties of geometry move from the philosophic method of the seventeenth century to the administrative method, at least in Bentham's case, of the eighteenth.

At the heart of Bentham's system of management was the idea of rational rules as paramount standards of administrative behavior. Far from the slipshod world of eighteenth-century English administration, especially Poor Law administration, Bentham looks forward to the rationalization of the nineteenth and twentieth, from whose embryo he took his inspiration by means of the imagination of its perfection. He may even have invented the word "rationalize," based (as will be seen later) on his translation of the French "raisonné": the Oxford English Dictionary records no earlier usage.

In administrative method his writing bristles with the advocacy of routine, or unchanging repetition of procedure. Established on his principles, no company, he argued, was likely to be inattentive to existing rules, and "change in the rules themselves is less to be apprehended."[105] The degree of publicity possible for a semipublic company meant the utmost "obedience paid to the rules—or reasons for the departure";[106] *"fixity"* or "steadiness" was a virtue peculiar to this kind of public management as opposed to private. Whatever was good in it could be "expected to continue: to continue unchanged unless any change has been discovered which would be for the better."[107] So effective did Bentham believe a rule-governed system of management to be, that even though he was fond of saying that in efficiency the race between government and private industry is "the race between the greyhound and the sloth," in this case he confessed that he had at first chosen "government management, . . . not mercantile management, not company management"; and even so he still thought that "even government under all its disadvantages might be trusted for the adhering to it."[108]

Rules reduced to principles were for Bentham almost magical instruments. Writing to Arthur Young, he spoke of "the names of my *principles* of management"; the names were nearly all his "own manufacture made out of so many rules":

> What I get by making them is this: a rule is a whole system: a principle is but a word: a word which though it would be like a German word or a tape-worm half an ell [an old measure varying from 27" to 45"] long, and made of a dozen words put together, is still but a word—a mere noun-substantive, and as such capable of entering like any other into the composition of a sentence. Cut down into a *principle*, a rule has a name by which it may be spoken of and called to mind without loss of time. You have thus and without quackery, the Iliad in a nutshell. . . .[109]

Management by fixed rules was like government through a legal code. Just as in the above passage rules could be reduced to concise principles and therefore retained by the mind, so also Bentham had long advocated the promulgation of law in its simplest and briefest form, published in legal "Digests," and fashioned into "catechisms" for easy learning. But once leave legal decision to individual discretion, to legal 'managers,' that is, to judges, and instantly one gets, in all its glory, that "labyrinth without a clue," the Common Law. That is why in Bentham's hands, the legal code itself actually became a rationalized system of administrative rules: the *Constitutional Code.*

The quality of managerial decision if left to individuals was equally precarious. Bentham argued that single enterprises were all too subject to degeneration once founders or founders' zeal died: "the spirit evaporates, and nothing but . . . indifference and negligence on the part of . . . management, relaxation and abuses in all its forms, remain behind." What was lacking was that "business practice," the "modes of proceeding," were not "consigned to any fixed and written general rules."[110] That, obviously, is what his large-scale system of management, with its catalogue of rules operating within a framework of central inspection, remedied. "In the case of an ordinary mercantile concern in private hands, a man follows without restraint the [bent] of his own inclination: accountable to nobody he may neither look at accounts, nor so much as keep any unless he pleases."[111] This was the freedom of the entrepreneur; but Bentham had in mind the systematic training of a very different economical animal, the manager.

Entrepreneurs are founders and innovators. They take risks for their business, make fundamental decisions, decide the kinds and amounts of services to be offered, and are not specially concerned with devising accounting methods. Managers, on the other hand, inherit going concerns. They carry out limited innovation, perpetuate rather than found enterprises, take limited decisions more like tactics than strategies, and tend to be subject to accounting.[112] They are administrators, as entrepreneurs are legislators. Now, Bentham sought to remain the sole entrepreneur-legislator of the National Charity Company, and his success depended on the quality of the Code of administrative rules he promulgated. Those who executed his managerial principles he properly called "managers." The large scale of the enterprise would, he believed, provide "the requisite facilities for obtaining a fit manager"—a man from the "superior ranks"[113]—but one who, by the nature of his position, could be no other than a manager: "Here accounts must be kept, must be published . . . regularly—and will be scrutinized . . . by many a benevolent, many a suspicious, many an envious eye; accounts under heads previously arranged with the declared purpose of giving the most perfect transparency to the whole management in every point of view imaginable."[114]

"In number they are few, and thence not only they are the more efficient and fertile in their operation," but they "will sit the lighter on the memory." This was Bentham's description of the "leading principles" of his "rules of management."[115] What were they? Most of them we already know. Foremost, of course, was the "Inspection Principle"—an idea for which he listed five synonyms.[116] There were also the separate-work and piece-work principles and the "peculiar premium" principle, the idea that a reward given to a few would more than compensate for the efforts of the many competitors. Wherever possible (children were the most likely prospects), rewards should be honorary ("Honorary-reward principle") to spare expense to the Company.[117] Distinction in dress, superiority in table seating, precedence in processions, promotion of children to a class of a higher age all were techniques of honorary reward; but reward for natural attributes alone—"beauty, stature &c."—was forbidden: for the excluded "it would be productive of humiliation without fruit."[118] (No doubt Bentham still felt the pain of his days as the puniest boy at Westminster School.) We are also familiar with the "standard presented by economy, justice, industry, morality, and genuine humanity," the "Neighbour's-fare" principle, a notion which he described as the *"Magna Charta"* and the "Sheet-Anchor," the "main pillar of public charity."[119] This principle, which had less to do with neighbors than it did with cutting costs, was, Bentham argued to those of over-nice moral or emotional sensibility, quite consistent with the Golden rule, "a mine not less of prudence than of beneficence" whose riches "have scarce yet been sufficiently explored."[120]

One rule as yet unfamiliar was the "Earn-first" principle. Quite simply, "earn-first" stipulated that no meal would be served before work was performed; it was designed especially for the lazy as reward-conditioning that would indelibly etch upon them the nexus between working and eating: no work—no eat, but work—eat. It was in this connection that he recommended the use of the device mentioned of precisely measured work like the turns of a wheel. The procedure was childishly easy—"You take your Raw or Lazy Hand and put him to [the task] at once—saying to him— *When you have performed such a number of turns, your meal is ready for you*."[121] For those recalcitrants who nevertheless refused to labor, there would be a compulsory two-day fast, after which, though the task were yet undone, a meal would be administered—"the effective powers of the principle might not be much impaired." Bentham tells us that he does not intend death by starvation for the lazy and that two days without food would do no harm. A worse application of the earn-first principle in Bentham's estimation was the practice of the Spartan school in which a boy "did not get his breakfast, till he had shot it off a tree." "This it must be confessed, was discipline with a vengeance. It was making it [a] felony without benefit of clergy not to be a good shot."[122] His own methods were milder.

These rules and others formed an harmonious and interdependent system and were extended to be applied in tandem. Thus, the piece-work (sometimes redefined into the more euphemistic "proportional pay") and peculiar-premium principles would be applied together whenever possible; and only insofar as the separate-work rule was followed could the earn-first, self-liberation, piece-work, peculiar-premium, and honorary-reward principles be applied.[123] And overarching all these facets of management, of course, was the brooding, somber figure of Panopticon itself.

Finally, the plan of management incorporated Bentham's famous imperative that duty and interest be joined together. "In the instance of the Manager of each local establishment," he wrote, "neglect no means of strengthening the connection between personal interest and public duty: in other words of establishing a community of interest between the public in respect of this branch of service."[124] All the means of acting on a man's interest, he argued in *Pauper Management Improved*, are "reduceable to the two heads of *reward* and *punishment*."[125] He made extraordinary claims for the perfection of such a system: the completion of the junction of interest and duty "in every line of conduct is neither more nor less than to bring the science and art of government to perfection, to have established a perfect system of law." The term "government" in this passage was remarkably inclusive—"The art of government is as yet but in its infancy even at the capital manufactories: no wonder it should have made but small advance in the petty establishment of a country Poor-house."[126] Quite appropriately, this suggests that *"government"* as used here was synonymous with *management*. Bentham again more than hints that the way to make the social world knowable and therefore controllable is through administrative unity: "In a cluster of small pauper establishments straggling over England, dispersed and unconnected . . . all is opacity and obscurity." His system "connected together by one authority" was, in stark contrast, "as transparent in the figurative sense, as each House, if constructed in the Inspection Architecture principle, would be in the literal sense."[127]

One paramount question had to be answered: what motive could be depended upon so that when interest and duty were joined, they would *stay* joined? One possibility was shame: since managers would be ashamed to be found in dereliction of duty, they would have an interest in performing it: ". . . the eye of the public is drawn upon the subject, and operates as a check [upon] personal interest and favouritism." This, however, was unsatisfactory, for once public zeal cools, once "the eye of the public is taken off," Industry Houses, like government departments would be considered as a "fund of patronage—as a means of providing for friends, relatives, and dependents."[128] Other possibilities were likewise dismissed:

> To suppose that a man will not by fits and starts, but for a constancy and for ever bestow the same measure of attention upon a concern by which he can neither gain nor lose, as upon a concern in which he may profit by diligence and [lose] by negligence—to suppose that he will be led to bestow the same measure of attention by the principle of pure benevolence alone, or by the principle of benevolence and the love of reputation together, or by both with the principle of religion to add strength to them, or by . . . all together without the aid of personal and worldly interest as with that aid, would be a supposition altogether repugnant to the known constititution of human nature.[129]

Systems of management, he said in the *Annals*, which have "disinterestedness, pretended or real" for their foundations are "rotten at the root . . . sure to perish [in] the long run."[130] There was one and only one motive that could master the contingencies of human emotion, one which was "of all others the most potent and efficacious, the only one which can be depended upon in the instances of all persons and at all times,"[131] one which "may be depended upon to the end of time"—the "pecuniary interest otherwise known as the love of money."[132]

The "pecuniary interest" was therefore the motive seized upon to bind interest and duty in this "mercantile concern, as thoroughly mercantile as any that can be imagined."[133] The "life assurance" or "life warranting" principle guaranteed that if the health or even life itself of inmates failed, administrators' emoluments would be adversely affected. Salaries were decidedly out; payment by the head was in—piece rates for the inmates; piece rates for the governors too. Money as reward, for example, would be provided annually to administrators for every child who survived; money as punishment would be docked for every woman who failed to survive childbirth.[134]

The last of Bentham's principles of management that will be considered is that of bookkeeping, which he called "an indispensable basis to good management" of "peculiar extent and importance" to his system. "Extent" is, in fact, the quality that most characterized bookkeeping in poor-Panopticon. "The supposition to set out upon," he wrote, "is—that everything is to be registered, for the registration of which any use whatever can be found."[135] If the purpose of bookkeeping is in any case regulatory, it was quintessentially Benthamite to carry such regulation to its furthest extremes; it was an example, in his words, of a "variety of minute regulations, absolutely necessary to carry the principle of the measure into effect."[136] Next to the Panopticon principle itself, it was the supreme measure of control. It was an integral part, indeed a *sine qua non* of the inspection system itself; and as such it was a powerful vehicle for the removal of the last vestiges of contingency from the Company as a whole. Bookkeeping in the Company's "frugality bank," for example, afforded a "degree of competency, which at present is exposed everywhere to contingencies," that would be "certain and universal."[137]

For the purposes of more extensive control, Bentham proposed the multiplication of books, an operation which, he argued, so far from making accounting more complex, would actually simplify it.[138] And an addition would be made to ordinary accounting—the "Tabular Statement Principle." (Tables and tabulations were a lifelong preoccupation for Bentham.) Tables which afforded comparative analysis between House and House would mark out the most successful enterprises and therefore make for uniform modes of operation. Uniform, *methodical* behavior, such was the triumph of Benthamite management: "The importance of this principle is greater than at first sight might be apprehended. Tabular Statement is methodical, uniform, distinct, all comprehensive statement"[139]—rather like a legal code. The methodical statement made for methodical control. "The Tabular-Statement principle," he said, "is an instrument in the hand of the principle of publicity. It is bookkeeping reduced to a quintessence."[140]

Bentham believed that the determination of the *"heads"* of books to be kept should be guided by the *"ends* or *objects"* in view, which in this case were health, comfort, industry, morality, discipline, and "pecuniary economy." The general categories of books were accordingly population, health, stock, and correspondence books. A fifth category, for discipline and morality, involved that most Protestant of activities, moral bookkeeping. These were the "Behaviour-books."[141] All of these categories were subsumed under more general headings: *"Chronological* and *Methodical— Elementary* and Aggregate." "Chronological" books recorded each discrete particle of information or "elementary" datum, which data, when appropriate, were totaled as "aggregate" data and entered according to subject matter in "methodical" books.[142] The range and detail of these books was truly monumental,[143] but the procedure had a simple defense: because of the large scale of the system, "the minutest article may swell into importance."[144] Again the legal analogy is apposite—he made precisely the same defense of his legal codes.

Detail is also the catchword for any description of the moral bookkeeping in this pauper kingdom. Time and "method" were of its essence. For the "methodical relief" of paupers, "an appendage . . . obvious and necessary, [is] the prescribing a system of book-keeping for composing and preserving upon record a *methodical history* of the proceedings of all those by whose instrumentality the relief is to be administered."[145] This referred to the authorities, but the same "methodical history" applied to the moral behavior of inmates. In Bentham's Utopia the idea of a "complaint book," one of several kinds of moral bookkeeping books—there were red and black (reward and punishment) and misbehavior books as well—involved capturing every relevant and irrelevant particular:

> Heads for a complaint book—1. Time (day, hour, minute)—2. By whom—3. Against whom, or what—4. Concerning what—5. To whom—6. By whom examined into—7. Witness or witnesses examined—8. By whom decided upon—9. Time when decided upon—10. Time employed in the examination—11. Decision—12. Decision, by whom executed—(if it be a case calling for execution)—13. Time, &c., when executed.[146]

For Bentham, bookkeeping *freezes history*, captures every moment. It was as close as he could come to photography. Even as I am watched by others now, through moral bookkeeping I am watched in the future by others still. The "moral" books were the guards that watched over the guardians. "Bookkeeping *rationalized*," Bentham wrote to Arthur Young, "if thus I may have leave to translate your French-imported *raisonné*—Book-keeping extended in its limits as well as corrected in its language by human reason, is one of the main pillars of my system. . . ." "I had all along," he went on, "said to myself, that while the Penitentiary House was building, Book-keeping was among the arts which I should have to learn for it."[147] Bookkeeping perfected, inspection perfected; at last these two objects of Bentham's desire, these two fetishes, coalesced into a yearly fetishistic rite—the "annual walk." In their Board Room, round a circular table sixty feet in diameter, set off by portrait tables and map tables three feet by three feet, the directors of the Company would view the Books and "obtain a simultaneous view of the state of the establishment . . . in the way of ocular demonstration."[148]

Bookkeeping perfected was the ultimate Utilitarian victory over the messy disorderliness of social reality. This victory lay in the capacity of bookkeeping to telescope all things and all events into categories which, once condensed, could be rigorously displayed in written form and made literally visual at a glance. (It was ironic that the only instance in which Bentham referred to those human beings who were to inhabit his "Houses of Industry" as "souls" rather than as "hands" occurred when they were literally ciphers, when he spoke of bookkeeping.)[149] Those subject to this regime, their actions, indeed their whole lives laid bare, could be expected to pattern their future behavior into exhaustively prescribed channels: so long as pain-avoiding animals refused certain punishment, the future, so far as it depended upon them, would cease to be unknown. Only one stimulus would bring forth systematic change, the technological change inherent in scientific experiment. This was the last word in social control.

Bentham's system of management, then, was anything but peripheral to his Poor Law reform; it was at its core. Among the most notable aspects of his thinking on management, as one writer has pointed out, are the extent to which he assumed the context of a factory system and the unambiguous way in which he saw "management" as a distinct function of an enterprise.[150] If the broad outline of his recommendations was not necessarily original (uniformity of procedure, the establishment of methods of bookkeeping and inspection, and the centralization of authority were all commonly advocated in the last quarter of the eighteenth century),[151] the extent to which Bentham carried his proposed managerial system was surely unique: it formed the framework within which every aspect of life in Panopticon poorhouse was to be directed and evaluated. And, coupled with the value of child labor, it was the principal defense of his assurance to a skeptical public that the poor could more than pay for their own relief. With its adoption, the hit-or-miss whimsy that characterized eighteenth-century Poor Law administration would be transformed at a single stroke. This, too, formed part of his silent revolution.

5. An Experimental Laboratory: Social Engineering

"Observation and experiment compose the basis of all knowledge," Bentham wrote in *Pauper Management Improved*. Not the least of the "collateral benefits" of the Company's establishments was their use as a vast experimental laboratory for the augmentation and dissemination of useful knowledge; even if this were the sole "collateral use" of the system, could Panotpicon not, he asked, "be styled a *polychrest—an instrument of many uses?*" The word was taken from Bacon, the saint whom Bentham so often invoked, who "would not have regarded [Panopticon] with indifference."[152] Just as the Company's establishments gathered together the scattered fragments of men's labor for systematic exploitation, so they collected the means for the growth of scientific knowledge, *data*. Data had hitherto been "scanty, accidental, irregular, incomplete . . . the scattered fruit of the uncombined exertions of unconnected individuals." The Company gave the "first opportunity ever presented to mankind" to increase useful knowledge on a "regular and all-embracing plan" on a national scale; and the sciences would be "raised to a pitch of certainty, to which neither example, nor, till now, so much as conception, has perhaps ever reached."[153]

It was in its capacity as a tool for social research that bookkeeping acquired a double significance, for through it the relevant data would be collected and preserved. The range of possible experimentation was enormous. Mechanics and chemistry, husbandry and meteorology, manufacturing and "domestic economy," even logic (as the "art of communicating ideas") and bookkeeping itself would find improvement under the Company's guiding hands and watchful eyes.[154] Every improvement discovered, whether in technical or in managerial knowledge, would find "universal and immediate adoption in all the 250 Houses."[155]

A further field of experimentation, medicine, involved the paupers themselves. They were to be the unknowing, no doubt at times unwilling, subjects of "medical" experiment. Bentham listed four fields for such experiment from which knowledge might be reaped: food, drink, temperature, and "commencement of sexual intercourse." Different kinds and (as we have seen) amounts of food would be administered to the apprentices to determine which mix best promoted health. If some became sick or sickly, it was an indication that the diet had better be changed; that permanent damage might be inflicted was a question that Bentham seems not, in his euphoria, to have considered.

He did, however, give a specific defense of this policy against charges of its inhumanity to the subjects. The defense was ingenious and almost works. The objection he answered was that it was "inhuman to take human nature for the subject of the experiment," to "single out these whom their weakness and helplessness has laid at our mercy." He replied that it would indeed be inhuman deliberately and knowingly to put them "into a bad condition for the chance of bringing them out of it," just as it would be inhuman to inoculate a disease to test medicines. But, continuing the medical analogy, if the disease *already* exists, "if six different medicines present themselves as equally promising, there would be no sort of inhumanity, but on the contrary great humanity and great use to give to each of six patients a different one of the six medicines." The argument had force. This is almost precisely the procedure so often used today among cancer patients at institutions like the Mayo Clinic. But Bentham then used the disease analogy to defend the separate administration of six foods to *healthy* 'subjects' to find "which of them answers best": "By this means (the course of experiments gone through and the result ascertained) that only is practiced, which is best: without these helps, good and bad *take their chance together*. With these helps, practice is . . . the fruit of wisdom: without them, the offspring of *blind chance*."[156] Who could tolerate chance? It might have occurred to him to let nature take its course and allow his subjects, within some limits, to eat what foods they pleased; but nature was mere chance, and like his hero Bacon, Bentham's object was to *subdue* nature.

The remaining areas of human experiment are soon described. The "experiment" with "drink" was less an experiment than a morality lesson, a living advertisement that not even a walk on Beer Street was so healthy an exercise as a ride on the water wagon down the straight and narrow path of sobriety. The results of indulgence by "old-stagers" would be compared to the robust health of abstinent youth and others. As for ventilation, Bentham proposed to experiment by keeping some "apartments" hotter, others colder, others still alternating in temperature, which offered a chance to use the precise measurement of "thermometrical observations." However, the results of this experiment seem to have been predetermined, since Bentham remarked that "*Chilliness* will . . . suggest to charity the importance of warm *clothing*."[157] We have already discussed his plan for early apprentice marriage, due regard being paid to health. The question was, how early was healthy? To find the answer, he would experiment with marriages at puberty and compare them with respect to health with others delayed by three-month periods up to a delay of several years; the age of the youngest partners to retain their health would become the age that marriage would be permitted and encouraged. Bentham said nothing whatever of emotional maturity, though perhaps this was included in the "intellectual " maturity that he did think necessary. "*Fiat lux*," he wrote in the *Annals*, "were the words of the Almighty:—*Fiat experimentum*, were the words of the brightest genius he ever made. O chemists!—much have your crucibles shown us of dead matter;—but our industry-house is a crucible for men!"[158] Bentham the scientist augmented knowledge; Bentham the social scientist augmented the numbers of Utilitarian men.

This brings us to the other half of the program—the dissemination of "useful knowledge"—the increase in "the multitude of individuals, to whom any part of the existing stock of lights has been communicated."[159] By educating the paupers in Panopticon, Bentham hoped to educate the independent poor, spreading the good news of reformation and salvation through Utilitarian values. The poor had usually received a sort of non-education, via the trickle-down method, from the rich. "In the situation proposed, the conduct of the poor will depend—not upon the remote and casual influence of the rich, . . . but upon the direct and constant exercise of plastic power." Compared with the "influence exercised by the Company over these its wards," he went on, the influence of the schoolmaster over the ordinary pupil "is as nothing." The poor were nineteen-twentieths of the population—"in the condition of one of these twentieths, the plan in question would exercise a direct and all-commanding authority; and over the remainder a very considerable,—and finally, perhaps, an all-prevailing—though less certain and immediate, influence."[160] Both from direct instruction and from the results of management, knowledge acquired "would, upon the emancipation of the apprentice-stock, be disseminated, along with them, through the community at large." The dissemination would, again, be "a less direct and certain way," but knowledge and habit might insinuate themselves more or less "in the way of adoption and imitation, through the bulk of the self-maintaining poor."[161] Through such means, and through the influence of the whole range of services the Company offered, from banking and insurance to the employment bureau, the system would act as a Utilitarian Trojan Horse strategically poised within a society governed traditionally and aristocratically, in mores as in Parliament.

This 'subversive' aspect of the Company is even more apparent in Bentham's treatment of religion, for he attempted to co-opt religious habit and even the church itself to the Utilitarian cause. We saw before how, if all went well, the poor box would move from the parish church to the local House of Industry.[162] That was one small step; there were many others. He suggested, for example, that honors such as church sinecures be given to the most successful House managers—this would neatly infiltrate, as it were, Utilitarian men into otherwise useless positions and suggest to society which values were in the ascendant. "Might not an arrangement of this sort," he inquired with feigned innocence, "help to protect the church establishment from obloquy?"[163]

More important, Bentham set out to incorporate the more useful affairs of the National Charity Company into Sunday activity, both inside and outside the Inspection Houses, even into religious liturgy itself. In *Pauper Management Improved*, he proposed that the parish clerk receive the *Employment Gazette* and post it "in a certain place within or without the church." Moreover, "by means of suitable comments and offices," the "Pauper-Population Report" might be read by the minister, having been "ingrafted into the liturgy." This was all quite proper—"it would be congenial to the gospel, in which the concerns of the poor are the objects of such anxious and distinguished notice." After all, he argued, "the gospel itself means, in the original, *good news*: this would be truly gospel news."[164] (He neglected to mention that the "gospel" of work and save is not exactly the essence of religiosity.) In his manuscripts, he went even further in defending this practice. Sounding like a footnote in Weber, he remarked that the minister might comment on the Report, showing those "successes or miscarriages considered as indications of the divine blessing in the endeavours of the Company, or warning to redouble their diligence in the correction of whatever might be found amiss." He continued:

> Thanksgivings for any remarkable diminution in the rate of Infant mortality, or in the number of committments among the number of Ill-famed and Unavowed Employment Hands:—prayers for the speedy reformation of these degraded classes, and for their happy return into the bosom of society: applications of this nature, while strengthening their connection between charity and religion, would naturally contribute to interest the affection of the lower classes in the prosperity of the institution. . . .

He confessed that he could not see why "communications and comments of this nature" should not be admitted into "the celebrations of the Lord's Day."[165] Elsewhere, he noted that he could not see why "the rigorous observation of the Sabbath" should interrupt harvest work.[166]

Another way to transform the church (he was thinking exclusively of the Church of England) into a more Utilitarian institution was to turn it into a bank. Sunday would be banking day—for the poor to use any other day would amount to an onerous tax on them—and the parish clerk and vestry room would serve as banking officer and office, respectively.[167] Alternatively, the congregation might be served at their seats after the service—"none to be admitted who have not been present at the service." Here was an instance in which direct rather than indirect legislation was more effective: "By this means Sabbath-keeping is promoted in a direct way: by the customary and established means in a way very indirect and than which nothing can be more inefficient." Again Bentham needed to defend this rather daring departure from custom, preferably without provoking memories of Jesus driving the money-changers from the temple. "The Sabbath of the Church of England," he said, "so far from being prohibitive of all pecuniary business, is in its own way a day of great pecuniary business. Money received for Burials, Marriages, and Christenings."[168] His reasoning in the *Annals* was quite ingenious, not to say disingenuous: "if a money transaction be sanctified by charity, why not by a virtue which stands paramount to charity herself, by preventing the mischiefs for which her best exertions are but a palliative?"[169]

Within Panopticon, the nexus between utility and religion was more open. Sunday was a day for better things than prayers in the chapel and pints in the pub. The navy would be trained, the militia would be drilled,[170] and science would be reconciled with religion in a way Paul Tillich never dreamed of. In particular, there would be courses of scientific lectures infused with religious overtones: they would not be "merely *physical* but *physico-theological*," "impregnated by the spirit, and rendered subservient to the sacred purpose of the day."[171] This, however, stood the matter on its head, for "the sacred purpose of the day" was obviously being made subservient to the dissemination of useful knowledge—all the rest was window-dressing, as Bentham very well knew.

This is not to say, however, that he would have eliminated religion from poor-Panopticon if he were able. If he was somewhat less than candid in listing "uninterrupted benefit of divine services" as a "pauper comfort," the pauper's "clear conscience brightened by religious hopes"[172] was an objective of no small importance, for with his heart lightened by religious hope, the pauper would be more likely to accept his station and its duties. And religion, of course, was one of the four "sanctions" for promoting desired behavior listed in *An Introduction to the Principles of Morals and Legislation* (1789).

To complete this view of religion in Panopticon poorhouse, let us glimpse the spectacle presented to us just before worship has begun:

A Sunday Scene

The Dome [is] let down upon the Inspection Room. The Dome with the Pulpit, Reading Desk, Clerk Seat, . . . let down upon the Inspection Room—The Galleries above the Dome for Visitors disclosed to view. The circumferential [screens] composed of the several pairs of partitions bounding the Apartments of the Married Couples, with the respective Middle Pieces, put up all round—The Sleeping Stages lowered so as not to exclude the light—so as not to diminish the zone of light, which will thus have its two feet of breadth throughout the whole of its circuit, the officers' Division and the parts occupied by the Radial walls excepted.[173]

Here Bentham breaks off—and we shall also.

What is most striking in Bentham's projected 'social engineering' as revealed in his Poor Law reform writings is that even in his most conservative phase he was intensely dissatisfied with social institutions and habits as he found them, and he therefore formed a strategy, though only a partial one, for their renovation. Years before he set about attacking the Church of England in extended essays, he had formed a plan subtly to undermine it; and long before he advocated suffrage for the great mass of Englishmen, he had seized upon the lower classes, especially the young, as the vehicle for the transformation of the habits and mores of future generations. These 'new' men and women were, of course, to be directed from above; but later theorists of social transformation—notably Marx and Lenin—in their varying ways also found a special role in the revolutionary process for those better educated and more farsighted than the poor usually are. In Bentham's case, he was subsequently (after the end of the revolutionary turmoil in France) to become more explicit about the leading place he accorded the middle (rather than the working) classes in a struggle to wrest social, political, and economic power from what he considered a corrupt aristocracy. He expected the working classes to follow a middle-class lead. In his writings on poverty, all of this was no more than embryonic; but the germinating seeds of a radicalism which years later burst into full bloom are already visible.

Conclusion

This is not the place to attempt a complete description of Bentham's view of the components of a social order. A thumbnail sketch may nevertheless be useful as a perspective for his views on poverty. Such an account, however, will necessarily be overly compressed, and it should be borne in mind that a good deal of flesh must be added to this skeletal version before the body of Bentham's social thought is true to life. A summary of his argument, then, is as follows.

The proper end of any society is the happiness or "well-being" of its members, and it is the function of government to pursue this end. Well-being or welfare consists in a maximum of pleasure and a minimum of pain; happiness consists in this and in nothing else. The duty of the state is to ensure the welfare of all of its members, each counting equally; the happiness of the lowest peasant is of as much concern to the state as that of the highest prince. But it is not always possible to maximize the happiness of every member of society; often one man's happiness must be sacrificed to others, and the most that can be expected of the state is that the happiness of the greatest number be maximized. This is accomplished through the pursuit of several subordinate ends, the first of which is the security of the subject: he is to be protected from force and fraud or any other source of pain, for example hunger. Thus, a guarantee of sheer material subsistence is properly the object of state policy, and so is material abundance, since abundance is a guarantee of subsistence. But if abundance is to guarantee subsistence, one man's surplus must be transferable and when necessary transferred to provide another man's subsistence. Private agency is inadequate to accomplish this because of the uncertainty of its will to transfer, its insufficient knowledge with respect to recipients of transfer, and the uncertainty of its capacity to supply enough goods to satisfy need; therefore public agency must bear the primary responsibility in ensuring every subject's subsistence. We will return to this theme later on.

To this list of state ends, a fourth must be added—equality of wealth and equality of consideration in the eyes of the state. Equality of wealth is desirable because it maximizes happiness. This is so because every normal person has an equal capacity to feel pleasure and pain, though not necessarily an equal capacity to feel the same kind of pleasure or pain. All will equally feel the pain of hunger or a burn, but all may not equally feel the pain of sympathy for the hungry or burned, just as they may not derive equal pleasure from listening to Mozart or from an evening in a Public House. Equality of wealth maximizes the overall happiness of a community (insofar as happiness depends on wealth) because, first, each additional unit of wealth which an individual gains brings a diminishing amount of pleasure; secondly, those who are poorer will gain greater pleasure or utility from an additional unit of wealth than can be gained from that same unit by the rich. Ten pounds gained by a man who has only fifty pounds yields greater utility than ten pounds gained by a man with one hundred thousand pounds. Thus, subtracting wealth from the rich will continue to increase overall pleasure or happiness until everyone's wealth is equal.

However, since human nature is what it is—some are more industrious, more intelligent, or more greedy than others—absolute equality cannot be realized, for even if all were equally wealthy one day, they would not be so the next. The goal of equality can only be that of an approximate equality, and there ought to be limitations placed on this more modest aim. Wholesale confiscation of the property of the rich (as opposed to a partial tax on wealth) cannot maximize utility or pleasure due to the pain felt by losers combined with the general alarm spread in the community that all property is unsafe and not just the property of the rich: peasants might come to be called Kulaks and treated like princes. The community's alarm creates the pain of insecurity, which, added to the pain of the losers, always outweighs the pleasure of the gainers—pain hurts worse than pleasure pleases. This is a case of the objective of equality conflicting with the objective of security, which always takes precedence. Nor, as will be seen, can equality rightly be approximated unless and until all are equally productive. Gross inequalities should be gradually diminished over time, especially through taxation of the estates of the deceased, for the dead have no expectations; they feel no pain. Estate taxation is known in advance, and inheritors will lower their expectations accordingly; no legitimate expectations will be dashed.

Attacks on security are attacks on expectation. Expectation creates the possibility of the pain of loss. It also binds the present to the future and makes life an intelligible whole. Expectation is the faculty of foreseeing certain features of the future, with the reasonable hope that these features will in fact obtain—for example, the expectation that a year hence one will not be without the ordinary necessaries of life. Thus secure expectations allow us to plan our lives without the constant threat that contingent events will interrupt them to our disadvantage; securing expectation is a primary function of government.

Now, expectation is secure only when men behave in certain ways. Human beings are pleasure seekers and pain avoiders, and their behavior, unavoidably governed by the sovereign masters of pleasure and pain, will always follow their interpretation of how best to satisfy their desires. But pleasure-seeking men and women are apt to clash in their pursuits, and it is the duty of government to create a system which harmonizes interests— individuals are liable to misperceive their true interests or to substitute their selfish interests for social ones, thereby giving rise to general insecurity. In fulfilling its task of harmonizing interests, government uses the agency of law to ensure the conjunction of interest and duty; benevolence, because it predominates in only a few individuals, cannot be relied upon for social stability. To be effective laws must attach themselves to human motives, the source of outward behavior. That is why motives—the "springs of action"—must be fully analyzed and properly classified.

Sources of pleasure or pain that bind us to act in certain ways and to forbear acting in others are called sanctions. Of these there are five—the physical, the political, the moral (or popular), the religious, and the sympathetic. The physical is a source of actual or expected pleasure or pain stemming directly from the hand of nature without human or divine intervention; the political is exercised by agents of the state through courts; and the religious sanction is exercised, or expected by believers to be exercised, now or in the hereafter by a supreme being. A fifth sanction, the sympathetic sanction, binds us to aid those of our fellow creatures, human or animal, whom we find suffering or, but for our intervention, about to suffer;[1] this is why in discussing poverty we spoke of the "pain of sympathy."

Any sanction is capable of giving binding force to a law or rule of conduct, but only the political sanction is directly in the hands of government. Still, government can use indirect means to influence the other sanctions; for example, public opinion (the moral sanction) can be tutored indirectly. To some extent even the religious sanction can be influenced by giving or withholding the support of the political sanction; and the physical sanction can be utilized by the simple expedient of not interfering with it, as in the case of allowing hunger to occur.

In its use of the moral sanction the aim of government is not necessarily to deliver individual subjects over to the influence or rule of any existing popular opinion, without regard to its content, for much public opinion is ignorant of what kind of behavior is required to maximize utility. Religion in particular has often misled public opinion, encouraging widows to leap onto their husbands' funeral pyres, as in Hinduism; brutal punishments to be exacted for trivial offenses, as in Islam; sexual minorities to be persecuted, as in Judaism and Christianity (the so-called "religion of love" corrupted by Paul); and men to tyrannize over women, as in Hinduism, Islam, Judaism, and Christianity.

By the same token, government needs to be restrained from an unlimited power over its subjects; it needs to be watched just as individuals do. Publicity of all its actions and a requirement that a statement of reasons, backed whenever possible by scientifically collected data, justify those actions are means to ensure subjects against misrule. The closer government is watched, the better it too behaves.

Education and social discipline, with the former standing as a means to the latter, are the twin pillars on which, in Bentham's view, society, and therefore civilization itself, rest. Society is a system of rewards and punishments, and the task of government is to provide a framework of punishment and to clear the way for individuals to reap rewards by their own positive effort. It is through this sytem of rewards and punishments that disparate interests can be harmonized. Everyone knows his own interest; that is, he knows what gives him pleasure and pain. Pleasure seekers will always seek rewards, since rewards, as immediate sensual or other gratification and as the present means to future gratification, are the very stuff of pleasure. Similarly, everyone avoids punishment, since punishment is pain. But uneducated or improperly educated men and women often seek the opportunity to steal away the rewards of others or squander their own legitimately gotten gains without regard to future pleasure and pain. Such individuals (or even, when they are predatory, whole societies) are in an elemental way improperly disciplined: they are like small children who grab at immediate pleasure without regard to future consequences, that is, without the moderating forces of prudence and foresight. Taking no thought for the morrow, they become barbarians unless they are educated. It is therefore the necessary function of law to educate and discipline its subjects.

Law is primarily a system of social control. Properly written and enforced, law educates men to prudence, to future-regarding behavior. So when considering a course of action, a murder for instance, a man will ideally have this order of thoughts—the crime, the officer, the prison, the judge, and the gallows, or, rather, a long term in a penitentiary. This is how that foremost principle of mental activity, the association of ideas, works in pleasure-seeking, pain-avoiding men. But for this to occur law must be both knowable and known: to be knowable, it must be clearly written and capable of concise statement for easy commitment to memory; to be known, law must be promulgated with maximum publicity, making use of every means at hand to inculcate its message into its subjects. Subjects must be assured that infractions will be detected and punished—legal niceties such as rules of evidence and procedure should not be permitted to undermine this assurance. Since subjects of the law are pain-avoiding animals, they will refrain from illegalities, and insofar as the system is perfected, so far will punishment be nonexistent. So it is that the more closely we are watched, the better we behave. This assumes that laws are in fact well-written in the sense that legal behavior is good behavior; and it also assumes an effective police force. Auxiliary to a police force is a foolproof means of individual identification; Bentham's suggestion of a unique tattoo for each person was an eighteenth-century version of twentieth-century fingerprinting.

Enough of punishment, but more needs to be said of reward. Government, Bentham would assert, ought to be sparing in its dissemination of rewards for the behavior it requires of its subjects. We all ought to be good, but if we presented our *bill* for good behavior, there would be no end to expenditure. To reward is to take the substance of reward from one man for the sake of another; this is as true of honorary reward as it is of money or money's worth, since to raise up one man lowers the rest. In the case of taxation, taking from one to give to another, all other things being equal, is inherently unjust; it appropriates from the taxpayer the fruit of his labor, and the fruit of a man's labor is properly his own. This is a fundamental principle of natural justice. Thus the law does not say "work and I will reward you," but rather, "work, and by staying the hand that would rob you, I will safeguard the reward that you yourself earned." But this principle of natural justice can be overridden by another which properly is the first principle of any system of right, the utility principle. According to it, the state ought to maximize pleasure and minimize pain of its own subjects (and not, we should notice, everyone in the world). Utility supersedes natural justice whenever subsistence (that is, survival itself) is at stake, for allowing primacy to natural justice would yield more misery than enjoyment. We recall that the happiness of one subject counts as much as any other and that pain hurts worse than pleasure pleases: the pleasure of producers in the enjoyment of their goods cannot outweigh the ultimate pain of losing one's life. (Such propositions must be accepted axiomatically, but they also accord with common moral sentiment.) But this seems to be the only instance in which redistribution is justified during the owner's lifetime, and only the minimum required for the most efficient system for saving life is warranted by the utility principle; more than that is unjust expropriation. If taxation is forced labor, in this instance it is justified by the utility principle, but this justification limits the scope of transference and the amount to be transferred.

So much for a brief account of Bentham's social theory. A great deal of it can be seen at work in his Poor Law reform writings. Since, as we have seen, he called Panopticon poorhouse his "Utopia," we should ask ourselves *why* for Bentham is this Utopian? The answer, I think, is that here he could indulge his fantasy of possessing total control; here he could dream his dream of taking complete power over a social system. In the preface to *Panopticon* ... he described his novel architectural principle as "a new mode of obtaining power of mind over mind, in a quantity hitherto without example: and that, to a degree equally without example. . . ."[2] As a social scientist, as an engineer applying technology to social problems, Bentham at last had the stage on which to create a miniature society where a system of rewards and punishments worked in practice as it did in theory; where "not a wink, not a whisper" escaped notice; where 'crime' would be instantly detected and punished. He fully expected there to be no punishment. It was also a golden opportunity to tutor "public opinion," to create afresh the moral sanction among the large number of pauper youth he expected to govern, to inculcate the Utilitarian point of view without the interference of contingent events and contradictory ideas or behavior. It also had the virtue of following with a vengeance the rule that only the minimum necessary to save the life and health of the indigent be forcibly expropriated from producers by taxation; and if all went well, none at all would be expropriated for this purpose, which was even better.

"Charity is the end; economy is but the means": this claim of Bentham's, as mentioned before, was disingenuous at best. Economy and charity did not bear the relationship of means and end but rather of competing ends. And in that competition economy invariably took precedence. Charity could have been infinitely better served by giving up the "golden dream" of the indigents' self-support, not to mention the impossible dream of their actually turning a profit for their keepers. Utility may have taken precedence in its conflict with "natural justice," but the latter retained enormous influence: without this second standard of right, Bentham's justification for the ending of home relief, for the minimization and coarsening of food, for the extraction of a maximum of labor from children, the sick, and everyone else, collapses—collapses, that is to say, insofar as it is separable from "less eligibility." If the happiness of the indigent had any real standing in this system, which manifestly it did not, relief would have been dispensed at home, and a middle course charted between the squandering of public money on the one hand, and the utter minimum of Panopticon on the other.

Does the necessity or supposed necessity of less eligibility justify Bentham's plan, quite apart from the natural justice argument; is the "less eligible" nature of Panopticon poorhouse necessary to ward off a catastrophic decline in a workforce which prefers the dole to exertion? But we already know the answer to this. Something like less eligibility is practiced, or attempted to be practiced, by many governments today and no doubt will always be practiced: but there is a great difference between a policy of mere *less* eligibility and the one proposed by Bentham of *least possible* eligibility consistent with the absence of human abuse and the presence of health—as large a difference as there is between supervised probation for minor offenses and consignment to a well-run labor camp.

We come now to a fuller accounting of Bentham's writings on poverty and the Poor Law. If they are judged by his own method, a balance sheet can be drawn up weighing their positive and negative features. The content of his proposed set of reforms requires one kind of judgment; other parts of his work on poverty require separate consideration. Had the National Charity Company come into being, a substantial number of the poor would have derived certain benefits if they chose to avail themselves of the facilities, especially the "collateral uses," of Bentham's semi-public corporation. These are by now familiar. The mobility of the poor would be enhanced through Panopticon's function as "Poor man's Inn"; and employment would be facilitated by publication of vacant positions. Saving would be made easier by acceptance of small sums by a banking system the Company provided, and pawn brokerage would be available at attractive rates. All of these benefits were available to the working poor and were designed to maintain their independence.

There were other benefits. One was that a special effort would be made to improve the disastrous mortality rates among the infant children of the poor. By means of cleanliness, properly trained midwives, immediate medical attention, and other improvements infant lives would unquestionably have been saved, though how many can hardly be estimated. Another advantage was the rationalized system of Poor Law administration itself; thousands of sometimes arbitrarily and often inefficiently managed pauper princedoms would have been transformed by a single revolutionary stroke into one pauper "kingdom," rationalized and centralized, with evenhanded treatment for all, as much in London or Torquay as in Berwick-on-Tweed or Carlisle. Added to all of this was the end spelled out to pauper illiteracy by the Company's education of Panopticon's non-adult population. Even if the schooling of pauper youth was not all Bentham made it out to be (and it was not), the halt called to the illiteracy of tens, perhaps hundreds, of thousands who would otherwise have reached adulthood without the capacity to write more than their names or to read at all must be accounted no inconsiderable advantage of Bentham's scheme. A further benefit would have accrued to those children who would otherwise have been abused by parents and guardians; the thorough responsibility of Panopticon's management ensured that mistreatment could not go unnoticed.

One more feature of Bentham's plan as yet unmentioned is more difficult to judge. No one in need of relief who possessed saleable property, especially real property, would be permitted to enter Panopticon without its prior disposal and payment to the Company of the proceeds, half of which became Company property and the other half returned to the pauper in the form of small annuities. At first glance, this might seem a callous seizure of a widow's mite to extract from the poor every iota of value to be had. But a closer look beclouds the issue, for contemporary law required that no relief be extended to those who owned real property: such indigent owners were required to deplete their resources entirely before being eligible for public assistance. It is therefore unhistorical simply to condemn out of hand Bentham's version of this policy; at least under his rules the otherwise indigent owners of property would be allowed to retain half of its value. Still, his view of the matter was not the most humane that contemporary opinion adopted, since Pitt's bill allowed owners full retention of real property up to a value of £30.

In defending his policy Bentham ignored Pitt's bill entirely; in fact he felt called upon to justify allowing the otherwise indigent anything for their property. He argued, first, that it was a matter of justice to the pauper since there is an "evident hardship in taking a man's property from him and giving him nothing"; and secondly, there was a benefit for the Company since if the pauper received nothing for his property, he would give it away, dissipate it, or otherwise dispose of it.[3] Between harshness and humanity, in this case Bentham sat squarely in the middle upon the rock of 'economy,' which meant the maximum income for the company and a measure of justice for the pauper. But lurking behind the humane or 'just' aspect of his policy was the realization that without it the Company would be the financial loser.

A final benefit to the poor provided by Bentham's scheme was the most fundamental guarantee of any Welfare State: the poor would enjoy the secure expectation that under no circumstances would they be abandoned to starvation.

On the other hand, they already had that expectation, legally assured by the Poor Law. Moreover, all of the other benefits which Bentham's plan provided were possible without the termination of outdoor relief and the introduction of enforced incarceration in an institution that would have been overwhelmingly humiliating for its inmates. One need not be too shrewd to guess what the poor themselves would have thought of Bentham's revolution, but guessing is unnecessary since during the riotous week in Suffolk thirty years earlier which we have already cited, the poor expressed themselves clearly enough, smashing workhouses and demanding relief in the usual manner.[4]

As for humiliation, it began the moment paupers were required to wear distinctive dress which stigmatized them as public burdens, which according to Bentham's own showing they would not have been. And what would one say of a society that collectively jeered at its weakest members even if they were burdensome? It was to Pitt's credit that he called for a reversal of traditional attitudes which marked the pauper a lazy parasite, as if every circumstance that found a man impoverished should also brand him a cur. But under Bentham's system the humiliation that began with a novel form of the ancient practice of badging continued with the jail-like contrivances of Panopticon—its cells (albeit without bars), its ubiquitous rules and punishments for their infraction, its formalized procedures for doing everything, with virtually no choice whatever left to the pauper himself. The activities of each moment of every day, with the exception of one period on Sunday (for only some of the adults) would be predetermined for the pauper by his guardians and guards.

Equally humiliating was the constant possibility of observation that Bentham trumpeted so loudly and so often. Privacy was wiped out, but privacy is a *sine qua non* without which there is no human dignity, and so is the possibility of making at least some choices for oneself. A day in the life of a Panopticon pauper was never once without the threat of governing eyes suddenly appearing; even during the most private of natural functions, Bentham had ensured a but incomplete and tenuous solitude. In ordinary society even children beyond a certain age are treated with more respect, but in this regard under Bentham's rule the indigent were managed less as if they were the children of the state than as if they were its infants. Not even paupers' letters traveling between the islands of this chain of pauper prisons would escape the eternal gaze of authority. Presumably private ridicule of the Best Friend of Paupers carried through such channels would not result in actual punishment (though one cannot be certain), but at the least one could confidently expect the perpetrator to have been subjected to increased surveillance. We saw earlier that pauper communication was strictly controlled as part of a policy that ensured political quietism; scattered among so many Panopticons, the poor were quite literally ruled by division.

All of this underlined the extent to which the indigent in Panopticon were to be divested of personality and formed into a common mold, much like soldiers upon joining an army. Bentham treated the pauper not only as less than an adult but also as less than a human being. In any other situation the normal adult is routinely granted at least some degree of moral autonomy, but not here: the indigent were viewed instead primarily as living productive capital, capable, to be sure, of pain—but so were all animals, not excluding "that part of the national live stock which has no feathers to it and walks with two legs."[5]

The loss of human dignity was paralleled by the loss of hitherto existing legal protection. For the sake of grappling with a momentary crisis and the chronic agony of ratepayers, the poor were to have been stripped of positive rights which had taken centuries to accumulate. For those accused of begging, the Habeas Corpus Act (1679) would have been effectively nullified: courts were to be excluded from appeal for legal redress. The Company's power to seize, try, and sentence an accused beggar would have amounted to a great menace to the poor, threatening every laborer who wandered abroad in search of work and every child who sought a farthing from passersby. We recall that no "convicted" beggar would be released until his lengthy "self-liberation" account was paid with labor (and not with money) and that no child would be released before his majority. Imprisonment also unavoidably awaited anyone who seemed suspicious, who could not "give a good account" of himself, as well as discharged prisoners and even those of the acquitted who lacked an employer. One can only guess at the abuses and corresponding anxiety among the independent poor that such procedures would have given rise to.

An equally grievous loss to the impoverished would, of course, have been the abolition of home relief, with the possible exception of a few of the old. Here again, a gnawing anguish lest the same fate await them would undoubtedly have haunted the working poor; this seems indeed to have been consciously intended—it was Bentham's way of applying Townsend's exhortation to apply "pressure" to the poor. Whatever the ultimate advantages Panopticon may have held out to taxpayers, the poor themselves were obviously worse off by far than they were under the present "system." This may not have been true for certain individuals, but it was for the poor as a whole: since the poor were harassed by anxiety on the outside or humiliated and degraded, subjected to a minute control of their every action on the inside, their freedom of movement, expression, and association having been withdrawn entirely, one wonders how anyone with even the slightest sympathy for the poor could be other than horrified by Bentham's plan.

But can the same be said of the children and adolescents in this version of Panopticon? Bentham claimed that their situation would actually be more "eligible" than those living at large. Besides the benefits of rudimentary literacy, of the absence of abuse for the minority that would otherwise have been abused, of life itself for those who would have died in childhood or infancy, of a diet which, once settled upon, would have provided health, what would their condition have been?

What, first of all, does one say of a serious proposal that more than half a million children, or by a conservative estimate more than 10 percent (and perhaps as many as 15 to 20 percent) of the children of England and

Wales, be reared without even once being out of the sight of adults? The very thought is a monstrosity. No playing of traditional childhood games, no fishing in the stream or tramping in the woods and fields, no secret cabals and intrigues that children so delight in, and none of the many other childhood and adolescent activities without which the growth and exuberance of early life cannot be what they usually are and from which adults are so rightly excluded.

There would be none of this in Panopticon. Instead, from the age of four until release to the world at large at the age of twenty-one, there would be unremitting labor for up to twelve hours a day for pauper children and youth and shameless exploitation of their efforts, without so much as token payment when they left. Food would be insufficient to satisfy them fully (hence Bentham's comment that the quantity of food would not be enough to produce "excess" energy); clothing would not completely protect against a winter chill (more would have to be provided by private charity); and even sleep would be cut to a minimum ("the least that can be made sufficient for health and strength").[6] Similar material conditions obtained for adults, but children would have borne an even greater burden in Panopticon, for few would experience parental love. Bentham's defense of this circumstance—that the dependable evenhanded rule of an artificial father more than compensated the child for the absence of natural affection—was transparently flimsy; and whatever the benefits of an education which we have shown to be far more modest and inconsequential than Bentham made it out to be, it hardly indemnified the child for the warped emotional development that must inevitably have resulted from life in this peculiar version of an orphanage. A further advantage claimed for the pauper child was also suspect. Bentham argued that "sequestered from the world at large" the pauper child would not fall victim to its vices, especially its expensive ones. But sequestration was not necessarily an unmixed blessing. Innocent of the world's vices, newly released youth were also defenseless against them: what might the fate of many of them have been amongst the sharpers of the Metropolis?

From what we have concluded the character of Bentham's reform to be, it seems clear that no Utilitarian, in Bentham's time or afterward, can necessarily be expected to embrace his solution to the problems of indigence on the basis of common philosophical persuasion. The National Charity Company, obviously enough, was Bentham's own idiosyncratic application of his philosophy, not the voice of Utilitarianism itself, however much its enemies would like to think so. It is perverse to imagine as good a society whose weakest members are stripped of the most basic civil liberties and locked up in institutions suffused with inescapable, everwatchful authority.

Perhaps enough has been said of the repressive and exploitative nature of many of the features of Bentham's Poor Law reform to show that to call it historically "progressive" mocks any notion of progress worthy of the name. The enforced incarceration of hundreds of thousands in the drab and emotionally barren circumstances of Panopticon is not, one thinks, the excellence of human invention on the march. Nor can Bentham be defended by pointing to the necessity of these measures for the poor's very survival. The situation of the poorest Englishmen in the years of scarcity we have been discussing was not one of utter starvation—it bore little resemblance to the tragedy which engulfed Ireland fifty years later. Necessity, the proverb has it, knows no law, knows no bounds to action when life hangs in the balance. This is emphatically not true for the English poor during these years of misery. Emigration or starvation were not the sole alternatives.[7]

The means Bentham advocated to promote saving do have some merit. It is obvious that emotional anguish at the prospect of sickness or unemployment is attenuated by personal and social reserves. But in Bentham's writings on poverty, saving becomes a *mania*, a pathological pursuit whose ascetic nature gives the lie to promoting what anyone else would call happiness: how could the indigent—or anybody else—find anything like happiness when nearly every pleasure, as the idea of pleasure is generally understood, and all of their freedom was denied them? Bentham's portrait of England without the Public House was about as realistic as Rousseau's Poland without the Catholic Church. Critics may remind us that for economic development to proceed, somebody has to pay. That is correct—but how much, by how many, for how long? It is not obvious that one generation 'owes' to the unborn the maximum sacrifice in deferred consumption. In any case that is not the argument Bentham made. The life of unceasing work and vigilant parsimony was in his view the good life for the poor, quite apart from its effect on national wealth, though no doubt he thought that effect a good one. It was a vision of life devoid of both joy and every other form of spontaneity; both were too dangerous to be sanctioned in a social world so devoted to the elimination of contingency: but surely a more attractive ideal can be imagined than life as unremitting self-control and denial.

But having said all of this, it should not be forgotten that in the course of his writings on the Poor Law, Bentham was the first important systematic defender of the Welfare State, especially in the context of a market economy with all its vicissitudes and uncertainties. Is it right, and if so, why is it right, to take from the productive and give to the unproductive? Or (what is a different question) is it right, and if so, why is it right, to take from the richer and give to the poorer? It is to Bentham's credit that he answered these questions (at least partially) and answered them affirmatively. The main direction of his answer is that the Welfare State is justified because it is the most effective means available to relieve and to prevent suffering. It does this in two ways: it provides benefits to those who need them, and it creates security of expectation that *in extremis* (and sometimes long before *extremis* arrives) one will not be allowed to starve, go homeless, or lack medical care. Insecurity is suffering *too*—and it is preventable. Private, voluntary charity is unequal to the task because of its uncertainty. It may lack the knowledge of suffering; and it may lack the means or the will to relieve it. The Irish and other tragedies should convince anyone of that. Furthermore, neither prodigality nor the lack of foresight in providing against incapacity or unemployment can rightly, Bentham urged, be treated as crimes, or even if they are, as capital crimes. Punishments should fit crimes: whatever else laziness and imprudence may be, they are not akin to murder. Voluntary charity cannot in any case provide a just solution, for in the face of starvation it is not even voluntary. It is rather a tax on the humane, leaving the hard-hearted untouched: the relief of poverty ought first of all to be a *community* responsibility and not solely the burden of the sensitive and generous. Indeed, a decent and adequate provision for the poor is the first test of civilization: some degrees of poverty are positively barbarous.

These are not trivial arguments, and the enemies of the Welfare State have not made their case unless they have answered them. If they lack some of the polish and sophistication of those now available, it should be remembered that Bentham did not have the benefit of a long philosophical tradition which minutely dissected the issues involved. The Welfare State is a modern invention. It is not simply half of the Roman formula of *panem et circenses*. A fully reasoned set of arguments backed by the research of one or more of the social sciences was not available to him in 1797.

As for Bentham's peculiar version of the Welfare State, history did not deal kindly with this or with any other of his grandiose schemes. It attracted little attention, and there is no evidence that Pitt ever seriously considered it. Its historical influence seems to be limited to the transmission, through Edwin Chadwick, of the "less eligibility" principle to the 1834 Poor Law Amendment Act.

It has been argued that Bentham did not adopt a policy of "less eligibility" but opted rather for the less harsh policy of maintaining paupers in a condition that was "not more eligible."[8] This is significantly different from "less eligibility," and in one place Bentham does seem to favor a principle of "not more eligible," but the context of his argument must be considered. That context in his *Essays relative to the subject of the Poor Law* is a discussion of diet. He knew that a diet worse than the worst diet of the poorest working poor might be, no doubt would be, unhealthy. He therefore sometimes spoke of a "Neighbors' Fare Principle" which would fulfill the conditions of "not more eligible." Food would be the cheapest and coarsest possible consistent with health; worse food than that Bentham could not recommend. But the overall conditions of Panopticon's adult population were meant to be "less eligible." That this was his intention is strongly suggested by comments he made on the clause of Pitt's bill which allowed making up a laborer's deficient wage to "the full rate or wages usually given." The effect of this clause, Bentham argued, "seems to be putting the *idle* and *negligent* exactly upon a footing in point of prosperity and reward with the *diligent* and *industrious*"; the effect of the clause would frequently, not to say generally, be that idleness would "find itself in as *good* [a] plight as *industry*."[9] That was precisely what he intended not to do. As we have said, one of poor-Panopticon's functions was as a deterrent—as a means to pressure the poor into labor and prudent behavior. Now, a condition that is not worse than the worst-off independent laborer is no deterrent. Bentham knew this very well and therefore adopted in practice if not in name the principle of "less eligibility." Badging the poor by forcing them to wear distinctive uniforms was one form of less eligibility, and 'paying' them less than the independent laborer was another ('pay' was credited against their accounts, not given in cash). So was the termination, or near termination, of home relief and the total control of his life that greeted the pauper upon admittance. And if, as one critic has argued, this was meant merely to *appear* less eligible to free laborers but not actually to *be* so,[10] why were there so many pains taken to prevent escape, including the use of watchtowers and, for beggars and other categories of inmates, escape lists? And why humiliate the poor by badging them with uniforms? That was not a condition of "not more eligible"; or are we to believe that watchtowers, escape lists, lower pay, and badging were only camouflage to mislead outsiders, and that Panopticon's residents, having sampled the new regime, having enjoyed its "comforts," would actually have been indifferent as between independence and their new abode? that they would have found life in Panopticon novel but nevertheless not less desirable? But this is quite unbelievable.

What did concern Bentham was that his audience, the literate public, who hadn't the slightest hope of ever needing the National Charity Company, might find Panopticon 'not desirable enough,' might find their inferiors being dealt with too harshly, and so he inflated his list of pauper "comforts" far beyond what was warranted. If he could convince careful, sensitive readers of the *Annals of Agriculture*, readers who were sympathetic to the poor, that Panopticon would be no real hardship, he would have made his case and won the day. But if he could have done that, he could also have squared the circle. In appearance and in fact, incarceration is less desirable, less "eligible," than freedom. Bentham knew it, the poor knew it, everyone knows it.

Bentham never repudiated his Poor Law reform. *Pauper Management Improved* was reprinted twice in his lifetime, in French in 1800 and in English in 1812. He believed that George III was responsible for the failure of his scheme to be adopted, just as he believed that the King, the pinnacle of "Matchless Constitution," had vetoed Panopticon prison. (There is no evidence whatever for either view.) As late as 1828 and 1831 Bentham was preparing a new edition of *Pauper Management Improved*, whose revised subtitle advertised an "acceptance" given the plan by "Pitt II^d and the VETO put upon it by George the III^d."[11] In the Preface he alleged that "but for one man, for the last 20 or [so] years all the paupers in England would have been under the management of the Author of these pages. That one man was *George the Third*."[12] To the end he remained bitterly disappointed. "Never does the current of my thoughts alight upon the Panopticon and its fate," he wrote in 1830, "but my heart sinks within me: upon the Panopticon and both its branches—the prison branch and the pauper branch: upon what they are now, and what they ought to have been."[13] A period had been put to his Panopticon hopes in its prison and pauper branches nearly twenty years before when in 1811 a Parliamentary committee had rejected them, paying him £23,000 in compensation. La-ment and anger never having left him, in his sketchy *History of the War between Jeremy Bentham and George III written by one of the Belligerents*, we find him unreconciled to his inability to maximize labor: "J. B. never thinks of Panopticon without grief—Relative pecuniary value of a new born child under that and the existing system."[14] Panopticon was Bentham's trail of tears. But at least in its pauper branch, it is better that it was a trial for one man than a trail of tears for millions.

Notes

Introduction

1. See J. H. Burns, "Bentham and the French Revolution," *Transactions of the Royal Historical Society*, 5th series, vol. 16 (1966) pp. 95–114.

2. See Gertrude Himmelfarb, "Bentham's Utopia: The National Charity Company," *The Journal of British Studies*, vol. X, no. 1 (November 1970) pp. 80-125. This insightful essay should be read with her earlier study of Panopticon, "The Haunted House of Jeremy Bentham," in *Victorian Minds* (New York, 1968) pp. 32-81. And see J. R. Poynter, *Society and Pauperism* (London and Toronto, 1968).

3. See the discussion of idleness in Chapter Seven, pp. 164ff.

4. This distinction is made by Locke in the *Second Treatise*: "The *Labour* of his Body, and the *Work* of his Hands . . . are properly his" (ch. 5, sec. 27). The full (and seldom cited) title of the second of Locke's *Two Treatises of Government* . . . is *An Essay Concerning the True Original, Extent and End of Civil Government*.

5. See Chapter Seven, pp. 198–199.

6. See Chapter Seven, p. 189.

7. The manuscripts of Jeremy Bentham in the Library of University College London (hereinafter cited as U.C.), Box cli, 361.

8. U.C. cliib, 513.

9. See Chapter Six, pp. 156ff.

10. U.C. cli, 358. See also U.C. cliia, 217, where Bentham spoke of "a *connected* and *constant* system of relief, all along the coast against the calamity of *shipwreck*."

11. U.C. lxxxvii, 172. The edition of the *Essay on Indirect Legislation* ed. C. F. Bahmueller and Hardy Wieting, Jr., in *The Collected Works of Jeremy Bentham* (hereinafter cited as *CW*) is scheduled to appear in 1982.

12. *Ibid*., 110 and 19.

13. *The Works of Jeremy Bentham*, ed. John Bowring, 11 vols. (Edinburgh, 1843; hereinafter cited as Bowring), i, 308.

14. U.C. cliiib, 330. And see Bowring, viii, 375, 411–12 and 421 for further use of the chain image.

15. U.C. cli, 360.

16. U.C. lxix, 166.

17. See *CW, An Introduction to the Principles of Morals and Legislation*, ed. J. H. Burns and H. L. A. Hart (London, 1970) p. 21. And see p. 15 and n. where the word "caprice" was italicized because Bentham had himself underlined it in his copy, now in the British Museum. Bentham's fear of contingency extended even to the possible evanescense of brotherly love. Faced with the possibility of being disinherited if he carried out his wish to marry Mary Dunkley, Jeremy was assured by his brother, Samuel, that he, Samuel, would provide for him if their father carried out his threat. Jeremy replied, *inter alia*, that ". . . though I can trust entirely to what you *are now*, I cannot trust to what you may be hereafter" (Jeremy Bentham to Samuel Bentham, 12 September 1775, in *CW, The Correspondence of Jeremy Bentham*, ed. T. L. S. Sprigge [London, 1968; hereinafter cited as *Correspondence*], i, pp. 252–53). Citations below to Bentham's unpublished correspondence refer to British Museum Additional mss. 33537–64, whose volumes are numbered I–XXVIII. The roman numerals are used for citation.

18. U.C. c, 18. Richard Smith, who edited the incomplete and often erroneous version for Bowring's *Works*, mistitled it as *The Influence of Time and Place.* . . . The text to be published was established by the present writer. Every ms. for it bears the heading "Place and Time," and there can be no doubt but that *The Influence of Place and Time* . . . is the correct title.

19. U.C. xcix, 174.

20. U.C. lxxxvii, 139–40; and see Chapter One, p. 17.

21. *Ibid.*, 97.

22. U.C. xlix, 45.

23. Bowring, v, 233.

24. U.C. cliib, 564.

25. *Ibid.*, 370. And see U.C. cliiib, 303, where Bentham spoke of "local establishments scattered over the surface of the country by the hand of chance."

26. U.C. clivb, 340.

27. U.C. cliva, 107.

28. U.C. cli, 301.

29. *Ibid.*, 420.

Chapter One

1. For a detailed treatment of Bentham's involvement in French affairs, see J. H. Burns, "Bentham and the French Revolution," *Transactions of the Royal Historical Society*, 5th series, vol. 16 (1966) pp. 95–114. "Anarchical Fallacies" is not Bentham's title, but is an English translation of Dumont's *Sophismes Anarchiques*. Bentham used other titles, such as *Pestilential Nonsense Unmasked*.

2. *A Protest Against Law Taxes* (Bowring, ii, 573–583) was printed in 1793 and published two years later; but *Truth versus Ashurst* (Bowring, v, 231–37), although written in December, 1792, was not published until 1823, when Bentham accidentally discovered it, he tells us, "digging for other papers." Bentham may well have not

thought it prudent to publish such a scathing attack on the legal system amid the growing panic over the French Revolution.

3. This list is by no means exhaustive. Besides various fragments which survive among the Bentham Papers at University College, there are other works on economics published by Werner Stark, *Jeremy Bentham's Economic Writings*, 3 vols. (London, 1952; hereinafter cited as Stark). See vols. 1–2.

4. *Pauper Management Improved*, Bowring, viii, 432n.

5. Bowring, x, 85. Bowring prints several extracts from what he calls Bentham's "Commonplace Book" for 1776, but such a work, assuming that it ever existed, has not survived. It is possible that Bowring was quoting from early miscellaneous materials such as U.C. lxix, lxxiv, xcvi, xcvii, and v. James Steintrager has suggested that Bentham's commonplace-book "was not a book at all"; his examination of the early manuscript materials inclined him "to the opinion that this material is the missing 'book'." James Steintrager, "Report on the Problems of Editing Bentham's Writings on Religion," Appendix B to "Report" by General Editor to the Bentham Committee, June 12, 1967 (not published), p. 10.

6. *Ibid*.

7. See, for example, Sidney and Beatrice Webb, *English Local Government*, vol. 7, *English Poor Law History: Part I, The Old Poor Law* (London, 1927) pp. 425ff. This work is still indispensable to the student of the English Poor Law.

8. Bentham had corresponded with Shelburne but avoided meeting him. See *Correspondence* (*supra*, Introduction, n. 17) ii, 504n; and *Correspondence* iii, 24n.

9. James Anderson was a Scottish farmer, journalist, and economist whom Bentham had met several years before through their mutual friend George Wilson. See *Correspondence* iii, 25n.

10. Anderson's letter is dated March, 1781, and recalls a conversation between them "of a very interesting nature concerning the Poor Laws in England. . . ." See *Correspondence* iii, 30.

11. *Ibid*., 30–43.

12. These donations were collected in church and were supplemented from several sources. Fines for fornication, which according to Anderson were sometimes considerable, were added to the fund together with interest from loans from the poor fund and the proceeds from seat rents in churches, and the rentals of parish-owned hearses and "mort cloths" (cloths draped over corpses). Such additions varied from place to place. *Ibid*., 31–34; 37–38.

13. *Ibid*., 30–31 and 38.

14. *Ibid*., 40–41.

15. *Ibid*., 25. The following year Bentham added to his argument. "I should be sorry," he wrote, "to see the English poor-laws made general in Scotland. But once established they must be continued: otherwise half the poor would perish before the requisite habits of benevolence and frugality could take root" (U.C. lxxxvii, 79–80).

16. No accurate reports on Poor Law expenditure were available until 1776, when Thomas Gilbert, author of a number of bills for Poor Law reform, induced Parliament to require Overseers to report on the amount raised by the poor rates and the amount spent on poor relief for the year 1776 and then for the three years 1783–85. These returns showed an expenditure on the poor of about £1,500,000 in 1776 and about £1,900,000, on the average, in 1783–85—thus justifying (roughly at least) Bentham's reported estimate in 1782 of "upwards of 2 million a year (U.C. lxxxvii, 79). In 1778, The Rev. J. Howlett argued that the increase of the 1780's was unusual and no cause for general alarm; it was the result of general inflation and certainly not

from any increase in the "wickedness" of the poor—a very favorite cause given by alarmists. Nevertheless, the rate continued to rise, especially after 1794, and reached well over £4,000,000 by 1802–03. The poor rates were levied only, with a few exceptions, on the occupiers (rather than owners) of houses and land—hardly an equable system. It is hard to know why Bentham described this system as "as equable a mode as could have been devised" (U.C. cli, 12). See the Webbs, *op. cit.*, pp. 152–54; J. R. Poynter, *Society and Pauperism* (London, 1969) pp. 17–20; and J. Howlett, *The insufficiency of the Cause to which the Increase of our Poor and of the Poor Rates have been commonly ascribed* . . . (London, 1788) p. 66 and *passim*. See also J. L. and Barbara Hammond, *The Village Labourer, 1760–1832* (London, 1921).

17. These demands reached their climax after 1815 but were voiced in the eighteenth century most notably by the Rev. Thomas Alcock in 1752 in *Observations on the Defects of the Poor Laws* . . . and, of course, by the famous precursor of Malthus, the Rev. Joseph Townsend, in *A Dissertation on the Poor Laws by a Well-wisher to Mankind* (London, 1786). See J. R. Poynter, *op. cit.*, pp. 39–44; 223–48.

18. U.C. lxxxvii, 79–84.

19. *Ibid.*, 80.

20. *Ibid.*

21. *Ibid.*

22. *Ibid.* Elsewhere in *Indirect Legislation*, Bentham argued for the complete abolition of legal penalties against prostitution, but he was not sanguine about the chances for adoption of such a policy in England. See *ibid.*, 77.

23. *Ibid.*, 79.

24. *Ibid.*, 81.

25. *Ibid.*

26. *Ibid.*, 82.

27. *Ibid.*

28. *Ibid.*, 82–83.

29. See *An Introduction to the Principles of Morals and Legislation*, ch. VIII, para. 13; *CW*, 88–89.

30. U.C. lxxxvii, 82.

31. 17 George II c.5.

32. Quoted in the Webbs, *op. cit.*, p. 354. The basis of the eighteenth-century vagrancy laws was an act of 1597 (39, 40 Elizabeth c.4). A myriad of supplementary acts followed; and the Webbs remark that as often as the Commons took a dislike to some irregular way of life, it included its followers in the category of "rogues and vagabonds." The laws became so confused that they had to be recodified in 1714 (13 Ann3 c.26), but many more amendments followed. Bentham was surely right in castigating the confused state of the law. See S. and B. Webb, *op. cit.*, pp. 352–55; and William Holdsworth, *A History of English Law* (London, 1938) vol. X, pp. 177–180.

33. 11 Henry VII c.2.

34. See S. and B. Webb, *op. cit.*, pp. 361–67.

35. Bowring, viii, *Pauper Management Improved*, 405–06 (emphasis added). Bentham specifically referred to 17 George II c.5; but he did not specify which of the classes in the act he considered "unpernicious." The act itself divided vagrants into three classes: idle and disorderly persons; rogues and vagabonds; and incorrigible rogues. Among those liable for punishment were tipplers who did not adequately provide for their families, fencers, bear wards, strolling players, minstrels (except those licensed by Lord Dutton in Cheshire), fortune tellers, those pretending skill in palmistry, those pretending to be gypsies, and others. Punishments ranged from up to one month in prison, to

a public whipping and six months imprisonment; or, for the worst offenders, up to seven years transportation. See Sir Frederic Morton Eden, *The State of the Poor: or An History of the Labouring Classes in England* . . . , 3 vols. (London, 1797) vol. 1, pp. 307–09. For the history of the exemption of Lord Dutton and his heirs, see S. and B. Webb, *op. cit.*, p. 354 n. 1. Gypsies were evidently one of the "pernicious" classes, since in 1797 Bentham used the phrase "gypsies and other vagrants" (U.C. cliib, 457). Gypsies were, of course, a favorite subject of vagrancy law, not to say persecution. Banished from the Kingdom under Henry VIII, they were subject (under certain circumstances) to the death penalty during the next century. A few years before the Restoration, thirteen gypsies were executed at Suffolk Assizes. In present-day England, gypsies are still the subjects of legal harassment. See Eden, *op. cit.*, vol. 1, pp. 308–09.

36. Bowring, viii, 402.

37. Bentham's letter of "John Glynn, Esq., Sergeant-at-Law" in the *Gazetteer and New Daily Advertiser* of 3 December 1770 is reprinted in David Baumgardt, *Bentham and the Ethics of Today* (Princeton, 1952) Appendix III, pp. 552–54. For the context of the letter, see Douglas G. Long, *Bentham on Liberty* (Toronto, 1977) pp. 50–51. This valuable book is a welcome addition to Bentham scholarship.

38. See Chapter Two, pp. 52–53.

39. See, for example, "Quatre buts du droit distributif," U.C. xxxii, 125–31.

40. U.C. xxxii, 129.

41. *Ibid.*, 2.

42. *Ibid.*, 32 and 129.

43. *Ibid.*, 45.

44. *The Theory of Legislation*, trans. James Hildreth (London, 1876) p. 130. See also the discussion in James Steintraeger, *Bentham* (Ithaca, 1977) pp. 69–72. In his description of Bentham's Poor Law reforms of the 1790's, Professor Steintraeger speaks of "a system of agricultural communes and a system of Industry Houses" and refers to "both projects," leaving the impression that Bentham proposed two "systems" (p. 70). Bentham's proposals, however, called for a unitary system, no part of which was to be a "commune" in the ordinary sense. The agricultural activities of the system were designed to make the whole self-sufficient in food. On the unitary nature of his proposal, see, for example, Bowring, viii, 369, where Bentham speaks of "*one* authority," "*one* undivided authority" for the "management of the concerns of the poor" (emphasis in original). For a manuscript source of Bentham's 1780's attack on voluntary charity, see U.C. xcix, 50.

45. *The Theory of Legislation*, pp. 127–28.

46. The folder containing U.C. cli, 7–24 is marked in Bentham's hand "Poor Principles. 1786." Pages 7–8 are definitely the work of the 1780's and are headed "Poor's Cry Introd." and "Poor's Cry Liberty." The remaining pages in the folders are unquestionably (as indicated by the handwriting, the paper, and the content) part of the 1796–97 Poor Law reform mss. What Bentham intended by "Poor Principles" is not elucidated.

47. 13 & 14 Charles II c.12. The most readily available extensive treatment of the Law of Settlement and Removal is S. and B. Webb, *op. cit.*, ch. 5; for seventeenth-century practice see E. M. Leonard, *Early History of the Poor Law* (London, 1901). For a brief but valuable discussion, see J. L. and B. Hammond, *op. cit.*, pp. 112–20. For other short accounts, see Geoffrey Taylor, *The Problem of Poverty* (London, 1969) pp. 26–28 (Taylor prints several brief documents on pp. 93–94); and J. R. Poynter, *op. cit.*, pp. 3–7. The Webbs provide much additional bibliography.

48. The means of gaining a settlement become quite complex, and historians have generally found it useful to follow the summary given by Eden. Most of the poor were probably settled by one of four means. Bastards usually acquired settlement by birth, as did legitimate children if neither parent's settlement could be determined (but see Chapter One, p. 22). Women secured settlement by marriage; and residents of freeholds likewise acquired settlement. In addition, immigrants could gain a settlement by paying parish taxes, by holding a public annual office in the parish, or by being hired for one year (hence the practice of being hired for 364 days). Cf. Eden, *op. cit.*, vol. 1, p. 180; and J. L. and B. Hammond, *op. cit.*, p. 113.

49. 12 Richard II c.7. For this and other examples, see Eden, *op. cit.*, vol. 1, pp. 174ff.

50. S. and B. Webb, *op. cit.*, pp. 316 and 318.

51. "This cruelty to the poor was a subject of remonstrance by the Puritan party from the early days of King James; and Decker, in his *Seven Deadly Sins* (1606) refers to this as one of the causes of the Divine Judgement upon the City of London in visiting it annually with the plague" (F. C. Inderwick, *The Interregnum* [London, 1891] pp. 91-2, quoted in S. and B. Webb, *op. cit.*, p. 321).

52. Yearly expenditure was £35,000 in 1776; nearly £92,000 in 1783-85; £190,000 in 1802-03; and reached more than £327,000 in 1813-15. Cited in Poynter, *op. cit.*, p. 7.

53. William Hay, cited in S. and B. Webb, *op. cit.*, p. 322 n. 3.

54. The obvious answer was not to remove until appeals had been exhausted. When this was proposed in 1819, it was defeated—evidently because lawyers feared a decline in litigation. See S. and B. Webb, *op. cit.*, pp. 332-33 and n. 1.

55. Professor Poynter says that the Webbs' estimate was that "not more than a few tens of thousands" of removal orders were executed per year (Poynter, *op. cit.*, p. 6). What the Webbs actually wrote was: "And the law was enforced in tens of thousands of cases annually" (p. 322). The exact figure is unknown.

56. S. and B. Webb, *op. cit.*, p. 322.

57. J. L. and B. Hammond, *op. cit.*, pp. 114-15.

58. S. and B. Webb, *op. cit.*, p. 333.

59. *Ibid.*

60. J. L. and B. Hammond, *op. cit.*, pp. 117-18. The Hammonds also point out that it would also seem in the parish interest to allow slight relief to claimants rather than go to court; but this assumption is also incorrect.

61. John North, quoted in S. and B. Webb, *op. cit.*, p. 330.

62. See the discussion in Eden, *op. cit.*, vol. 1, pp. 196ff.

63. E. P. Thompson, *The Making of the English Working Class* (Pelican edition, London 1968) p. 102.

64. Adam Smith, *The Wealth of Nations*, 1776 (Pelican edition, London, 1970), p. 244.

65. *Ibid.*, p. 245.

66. *Ibid.*, p. 383.

67. *Ibid.*, p. 245.

68. For the effect of the Law of Settlement in London, see M. Dorothy George, *London Life in the Eighteenth Century* (London, 1925) as index; for the practical operations of the law, see Dorothy Marshall, *The English Poor in the Eighteenth Century* (London, 1926) pp. 161-245.

69. F. M. Eden, *op. cit.*, vol. 1, pp. 297-98.

70. S. and B. Webb, *op. cit.*, pp. 240-42.

71. J. R. Poynter, *op. cit.*, p. 5.

72. 35 George III c.101. Cited in Michael E. Rose, *The English Poor Law 1780–1930* (Newton Abbot, Engl. 1970) pp. 29–30.

73. U.C. cli, 8.

74. *Ibid.* Bentham's use of the term "the working class" is among the earliest one can find; but it is purely fortuitous since he used "working classes" far more often, just as he usually spoke of the "middle" or "middling" *classes* even late in his life.

75. Bowring, v, 234.

76. U.C. cli, 16.

77. *Ibid.*, 18–19.

78. *Ibid.*, 13.

79. Stark, vol. 1, pp. 380–82.

80. U.C. cli, 17.

81. *Ibid.*, 9.

82. *Ibid.*

83. *Ibid.*, 13.

84. *Ibid.*, 15.

85. *Ibid.* "An enumeration of these will be found in a separate paper." A note to himself adds: "Annex it in form of an Appendix—or rather make a separate publication of it." However, such a list, if it exists, has not been discovered.

86. *Ibid.*, 13.

Chapter Two

1. S. and B. Webb, *op. cit. (supra*, ch. 1, n. 7), p. 156.

2. An act of 1744 (17 George II c.3) attempted to stem corruption by allowing the rates to be inspected upon payment of a shilling. Through their unlimited power, said the Act, "overseers and churchwardens frequently, on frivolous pretenses, and for private ends, make unjust and illegal Rates in a secret and clandestine manner contrary to the intent and meaning of 43d Eliz." Improvements in accounting were suggested later in the century by Thomas Gilbert in his *Considerations on the Bills for the better relief and employment of the Poor . . .* (1787). However, little improvement was forthcoming. In 1796 Eden wrote that the "right to inspect Poor Accounts would amount to nothing but wasted time the way the accounts are usually kept" (F. M. Eden, *op. cit.* [*supra*, ch. 1, n. 35], vol. 1, p. 489).

3. One such boss ruled Bethnal Green for some fifty years after 1787 by organizing local weavers at the vestry meetings. See J. R. Poynter, *op. cit.* [*supra*, ch. 1, n. 16], p. 9. There was little wonder that Bentham castigated the Overseers as "persons without liberal education" (U.C. xli, 11) and complained that under the existing system "no accounts kept, or if kept, not published—or if published, scarce any body in the Parish, nobody out of it would look into them" (U.C. cliib, 350).

4. G. Taylor, *op. cit. (supra*, ch. 1, n. 47), p. 16.

5. *Ibid.*, p. 96.

6. S. and B. Webb, *op. cit.*, p. 143.

7. The Workhouse Act, 9. Geo. I c.7.

8. Popular, that is to say, among rate payers and overseers, not among the poor themselves. In Suffolk in 1765, a mob roamed the district for a week, demolishing workhouses and extorting promises from Poor Officials that more would not be built, that "the poor should be maintained as usual" and that they should "range at liberty and be their own masters." See S. and B. Webb, *op. cit.*, p. 141 and n.

9. *Ibid.*, p. 147.

10. F. M. Eden, *op. cit.*, vol. 1, pp. 270ff.

11. Perry Jones, *The Trade in Lunacy* (London, 1972) p. 84. See also his discussion of the private madhouse proprietor, pp. 74–95.

12. D. Marshall, *op. cit.* (*supra*, ch. 1, n. 68), pp. 135ff. For Bentham's views on the contract system, see Chapter Five, pp. 113ff.

13. The "roundsman" system underwent a number of modifications in the late eighteenth and early nineteenth centuries. In some places, men were simply auctioned off to local farmers for the day, but this resulted in the dismissal of unpauperized laborers. As a remedy, the "labour rate" was sometimes introduced: the year's wage bill for all "settled labourers" was calculated and each ratepayer agreed to pay his share (unless he was exempted). Any deficiency had to be paid to the Overseer. See S. and B. Webb, *op. cit.*, pp. 190–95.

14. J. R. Pretyman, *Dispauperization* (London, 1878) p. 27, cited in S. and B. Webb, *op. cit.*, p. 172.

15. *The Annual Register*, 1795, p. 135.

16. Rev. David Davies, *The Case of the Labourers in Husbandry* . . . (London, 1795) pp. 5–6. Written below the title, "The Labourer is worthy of his hire, Luke x.7."

17. See the discussion in J. L. and B. Hammond, *op. cit.* (*supra*, ch. 1, n. 16), pp. 120–22. Food "riots" were hardly unique in 1795. For example, such riots took place in Nottingham in 1764 (the "Great Cheese Riot"; whole cheeses were rolled down the street) and again in 1788; in Honiton in 1766; and in Halifax in 1763. See E. P. Thompson, *op. cit.* (*supra*, ch. 1, n. 63), pp. 68–70.

18. Select Committee on Poor Rate Returns, *Report*, V, Appendix A (1822), reprinted in Michael Rose, *op. cit.* (*supra*, ch. 1, n. 72), pp. 40–41.

19. E. P. Thompson, *op. cit.*, p. 157.

20. F. M. Eden, *op. cit.*, vol. 1, pp. 133–34.

21. E. P. Thompson, *op. cit.*, p. 153.

22. *Ibid.*, pp. 154–57. There is, of course, no way to check this estimation, but even if the lower estimate is exaggerated, the point obviously remains that the "King and Constitution" party were badly frightened by such gatherings.

23. *The Autobiography of Francis Place*, ed. Mary Thale (Cambridge, Engl., 1972) p. 146. Place was an eyewitness to the entire incident.

24. E. P. Thompson, *op. cit.*, p. 158.

25. *The Annual Register*, 1796, p. 16.

26. E. P. Thompson, *op. cit.*, pp. 158–59.

27. *The Annual Register*, 1796, p. 17.

28. D. Davies, *op. cit.*, p. 40.

29. *Parliamentary History*, vol. 32, 695–96.

30. Eden (*op. cit.*, vol. 1, p. 533) described the reaction of poor laborers to soup, even as served at the table of the rich: "This is washy stuff, that affords no nourishment: we will not be fed on meal, and chopped potatoes like hogs."

31. J. L. and B. Hammond, *op. cit.*, p. 124. The Hammonds make the very dubious argument that the laborer living on bread and tea "had too delicate a digestion to assimilate the coarser cereals." Their evidence for this assertion is almost nil (p. 126).

32. *Ibid.*, p. 127.

33. D. Davies, *op. cit.*, p. 37.

34. However, one must record Boswell's glee at finding oatmeal being eaten at Johnson's home village of Lichfield: "I saw there, for the first time, oat ale; and oat cakes, not hard as in Scotland, but soft like a Yorkshire cake, were served for breakfast. It

was pleasant for me to find, that 'Oats,' the 'food of horses,' were so much used as *food of the people* in Dr. Johnson's own town" (Boswell's *Life of Johnson*, ed. G. B. Hill [Oxford, 1934] vol. II, p. 463).

35. See R. N. Salaman. *The History and Social Influence of the Potato* (Cambridge, Engl., 1949), *passim*.

36. D. Davies, *op. cit.*, p. 40.

37. *Ibid.*, p. 39.

38. *Ibid.*, p. 38.

39. The Buckingham Justices made special mention of the inadequacies of the "Roundsman" system: ". . . the mode adopted of employing all poor laborers indescriminately as roundsmen at the under price hath been attended with great inconvenience and abuse, and requires a speedy and effective remedy . . ." (Ms. Minutes, Quarter Session, Buckinghamshire, January 1795). Cited in S. and B. Webb, *op. cit.*, p. 177.

40. The scale itself is reprinted in M. Rose, *op. cit.*, p. 34. Rose (p. 33) points out that a bread scale of the Speenhamland variety had in fact been introduced in Dorset as early as 1792.

41. See J. L. and B. Hammond, *op. cit.*, pp. 161ff. "The tables passed rapidly from county to county. The allowance system spread like a fever. . . ." (p. 164). The Webbs' concurring opinion is found in S. and B. Webb, *op. cit.*, pp. 180–81; and compare J. R. Poynter, *op. cit.*, p. 83: "The extent and continuity of the allowance system before (and indeed after) 1820 can only be guessed at." And see his discussion, pp. 76–85 *passim*. For a spirited denunciation of Speenhamland, see E. P. Thompson, *op. cit.*, pp. 247–48.

42. See E. J. Hobsbawm, *Industry and Empire* (Pelican edition, London, 1969) pp. 104–05.

43. F. M. Eden, *op. cit.*, vol. 1, pp. 575ff.

44. *Ibid.*, p. 580.

45. See the account given by Francis Place in *The Autobiography of Francis Place*, *op. cit.*, pp. 147-55. According to Place, the demise of the L.C.S. dates from the latter half of 1797 (p. 155). By 1799, its very name was proscribed and most of its leaders were in jail or exile. See E. P. Thompson, *op. cit.*, pp. 161–63; 183–91.

46. *The Annual Register*, 1796, p. 48.

47. Richard Burn, *The History of the Poor Laws: with Observations* (London, 1764) p. 8.

48. 13 Richard II c.8, cited in *ibid.*, p. 13.

49. See F. M. Eden, *op. cit.*, vol. 1, pp. 123–26 and 140. The Elizabethan Act (5 Elizabeth c.3) provided wage restriction (subject to annual review by JPs) for three categories—menial servants, laborers, and apprentices. Giving more than the maximum wage resulted in 10 days imprisonment, taking more in 21 days imprisonment. Also, it is perhaps noteworthy that the Act made "artificers" liable to be compelled to do harvest work.

50. *The Wealth of Nations*, (Pelican edition, London, 1970) p. 246 (bk. I, ch. x).

51. *Ibid.*, p. 235.

52. See J. L. and B. Hammond, *op. cit.*, p. 134. 5 Elizabeth c.4 noted that the maximum wage was often too small (Burn, *op. cit.*, p. 16). Bentham, however, believed that both a minimum and a maximum wage policy had been practiced (see Bowring, viii, 422).

53. *Parliamentary History*, vol. 32, 701–03, 713–14.

54. For accounts of the debate and Pitt's speech, see *ibid.*, 703ff; *The Annual Register*,

1796, p. 49. Eden (*op. cit.*, vol. 1, p. 483) quoted Pitt's speech with approval. For a more extensive account of Whitbread's defeat, see J. R. Poynter, *op. cit.*, pp. 55–62. Whitbread tried to resurrect his proposal in 1800, only to be defeated again; he omitted it altogether from his Poor Law reform proposal of 1807; by 1809, he had himself rejected it.

55. *Inter alia*, Pitt mentioned a number of further reforms which prefigured the proposals of his bill. The law which prohibited giving relief where any visible property remained should be abolished ("that degrading condition should be withdrawn"); small loans should be offered to the poor; larger families should receive more relief than smaller (a minimum wage would not make this important distinction); there should be "some new mode of inspection" of the parishes, partly via annual parish reports to Parliament and an annual Parliamentary Poor budget. See *Parliamentary History*, vol. 32, 705–712.

56. *Ibid.*, 1405–06.

57. Much of the literature criticizing the bill is well summarized by J. R. Poynter, *op. cit.*, pp. 66–76. Poynter (p. 62) also shows that Pitt's proposals fared little better in the estimation of later historians—including his own.

58. Thomas Ruggles to William Bray, 5 February 1797. A copy is preserved in U.C. cli, 44. Bentham obtained a copy of the letter on the condition that he neither show it or communicate its contents to any other person. See B.M. VI, 458, W. Robertson to A. Buchan, 11 February 1797.

59. F. M. Eden, *op. cit.*, vol. 1, p. 479.

60. The bill empowered the wardens, with the consent of two visitors and the guardian of the poor, to apprentice boys at the age of 14, girls at 12 "or an earlier age if it shall be thought fit" after they had served a term at the "School of Industry."

61. Pitt fulfilled his pledge in Parliament to abolish the law which prohibited relief for owners of "visible property"; his bill would have allowed relief for those owning property worth up to £30. Child allowances were to be provided for fathers with more than one child, widows with more than two. After the age of five, they could be requisitioned for the "School of Industry" unless they could be properly instructed at home in accordance with the directions of the "School's" manager.

62. Thomas Ruggles approved of the "cow money" clause; he did not agree with one correspondent who thought that a pig could be substituted for a cow. ". . . if so, 'other animal' must mean Cat, Dog, or what else." And that "would throw a *ridicule* where humanity meant a *benefit* . . ." (He was right: Bentham suggested a rattlesnake; see Chapter Two, p. 49. Ruggles to William Bray, U.C. cli, 44). Bentham was well prepared for an attack on the "cow money" clause, for he had seen it suggested by William Wilburforce and had drawn up his criticisms in February 1796. The same material was used to attack Pitt. See "Obs. on Wilb. Poor Bill," U.C. cliiib, 365. A copy in a copyist's hand (369–70) was dated 10 February 1796 by Bentham.

63. George Rose to Bentham, 3 May 1796, B.M. VI, 177–78; Bentham to Charles Abbot, 4 May 1796, Public Record Office (PRO) 30/9–31 facing f. 78 of diary for 1796.

64. Bowring, viii, 440–461. It was not, as Professor Poynter thought, "addressed to Pitt" (J. R. Poynter, *op. cit.*, p. 68). The full title reads, *Observations on the Poor Bill, introduced by the Right Honourable William Pitt*.

65. Bowring, viii, 440.

66. J. L. and B. Hammond, *op. cit.*, p. 150.

67. Bentham to W. Baldwin, 13 January 1797 (B.M. VI, 440–41).

68. Rose to Bentham, 11 February 1797 (B.M. VI, 459).

69. Isaac Wood, *A Letter to Sir W. Pulteney, Bart . . . . containing some Observations on the Bill for the better Support and Maintenance of the Poor* (London, 1797).

70. Buchan to Bentham, 11 February 1797 (B.M. VI, 460). Alexander Peter Buchan (1764-1824) was not, however, "an influential member of the legislature." He was an eminent physician who had studied under Sir John Hunter and Dr. George Fordyce, and had settled in London in 1793.

71. U.C. cliiib, 353.

72. "Heads of Defect 1, Matter 2. Form" (U.C. cliiib, 352, dated 4 January 1796; Bentham made the common mistake of writing 1796 instead of 1797).

73. Bowring, viii, 440-41.

74. See *Correspondence* (*supra*, Introduction, n. 17) ii, 489n.

75. U.C. cliiib, 352-54.

76. Ruggles to Bray, 5 February 1797 (U.C. cli, 44).

77. U.C. cliiib, 354. The idea of a "secret history" of law was a recurring theme in Bentham's writings. For example, in the preface to *Indirect Legislation*, Bentham wrote that "[i]n most systems of law, there is a secret history which differs more or less widely from the public one. The laws are seldom so good or bad in effect as they seem to be upon paper" (U.C. lxxxvii, 6).

78. Bowring, viii, 421.

79. *Ibid.*, 441.

80. "Essay on the question,—Who are the person for whom the several bounties provided by this Bill are intended?" (*ibid.*, 457-60).

81. *Ibid.*, 459.

82. *Ibid.*

83. U.C. cliiib, 354; see also Bowring, viii, 458.

84. Bowring, viii, 461.

85. *Ibid.*, 455.

86. *Ibid.*, 448.

87. The other occasions include most of Bentham's popular pamphlets, such as *Truth versus Ashurst* and *A Protest Against Law Taxes*. For these, see above, Chapter One, n. 2, p. 220.

88. Bowring, viii, 445-46.

89. *Ibid.*, 447.

90. *Ibid.*, 444-46.

91. *Ibid.*, 454.

92. Adam Smith, *op. cit.*, pp. 225-26 (bk. 1, ch. 10). Smith remarked (*inter alia*) that an apprentice "is likely to be idle, and almost always is so." "A young man naturally conceives an aversion to labour when for a long time he receives no benefit from it."

93. Bowring, viii, 453 (emphasis in original).

94. *Ibid.*, 454.

95. *Ibid.*

96. *Parliamentary History*, vol. 32, 711.

97. Bowring, viii, 451.

98. *Ibid.* (emphasis in original).

99. *Ibid.* (emphasis deleted).

100. U.C. cliiib, 356 (dated 6 January 1797).

101. Bowring, viii, 451.

102. See above, Introduction, n. 17, p. 220.

103. U.C. cliib, 487.

104. Bowring, viii, 447.

105. U.C. cliib, 487.
106. Bowring, viii, 448.
107. *Ibid.*, 447. Here Bentham reprints the relevant section from Pitt's bill.
108. *Ibid.*, 449.
109. *Ibid.*, 460. A similar phrase is found at 459.
110. *Ibid.*, 449.
111. *Ibid.*, 442.
112. *Ibid.*, 441.
113. *Ibid.*, 444. Because he believed the act to compel making up wages to the "full rate," Bentham went to great lengths to show that the phrase was thoroughly ambiguous. He was successful, but his attack was quite beside the point. See 443–44.
114. *Ibid.*, 440–41.
115. U.C. cli, 171 (dated 1 January 1797), 175. Bentham repeated the argument in detail several times. See U.C. cliiia, 237 and 243–45; U.C. cxxxiii, 12-13; U.C. cliib, 450-52.
116. U.C. cliib, 452.
117. U.C. cliii, 248.
118. *Ibid.*, 238.
119. U.C. cxxxiii, 12.
120. Danial Defoe, *Giving Alms no Charity, And employing the Poor . . .* (London, 1704) p. 24.
121. The list of "Classes Mustered" was in fact omitted from Bowring's edition and from the 1812 edition. See also U.C. cli, 120ff. where Bentham discussed the 22 classes of paupers enlisted into service.
122. U.C. cliib, 452.
123. U.C. clivb, 534–35.
124. See Introduction, p. 5, and Chapter Four, pp. 86–87.
125. U.C. clivb, 345.
126. Ms. alt. "saved."
127. U.C. clivb, 534. The same point in nearly the same language is made at 345.
128. Bernard Mandeville, *The Fable of the Bees* (London, 1714), Remark Q (Pelican edition, ed. Phillip Harth, London, 1970) pp. 208–09.
129. Arthur Young, *A Tour through the East of England* (London, 1771) vol. IV, p. 361. Cited in S. and B. Webb, *op. cit.*, p. 428.
130. J. R. Poynter, *op. cit.*, p. 120.
131. U.C. cli, 20. The same material, in a copyist's hand, is found in U.C. clivb, 599–604.
132. *Ibid.*
133. U.C. cliii, 223.
134. *Ibid.*
135. U.C. cli, 20 (emphasis added).
136. *Ibid.*, 24. The same material, in a copyist's hand, is found in U.C. cliiib, 484.
137. Bowring, viii, 453.
138. U.C. lxxxvii, 63.
139. U.C. cli, 22.
140. *Ibid.*, 23.
141. U.C. cliiia, 150. The English economist Nassau Senior (1790–1864) faithfully followed Bentham's ideas in this respect (if not Bentham himself) in the well-known description of capital as "abstinence" in his *An Outline of the Science of Political Economy* (1836). Sheldon Wolin comments that "since abstinence was recognized as

self-inflicted pain, one might say that capitalist society was defined in terms of voluntary self-mutilation." He continues: "In Bentham's famous tract, *Defense of Usury* [sic], the usurer emerges as the symbol of self-denial: 'Those who have the resolution to sacrifice the present to future are natural objects of envy to those who have sacrificed future to the present.' The usurer, however, is identical with the liberal definition of a moral agent, and hence it is not extreme to characterize liberal moral theory as the catechizing of repression." Quite apart from the rather exaggerated language, what is bothersome in this passage is its incompleteness: Wolin might have added, first, that Senior's description of capital is correct—saving *does* mean abstaining from consumption, and it is perfectly legitimate to characterize such abstention as a kind of pain; second, that *any* society, and not just a "capitalist" one (leaving aside special cases such as possession of an especially scarce and desired raw material), which wishes to increase its wealth must practice some degree of abstinence from consumption; third, that any civil society worthy of the name requires of its members abstention from acting on certain impulses or desires, especially violent ones but also others, and therefore, fourth, that every decent moral theory, not just a "liberal" one, must require the suppression of certain desires and impulses. See Sheldon S. Wolin, *Politics and Vision* (Boston, 1960) pp. 333–34.

Chapter Three

1. Bowring, iv, 39. In mss. intended for a "preface" for a work identified only as "Poor Bill," Bentham reviewed the origins of the Panopticon idea and its potentially extensive application. He remarks that in his original "Letters" on Panopticon, "the Penitentiary system" was the "principal object and subject matter of these letters," and he mentions that they were published at the instance of John Parnell, the Irish government's Chancellor of Exchequer (U.C. cliib, 420–21). For discussions of Panopticon, see G. Himmelfarb, "The Haunted House of Jeremy Bentham" (*supra*, Introduction, n. 1) and D. G. Long, *Bentham on Liberty* (*supra*, ch. 1, n. 37) pp. 185ff. For Bentham's enthusiasm over the extensive application of Panopticon, see *Correspondence* iii, 503. Early in 1787 he had intended to approach Pitt on the Panopticon idea, but for some reason did not; see *Correspondence* iii, 534–36. For Bentham's use of the phrase "Panopticon in both its branches," see Bowring xi, 103. Bentham had been interested in how best to employ prisoners ever since he wrote his *View of the Hard Labour Bill* in 1778. In January of the previous year he visited a prison ship and made detailed notes on his observations. These included matters such as the hours and nature of work, the method of discipline, diet, clothing, and medical and "spiritual" assistance (see U.C. cxviia, 1–2). By the time of Panopticon, of course, these had become matters of intense concern. I am indebted to Professor Douglas Long for pointing these notes out to me.
2. For Bentham's initial defense of the contract ("farming") system, see Bowring, iv, 46–49; and see Chapter Five, "Farming the Poor." For the operation of the "subsidiary" institution, see Bowring, iv, 165–66.
3. For the rule of severity, see *ibid.*, pp. 122–23. The Webbs point out that the "less eligibility" principle could not always be enforced in practice, especially so far as food and shelter were concerned: making paupers' conditions "less eligible" in these items would often condemn them to malnutrition and inadequate shelter. For the vicissitudinary history of the principle, see their *English Local Government*, vol. 10 (London, 1910) pp. 260–63.

4. Bentham to Lord Spencer, 18 April 1796 (B.M. VI, 166–67). After two prodding letters (3 May and 24 May), Spencer finally consented to discuss the matter further. Such delays of weeks and months were typical of Bentham's Panopticon negotiations. In Spencer's case, Bentham had been negotiating since September 1793 (Bentham to Samuel Bentham, 2 July 1796 [B.M. VI, 210–11]; Lord Spencer to Bentham, 29 August 1796 [*Ibid.*, 264–65].

5. Lady Spencer Wilson, owner of an essential part of the Woolich site, refused to sell despite Bentham's offer of a life annuity of £500 if she would relent.

6. Bentham to George Rose, 16 November 1796 (B.M. VI, 344). Other parts of Tothill Fields were used as grounds for dumping rubbish. Bentham suggested that the school use Lords for its matches (Bentham to Bishop of Rochester, 31 October 1796 [B.M. VI, 314–17]).

7. Bentham to Samuel Bentham, 15 November 1796 (B.M. VI, 342–43).

8. Bentham to Samuel Bentham, 1 December 1796 (B.M. VI, 369); Bentham to Samuel and Mary Bentham, 2 December 1796 (B.M. VI, 370).

9. Colquhoun to Bentham, 4 December 1796 (B.M. VI, 373–74); Bentham to Colquhoun, 6 December 1796 (B.M. VI, 377–78). Colquhoun confused Jeremy with Samuel and addressed the letter to "General Bentham." Bentham diplomatically corrected him.

10. Bentham to Rose, 16 November 1796 (B.M. VI, 344–46).

11. Bentham to Samuel Bentham, 9 December 1796 (B.M. VI, 382–83).

12. Colquhoun to Bentham, 16 December 1796 (B.M. VI, 397–98).

13. Bentham to Baldwin, 13 January 1797 (B.M. VI, 440–41); Baldwin to Bentham, 14 January 1797 (B.M. VI, 442–43); Baldwin to Bentham, 23 January 1797 (B.M. VI, 446–47).

14. Samuel Bentham to Bentham, 29 October 1796 (B.M. VI, 309–10).

15. Bentham to Wilberforce, 28 February 1797 (Bodleian Library, Wilberforce Mss. d.13/41). On the same day, Bentham asked W. Morton Pitt to inquire of the Attorney General *"how it goes"* (B.M. VI, 448). The latter may not have been sent.

16. Bentham to Solicitor General, 25 March 1797 (B.M. VI, 463–64); J. Mitford (Sol. Gen.) to Bentham, 27 March 1797 (B.M. VI, 465–66).

17. Bentham to Solicitor General and Attorney General, 30 March 1797 (B.M. VI, 469–70).

18. Romilly to Bentham, 26 April 1797 (Bowring, xi, 116); C. Butler to Bentham 1 May 1797 (B.M. VI, 477–78).

19. Bentham to Samuel Bentham, 15 May 1795 (B.M. VI, 71–72).

20. Charles Long to White, sending contract for engrossing, 28 July 1796 (B.M. VI, 239).

21. Bentham to Pitt, 28 February 1796 (U.C. cliiib, 359). It is possible that this letter was not sent.

22. Bentham to Pitt, n.d. (1797; U.C. cxxxiii, 79).

23. U.C. cxlix, 118. This is a copy of part of the report.

24. See Bentham to Samuel Bentham, 10 December 1796 (B.M. VI, 284–86).

25. Bentham to Wilberforce, 1 September 1796 (Bodleian Library, Wilberforce Mss. d.13/35).

26. *Ibid.*

27. Wilberforce to Bentham, 3 September 1796 (Bowring, x, 318–19); St. Helens to Bentham, 10 September 1796 (B.M. VI, 281–82). Bentham had sent St. Helens a copy of his letter to Wilberforce. Jeremy subsequently summarized this spate of correspon-

dence to Samuel. Bentham to Samuel Bentham, 12 September 1796 (B.M. VI, 288–89).

28. Bentham to St. Helens, September 1796 (Bowring, x, 318–20).

29. Bentham to Wilberforce, 1 September 1796 (Bodleian Library, Wilberforce Mss. d.13f.35).

30. *Ibid.*

31. U.C. lxxxvii, 58–59.

32. Bentham to Society of Agriculture, n.d. (September 1797; U.C. cliv, 53).

33. *Luke* 21:1–3. One should notice the identity or near identity of Bentham's language and that of the biblical passages cited. In this case, the passage begins, "And he looked up, and saw the rich men casting their gifts into the Treasury." Bentham had written, "Now that your Treasury is open. . . ."

34. *Acts* 3:1–6.

35. *Luke* 10:37; *Matthew* 6:21.

36. Bentham to Samuel Bentham, 6 December 1790 (Bowring, x, 246).

37. F. Burton to Bentham, 2 August 1792 (B.M. V, 357–58); Burton to Bentham, 27 August 1792 (B.M. V, 361–63).

38. Bentham to Wilberforce and Morton Pitt, 1796 (U.C. cliiib, 361).

39. Bentham to Samuel Bentham, 24 February 1796 (B.M. VI, 150).

40. See, for example, U.C. cxxxiii, 2–65 *passim*.

41. See John MacFarlan, *Inquiries concerning the Poor* (Edinburgh, 1782).

42. See U.C. cli, 28 and 30. The material is in a copyist's hand, and is labeled by Bentham "Community Maintenance repulsive."

43. U.C. cvii, 48–49.

44. U.C. cli, 71.

45. *Ibid.*, 67–70.

46. Lansdowne to Bentham, 4 April 1796 (B.M. VI, 164–65).

47. *Ibid.*

48. See below, Chapter 5.

49. Powys to Bentham, 21 May 1796 (B.M. VI, 179–80).

50. Bentham to Samuel Bentham, 23 May 1796 (*ibid.*, 181–82).

51. *The Complete Works of Count Rumford*, 4 vols. (Boston, 1875) vol. 4, "An Account of an Establishment for the Poor at Munich," p. 233.

52. *Ibid.*, p. 243.

53. *Ibid.*, pp. 265–66.

54. *Ibid.*, p. 258.

55. *Ibid.*, pp. 261ff.

56. *Ibid.*, p. 289–90.

57. *Ibid.*, pp. 288–89.

58. "Of the Fundamental Principles on which General Establishments for the Relief of the Poor may be formed in all Countries." Count Rumford, *Works*, vol. 4, p. 357.

59. *Ibid.*, p. 305. See also p. 309, where more tears flowed upon Rumford's return to the workhouse after a long absence.

60. *Ibid.*, "Of the Fundamental Principles . . .", pp. 327–93 *passim*.

61. Bentham seems to have been unaware that the Munich House was not self-maintaining. In arguing that despite past experience the labor of the poor could be made sufficient for their expense, he asserted that "the experiments made by Count Rumford, in a situation that invested him with requisite powers, in a country more favourably circumstanced than England for the institution of political experiments,

seem to have already placed this out of doubt." (U.C. cliia, 66).

62. Rumford, *op. cit.*, "Of the Fundamental Principles . . .", p. 359.

63. *Ibid.*, p. 361. Bentham reports that the London Foundling Hospital reduced its fuel consumption by a third through the use of Rumford's suggestions. See U.C. cliib, 470.

64. Thomas Coram (1668–1751), immortalized by Hogarth, was a man of such kindly disposition and sensitivity that he was appalled at the practice of leaving unwanted babies on the dunghills in and around London. After years of campaigning (including the novel departure of appealing to great ladies), Coram obtained a royal Charter in 1739, and the hospital opened in 1741. It soon became a social and philanthropic center through the patronage of many of the greatest artists of the day such as Hogarth, Reynolds, and Gainsborough, who exhibited their works within its walls. (The enthusiasm for the arts thus generated, led, incidentally, to an annual general exhibition of art, the precursor of the Royal Academy.) George Handel raised vast sums for the Hospital through performance of his music, including the *Messiah*, and presented the Chapel with an organ. Bentham frequently mentions the Foundling Hospital, and its fame was at least partially responsible for the pains he took over the care of infants in poor-Panopticons. Although the Hospital itself was demolished in the 1920's, the site, adjacent to Mecklenburgh Square, still exists as Coram Fields, to which no adult may be admitted unless accompanied by a child. The nearby Coram Foundation still functions and preserves Hogarth's magnificent portrait. For an undigested but useful account, see R. H. Nichols and F. A. Wray, *The History of the Foundling Hospital* (London, 1935).

65. Rumford to Bentham, 10 July 1796 (B.M. VI, 214–15).

66. Rumford to Bentham, 10 December 1795 (B.M. VI, 124–25).

67. Bentham to Samuel Bentham, 20 February 1796 (B.M. VI, 149); Lansdowne to Bentham, 4 April 1796 (B.M. VI, 164–65): "Surely there is great merit in several of Count Rumford's Ideas about the poor."

68. Bowring, viii, 387.

69. See Bowring, viii, 387, where Bentham proposes experiments in the quantity of food for the poor and in the number of meals to be taken.

70. *Ibid.*, 430–39.

71. Colquhoun to Bentham, 31 December 1796 (B.M. VI, 423–24).

72. A circular for the subscription was drawn up and printed, but the scheme seems to have died a silent death. Bentham's draft for the advertisement of the plan is found at U.C. cli, 102–06. Bentham's influence on Colquhoun was a lasting one, as shown by the latter's *The State of Indigence* (London, 1806). Colquhoun sent Bentham details of his own plans for Poor Law reform together with correspondence seeking information on contemporary practice (U.C. cli, 102–06; U.C. cxlix, 112–17). The refusal of the parish of St. Giles, London (U.C. cxlix, 115) to provide such information was all too typical.

73. Colquhoun to Bentham, 20 January 1797 (B.M. VI, 444–45).

74. Bentham to Eden, 13 February 1797 (Eden Mss.); Eden to Bentham, 18 December 1797 (B.M. VI, 518–19).

75. "Observations on the Pauper Population Table Hereunto Annexed," Bowring, viii, 362–64.

76. *Ibid.*, 336. A proposal for taking a census had been made by Bentham's acquaintance William Morton Pitt (*ibid.*, 363). In 1800, a census bill sponsored by Bentham's half brother Charles Abbot (afterwards Speaker of the House of Commons and, in 1817, Lord Colchester) was enacted. The next year the first census was taken.

77. Bentham to Caroline Fox, 5 September 1797 (U.C. cxxxiii, 75).

78. *Ibid.*, 74. Sir John Sinclair, MP (1754–1835) was the author of a *Statistical Account of Scotland* (1791–99) and had founded the Board of Agriculture in 1793. In July 1795 he wrote to Bentham (the two had been acquainted since 1794 when Sinclair had given his blessing to Panopticon) for his thoughts on Poor Law reform, as he was sounding out "all the intelligent men of my acquaintance" and could not think of "overlooking so capitall a hand as Mr. Bentham." Bentham replied that he was already writing on the subject, and, complaining of his expenditures for Panopticon, remarked *"Pauper sum—paupertatis nihil a me alienum puto."* Sinclair to Bentham, 5 July 1797 (B.M. VI, 473–74); Bentham to Sinclair, 13 July 1797 (*The Correspondence of the Right Honourable Sir John Sinclair, Bart.*, 2 vols. [London, 1831] vol. 1, p. 483.

79. "Situation and Relief of the Poor," Bowring, viii, 361.

80. See, for example, Bentham to Arthur Young, 1797 (U.C. cli, 262); Young to Bentham, 2 April 1797 (B.M. VI, 471–72).

81. Young to Bentham, 31 October 1797 (B.M. VI, 498–99).

Chapter Four

1. See, for example, J. Acland, *A Plan for rendering the Poor independent of Public Contributions* . . . (London, 1786).

2. Dr. Porteus to P. Colquhoun, Glasgow, 18–23 October 1797 (B.M. VI, 490–95). Hereinafter cited as "Porteus letter." Page numbers refer to the typed copy in the possession of the Bentham Project at University College London.

3. See E. P. Thompson, *The Making of the English Working Class* (Pelican edition, London, 1962) p. 117n.

4. Porteus letter, p. 1.

5. *Ibid.*, p. 2.

6. *Ibid.*, pp. 3 and 9. Porteus did not know how such an estimate could be made or, indeed, how the "necessaries of life" could be defined. The humane clergyman added that it would "be unspeakably dangerous to have recourse to any theory for an answer to this question. We must not speculate with the lives of the people."

7. *Ibid.*, p. 9.

8. *Ibid.*, p. 4.

9. *Ibid.*

10. *Ibid.*, p. 6.

11. *Ibid.*, p. 3.

12. *Ibid.*, p. 10.

13. *Ibid.*, p. 8 (emphasis added).

14. *Ibid.* ". . . its [i.e., benevolence's] proper objects are surreptitiously monopolized by the law. . . ." Benevolence was "monopolized by a few public men to the unspeakable loss of the people and of the state" (p. 3).

15. *Ibid.*, p. 9.

16. London, 1786.

17. London, 1798. It is a curious fact that in a recent edition of this work (London, 1970) the editor, Mr. Anthony Flew, fails to give Townsend a single mention in the course of an extensive introduction.

18. Townsend, *op. cit.*, p. 55.

19. *Ibid.*, pp. 61–62.

20. *Ibid.*, p. 50.

21. *Ibid.*, p. 58. "Speculation apart, it is a fact that in England we have more than we can feed, and many more than we can profitably employ under the present system of our laws."

22. *Ibid.*, pp. 50–51.

23. *Ibid.*, pp. 67ff.

24. *Ibid.*, p. 87.

25. *Ibid.*, p. 84.

26. *Ibid.*, pp. 87–89.

27. *Ibid.*, p. 21.

28. *Ibid.*, p. 84.

29. *Ibid.*, p. 88.

30. *Ibid.*, pp. 79–81.

31. *Ibid.*, p. 98.

32. *Ibid.*, pp. 98–99.

33. U.C. cliia, 32. A similar argument can be found in U.C. cli, 2.

34. U.C. cliia, 33.

35. Bowring, viii, 428 (emphasis added).

36. U.C. cliia, 11. For Bentham's protests against "inefficient use of funds," see, for example, U.C. cliva, 2.

37. U.C. cliia, 8.

38. *Ibid.*, 10. For Bentham, charitable relief could be considered as a commodity with a certain supply and demand. ". . . the supply afforded by a rich proprietor would be proportional not to the demand but to his own conception of his own superfluities. . . ." In the case of a sweeping calamity, "what must be the lot of the most indigent class?" (*ibid.*, 9). What that lot might be was illustrated half a century later during the Irish potato famine, when English aid was a tragic case of too little too late.

39. Bowring, viii, 428, "Voluntary Charity assisted and directed."

40. U.C. cliia, 28.

41. *Ibid.*, 11. Cities, he wrote elsewhere, are "so many theatres for the display of talents dedicated to the vocation of begging." U.C. clivb, 327.

42. U.C. cliib, 428.

43. *Ibid.* In Greek and Roman mythology, Astraea, goddess of justice, was the last deity to leave the earth after the golden age; she became the constellation Virgo. Bentham later pencilled in a "Q" for *quere* through this paragraph. Certainly the idea that benevolence could be dispensed with would not have endeared him to many of his readers.

44. *Ibid.*

45. Bowring, ii, 579.

46. U.C. cxxxiii, 11.

47. *Ibid.*, U.C. cliia, 259–60.

48. *Ibid.*, 260.

49. In his manuscripts, Bentham suggests other roles for private charity. Many of them had nothing to do with poor relief. For example, rewards could be given for the "extension of useful knowledge" or simply presented to the treasury to reduce taxes. See U.C. cliva, 6; and U.C. cxxxiii, 22.

50. Bowring, viii, 429. Bentham gave several examples of the uses of such donations. One was for building the "outlying cottages" for the few who did not require constant observation. Two others are not reassuring: "Chilliness will thus suggest to charity the importance of warm *clothing.*—Good appetite . . . will propose additions under the head of *diet.*" The implications are obvious.

51. *Ibid.*

52. For an analysis of the various conflicting notions of poverty as traditionally debated, see Robert J. Lampman, *Ends and Means of Reducing Income Poverty* (Chicago, 1971) pp. 51ff.

53. U.C. cli, 7. "The poor are the objects of peculiar favour under the divine. Their title to favour is not less indisputable under the human. If of such is the *Kingdom of God*, of such too is the bulk of men."

54. U.C. cliiia, 21.

55. U.C. cli, 7.

56. U.C. cliiia, 22–23 (emphasis in original).

57. U.C. cli, 7.

58. Malthus' first *Essay* appeared in 1798, the year after Bentham published his articles in the *Annals of Agriculture*. An astute owner of Bentham's 1812 edition of *Pauper Management Improved*, preserved at University College London, observed that the final section, which seemed to encourage population growth, was omitted. That this may well have been occasioned by Malthus' impact has been remarked upon by Professor Himmelfarb. See her "Bentham's Utopia: The National Charity Company" (*supra*, Introduction, n. 2) p. 120.

59. U.C. cliib, 429.

60. U.C. cliia, 23–24. And see U.C. xxix, 6: "Expectation is the basis of every proprietary right: it is this which affords whatever occasion there can be for giving a thing to one man rather than another," and U.C. xxxii, 4, where Bentham described "the principle of expectation" as "the ground of civil rights" and as the "only true principle of civil justice." Cited by D. G. Long, *Bentham on Liberty*, p. 168.

61. U.C. cliia, 22–23; cliib, 429.

62. U.C. cliiia, 25, "Fundamental Positions in regard to the providing for the Indigent," dated 28 April 1796.

63. U.C. cliiia, 86.

64. *Ibid.*, 25 (emphasis in original).

65. U.C. cliia, 14.

66. See J. R. Poynter, *op. cit.* (*supra*, ch. 1, n. 16) xxiii.

67. U.C. cliiia, 23.

68. U.C. cliia, 61–62.

69. *Ibid.*, 62.

70. U.C. cli, 4.

71. *Ibid.*, 1 (emphasis omitted).

72. *Ibid.*

73. U.C. cliiia, 24.

74. U.C. cliia, 16.

75. See *Capital*, vol. 1 (Moscow, 1961) p. 616n. The *Essay*, according to Marx, plagiarizes "Defoe, Sir James Steuart, Townsend, Franklin, Wallace &c., and does not contain a single sentence thought out by himself." In his introduction to a new edition of Townsend's *Dissertation* . . . (Berkeley and Los Angeles, 1971) Ashley Montagu writes that this "harsh judgment need not be taken too seriously" (pp. 10–11) but allows that even if Malthus was not aware of it, his ideas "were not entirely underived from other sources." Marx very nearly calls Townsend a plagiarist as well, saying that "this delicate parson" from whom "Malthus often copies whole pages, himself borrowed the greater part of his doctrine from Sir James Steuart." *Capital*, vol. 1, *ed. cit.*, p. 647n.

76. Townsend, *op. cit.*, p. 55.

77. *Ibid.*, p. 37.
78. *Ibid.*, p. 55.
79. *Ibid.*, pp. 37–39.
80. Bowring, ix, 13.
81. See, for example, U.C. lxxii, 187–205 *passim*.
82. Stark, vol. 1, p. 207.
83. *Ibid.*, "Colonies and Navy," p. 216. And see also *Supply without Burthen*, *ibid.*, p. 366. For eighteenth-century opinion on the relation between population growth and the means of procuring subsistence, see, for example, Montesquieu, *The Spirit of the Laws*, bk. 18, ch. 10; David Hume, "Of the Populousness of Ancient Nations," in *Essays and Treatises on Several Subjects* (London and Edinburgh, 1758) p. 210; and Adam Smith, *An Inquiry into the Nature and Causes of the Wealth of Nations*, 3 vols. (Edinburgh, 1817) vol. 1, bk. I, ch. XI, pt. 2, pp. 226–27.
84. *Ibid.*, pp. 366–67.
85. U.C. cliia, 16.
86. Stark, vol. 3, p. 85.
87. In the Introduction, Bentham spoke of "offenses against population" as those offenses whose tendency is "to diminish the numbers. . . ." (see ch. 16, para. 17, *CW*, 201).
88. U.C. clivb, 544–45.
89. U.C. cli, 108.
90. "Method and leading principles of an Institute of Political Economy (Including finance) considered not only as a science but as an art" (1801–04); in Stark, vol. 3, p. 355.
91. U.C. cli, 108.
92. Stark, vol. 3, p. 301.
93. *Ibid.*, p. 302.
94. For *Emancipate Your Colonies!*, see Bowring, iv, 407–18. For the ms. sources of *Rid Yourself of Ultramaria!*, see A. Taylor Milne, *Catalogue of the Manuscripts of Jeremy Bentham* . . . (2nd ed. London, 1962) as index. A very helpful sketch of Bentham's shifting views on colonization on which I have partially relied is J. H. Burns, "Bentham on Colonial Problems: Summary Review" (April 1961 /January 1962), unpublished. A mimeographed copy is in my possession.
95. B.M. Add. Ms. 33550, f. 125 (autograph, 1828). Published as a part of "The Philosophy of Economic Science" in Stark, vol. 1, p. 110.
96. B.M. Add. Ms. 33550, f. 126, in *ibid.*, p. 111. Bentham's ambiguity on the colonial question continued at least until the summer before his death. In 1830, *Emancipate Your Colonies!* was republished without alteration, and at about the same time Bentham drafted his "Colonization Society Proposal." But on the other hand, in the summer of 1831, "he worked out in some detail" and "submitted to Gibbon Wakefield a scheme for colonising an unsettled area in south Australia. The key to this seems to be a revived awareness of the population problem and of the difficulties of the Poor Law administration in Britain" (J. H. Burns, "Bentham on Colonial Problems: Summary Review").
97. In *A Summary View of the Principle of Population* (1830), Malthus included in his list of vices which prevented population increases "improper arts to prevent the consequences of irregular connections." Contained in *An Essay on the Principle of Population*, ed. Anthony Flew (Pelican edition, London, 1970) p. 250.
98. When Archibald Prentice visited Bentham in 1831, he complained that Francis Place was a "bold bad man": bad because he was advocating contraception; bold be-

cause he did so openly. Bentham told Place that ". . . I took care not to let him know how my opinion stood; the fat would have been all in the fire, unless I succeeded in converting him, for which there was not time. . . ." (Bentham to Place, April 24, 1831; cited in Norman E. Himes, "Jeremy Bentham and the Genesis of English Neo-Malthusianism," *Economic History*, vol. 3, no. 2 (February 1936) p. 272.

99. Stark, vol. 1, 272–73.

100. Bowring, viii, 367–68.

101. Professor Himes was mistaken when he wrote that the most important observation on this passage is that "Bentham here recommends contraception as a means of reducing the poor rates" (Himes, *op. cit.*, p. 268). J. R. Poynter similarly disputes Himes' conclusion (Poynter, *op. cit.*, p. 125n.) Himes is confused in other matters as well. Bentham had written, speaking of the poor rates, that an illustrious friend was ". . . for limiting them.—Limit them?—Agreed. But how?—Not by a prohibitory act— a remedy which would neither be applied, nor, if applied, be effectual—not by a *dead letter*, but by a *living body*. . . ." (Bowring, viii, 367). Himes remarks that Bentham "declares that it would be folly to prohibit sexual relations by law." Bentham says no such thing: he says that he disagrees with Townsend's proposal for a legal prohibition that would limit poor rates. As for Bentham's remedy for pauperism, Himes says that Bentham "means to suggest that it will not be 'so rough,' not such a strain on human nature, as abstinence." But if Townsend was suggesting contraception, as Himes agrees (p. 270), how could he and Bentham be speaking of abstinence? Finally, Himes' suggestion that Bentham's use of the phrase "dead letter" might be a cryptic reference to the male sheath is patently absurd, even from the deepest depths of depth-psychology. Bentham *rejects* the "dead letter" of the *law* in favor of the "living body" of the National Charity Company.

102. U.C. cli, 108.

103. J. R. Poynter, *op. cit.*, p. 123.

104. But compare the further argument in this chapter, pp. 100–101.

105. Stark, vol. 3, p. 361. The ms. was dated 1801; mss. for the "Agenda and Non-Agenda" were dated 1804.

106. *Ibid.*, p. 362.

107. *Ibid.*

108. U.C. lxviii, 10; "Penal Code Appendix," dated January 1825.

109. Stark, vol. 3, pp. 362–63.

110. U.C. lxxiii, 94.

111. *Ibid.*, 97.

112. U.C. lxxii, 201.

113. *Ibid.*, 189.

114. U.C. lxviii, 12. In the 1780's, Bentham wrote, "It is wonderful that nobody has ever yet fancied it to be sinful to scratch where it itches: and that it had never been determined that the only way of scratching is with such and such a finger and that it is unnatural to scratch with any other" (U.C. lxxii, 189). Over the years Bentham became increasingly bitter towards religious asceticism, especially Christian asceticism, though brickbats were also hurled at Islam. In the chapter "Innocent aberations of the sexual appetite, why not included in the scheme of punishment" of the "Penal Code appendix" of 1824, he wrote that "For the establishment of evil in both these shapes"—eating and drinking on the one hand and sexuality on the other—"the practice has been the acquisition of the sympathies and the . . . antipathy of an Almighty being, who, by a self-contradicting proposition is at the [same time] stiled benevolent. In this race of mischief and absurdity, of moral and intellectual depravity, the fol-

lowers of Mahomet have outstript [?] the self stiled, and so falsely and manifestly falsely stiled, followers of Jesus: in that philosopher, for whether God or not, philosopher he was at any rate, asceticism in all its forms was an object of . . . scorn and ridicule. Asceticism is not *Christianity* but *Paulism*" (U.C. lxviii, 10). Bentham had previously published a savage pseudonymous attack on Paul in his *Not Paul but Jesus* by Gamaliel Smith, Esq., London, 1823. Francis Place stated that he compiled it for Bentham. For the duplicity in concealing his authorship from his editor Etienne Dumont, see the Dumont Manuscripts, Salle Naville, Bibliothèque Publique et Universitaire, Geneva (hereinafter cited as Mss. Dumont) 33 I, ff. 382–85, "Martha Colls" to Dumont, 29 November 1823.

115. U.C. lxviii, 13–14. In his writings on law and sexuality of 1814 and 1816 he argued that if "population be an evil, then every thing that operates towards the diminution of that evil must . . . be a good. Call it misery,—call it even vice, still in so far as this good effect is produced by it, the quality of goodness is not with the less propriety attributed to it" (U.C. lxxiv, 126).

116. Malthus, *A Summary View of the Principle of Population*, ed. cit., p. 250.

117. U.C. lxviii, 14. A decade earlier Bentham recommended active sexual practice among homosexuals on purely utilitarian grounds. The "solitary mode" of sexual gratification, he argued, is inferior to the "social mode" in countries where homosexuality is legally tolerated. (He made no argument for civil disobedience where it was not legally tolerated.) Human happiness would be greatly increased "if, instead of the solitary mode, all persons who from the gratification of their appetitie resort to irregular channels, resort to the social mode" (U.C. lxxiv, 142). As for the supposed immorality of the practice, he argued that it was no more immoral than smoking tobacco or drinking coffee and tea; all "unprolific" sexuality was on the same footing (*ibid.*, p. 69).

118. U.C. lxxiv, 6.

119. Edgeworth to Dumont, February 16, 1810 (Mss. Dumont, 33 II, f. 20). "Bentham is an extraordinary person—but I cannot conceive why you should work for him as Voltaire did the King of Prussia." Similarly, in September 1813, Richard Edgeworth told Dumont—with respect to a review of Dumont's editions of Bentham—that "if you were to forbid me to mention the editor, or to impress me with the idea that instead of working for him I was labouring for Mr. Bentham I would throw down my pen . . . Mr. Bentham!—what's he to me? or I to him?" (Mss. Dumont, 33 II, p. 94). For the rebuff of Edgeworth, see Bowring, x., 467.

120. *Ibid.*, p. 5 (Richard Edgeworth to Dumont, 18 September 1806).

121. See Amnon Goldworth, "The Meaning of Bentham's Greatest Happiness Principle," *Journal of the History of Philosophy* (July 1969) pp. 315–21. It is, however, on *prima facie* grounds rather dangerous to say, as Professor Goldworth does, that Bentham did not really mean what he said he meant—that he did not mean what he consistently said for more than fifty years. Thus, it is questionable to say that ". . . what Bentham meant by his greatest happiness principle is not the production of the greatest happiness of the greatest number but simply the production of the greatest happiness" (p. 321). But Bentham never distinguished between "greatest happiness" and "greatest happiness of the greatest number." On the contrary, he believed that the "greatest happiness" *always is—can only be*—the "greatest happiness of the greatest number": witness the many instances in which he says "the principle of the Greatest Happiness of the Greatest Number, or say, for short, the Greatest Happiness Principle." In one of his last published works, the *Parliamentary Candidates Proposed Declaration of Principles* . . . (1831), which was extracted from his

master work, the *Constitutional Code* (vol. 1, 1830), the only "right and proper end of government" is identified as "the greatest happiness of the Community in question: the greatest happiness—of all of them, without exception, in so far as possible." Bentham continues: "the greatest happiness of the greatest number of them, on every occasion on which the nature of the case renders the provision of an equal one of them impossible: it being a matter of necessity, to make sacrifice of a portion of the few, to the greater happiness of the rest" (p. 6). This appears to indicate, first, that at the end of his life Bentham had not abandoned the formula "the greatest happiness of the greatest number"; and secondly, that he viewed "greatest happiness" as a function of "greatest number," inseparable from it. That the formula might be logically untenable, as Edgeworth and Goldworth argue, is another matter. In any case, what Bentham is taken to have "meant" by it must not be at variance with his actual words.

122. Mss. Dumont, 33 II, p. 5.

123. Published by Bowring as "Pannomial Fragments" (iii, 211-30). Part of the material in Bowring was reproduced by Stark as part of "The Philosophy of Economic Science" (vol. 1, pp. 103-17). The material used by Stark is found at B.M. Add. Mss. 33550ff. and 113-44 and was accurately transcribed by Bowring. Most of the mss. are dated by Bentham as either January or February 1828 and are headed "Law Amendments"; ff. 140-41 are dated July 14, 1829. Both are headed "Law Amendment or Penal Code"; f. 140 is also labeled "Pannomion originally entitled Law Amendment or Penal Code"; f. 144 is dated April 29, 1831 and is headed "Pannomion or Penal Code."

124. Stark, vol. 1, pp. 111-12; Bowring, iii, 228; B.M. f. 127.

125. Stark, vol. 1, p. 112; Bowring, iii, 228; B.M. f. 128.

126. *Ibid.*

127. Stark, vol. 1, p. 109; Bowring, iii, 227; B.M. f. 124.

128. Stark, vol. 1, p. 112; Bowring, iii, 228; B.M. f. 128.

Chapter Five

1. Hobbes, however, did not so content himself. Accidents, he said, which left many unable to provide for themselves were inevitable, and such victims "ought not to be left to the charity of private persons" but provided for by the state. It is uncharitable of the sovereign "to expose them to the hazard of such uncertain charity" (*Leviathan,* ch. 30; Blackwell edition, ed. Michael Oakeshott [Oxford, 1960] p. 227). As we have seen, Bentham also pointed to the uncertainty of private charity in arguing for legally established poor relief. In some places on the continent, for example in some parts of Germany, poor relief was also legally established by the beginnning of the eighteenth century. In Brandenburg, almsgiving, though still practiced, "was really replaced by public charity and state-supported poor relief." See R. W. Dorwart, *The Prussian Welfare State before 1740* (Cambridge, Mass., 1971) p. 102; and pp. 100–05 *passim*. See also Frances Fox Piven and Richard A. Cloward, *Regulating the Poor: The Functions of Public Welfare* (New York, 1971) pp. 8ff.

2. G. Himmelfarb, "Bentham's Utopia: The National Charity Company" (*supra,* Introduction, n. 2) p. 114.

3. U.C. cli, 253.

4. Bowring, viii, 370.

5. U.C. cli, 308.

6. Bowring, viii, 369n.

7. U.C. cli, 253.

8. Bowring, viii, 392.

9. *Ibid.*, pp. 373–74. Gertrude Himmelfarb (*op. cit.*, pp. 123–24) cites a passage in Bentham's mss. (U.C. cliva, 231) in which, after speaking of the "trades of begging and depredation," he says that in working for their abolition, he is working for the destruction "of by far the greatest part of my own destined trade" and that in courting the trade it was "in the hope of ruining it"; ". . . many thousands a year, will not pay me for the loss." According to Himmelfarb, if the passage is taken seriously, the disjuncture between interest and duty implicitly vitiates the substance of plan, denies the long-term profitability of the Company, and suggests moral qualms on Bentham's part, and, perhaps, "doubts about the enterprise itself." But, quite apart from the rather shaky proposition that so much can in fact be implied, the passage need not be taken too seriously: this is merely another instance of Bentham's elephantine flaunting of his own self-sacrifice for the sake of others; his outburst was the product of a momentary passion which served to obscure, perhaps even from himself, his enormous drive for power and fame.

10. Josiah Tucker, *A Brief Essay on Trade* (3rd ed., 1753) pp. 70–71, cited in Sidney Pollard, *The Genesis of Modern Management* (Cambridge, Mass., 1965) p. 13.

11. Cited in S. Pollard, *loc. cit.*

12. Cited in *ibid.*, pp. 12–13.

13. Bowring, viii, 386. (A slightly different division of labor is mentioned in the manuscripts. See U.C. cliib, 306 and 309–10.)

14. Bowring, viii, 386.

15. *Ibid.*, 371.

16. See U.C. lxxix, 1–137; U.C. c, 1–4; U.C. cvii, 20–22. The first two citations date from the 1770's, and the third from 1793.

17. Bowring, viii, 371–72.

18. *Speech of Edmund Burke, esq. Member of Parliament for the City of Bristol, On presenting to the House of Commons (On the 11th of February, 1780) A Plan for the better Security of the Independence of Parliament, and the Oeconomical Reformation of the Civil and other Establishments* (3rd ed., London, 1780). We know that Bentham read the work before 1783, for he mentions it in his *Essay on Indirect Legislation* (1782).

19. E. Burke, *op. cit.*, pp. 82–86.

20. *Ibid.*, p. 84.

21. Bowring, viii, 370.

22. S. Pollard, *op. cit.*, pp. 202–03;

23. See Bowring, viii, 411.

24. *Ibid.*, 410–13.

25. *Ibid.*, 413.

26. *Ibid.*, 416.

27. *Ibid.* Because of the lack of data, which could not be supplied "without the aid of government" (410), Bentham hesitated to commit the Company to some form of insurance, particularly life insurance. The company's services in handling existing funds for such insurance would nevertheless still be available.

28. Bowring, iv, 66 (emphasis added). The suggestion that Panopticon is a model for Benthamite society at large was first made by Sheldon Wolin. A direct translation of Panopticon's scrutiny to the social order was obviously "too illiberal a notion to apply unaltered to normal existence, but with a slight change, say, substitute society for

the warden, would not the social non-conformist feel the same pressure for compliance as the prisoners, but with the added advantage of having no identifiable overseers?" (*Politics and Vision*, p. 348). This is a complex subject which cannot be resolved until Bentham's published writings are published accurately as at present they are not, and until his unknown writings see the light of day: how, for example, does Wolin's view square with the fact that Bentham quarreled violently and often with the immense social pressures for sexual conformity?

29. U.C. cli, 4.

30. U.C. cliia, 109.

31. *Ibid.*, 168. ". . . the dependent poor in general may be termed the spoilt children of the rich. . . ." (U.C. cli, 397).

32. Bowring, viii, 389.

33. G. Himmelfarb, *op. cit.*, p. 88.

34. U.C. cliia, 66; see also 42.

35. U.C. cliiia, 218.

36. U.C. cliib, 535.

37. *Ibid.*, 534–36.

38. Bowring, viii, 438.

39. Bentham to Samuel Bentham, 20 February 1796 (B.M. VI, 149).

40. U.C. cli, 393.

41. *Ibid.*, 394.

42. U.C. clii, 331.

43. *Hansard*, 13 June 1807.

44. Bentham may have had in mind the following passage: ". . . the overseers in many places having found out a method, of contracting with some obnoxious person, of savage disposition for the maintenance of their poor: not with any intention of the poor being better provided for, but to hang over them in terrorem, if they will not be satisfied with the pittance which the overseers think fit to allow them." Burn called such contractors "taskmasters." See Richard Burn, *The Justice of the Peace and Parish Officer*, 4 vols. (10th ed., London, 1776) vol. 3, p. 439.

45. U.C. cliib, 331. Bentham claimed to have drawn up his own "hobgoblin" portrait but to have thrown it in the fire.

46. *Ibid.*, 332.

47. *Ibid.*, 332–33.

48. *Ibid.*, 333.

49. *Ibid.*, 347.

50. *Ibid.*, 348.

51. The instance cited was meant to be a note to the main text, and so the only piece of empirical evidence was given subordinate status. See *ibid.*, pp. 340–41.

52. Identified only as "Bradford man."

53. U.C. cliib, 341.

54. D. Marshall, *The English Poor in the Eighteenth Century* (*supra*, ch. 1, n. 68) p. 135.

55. John Scott, *Observations on the Present State of the Parochial and Vagrant Poor* (London, 1773) p. 41, cited in *ibid.*, pp. 139–40.

56. *Ibid.*, p. 140. Leslie Stephen had a similar judgment: "The adoption of this principle of 'farming' had in fact led to gross abuses both in gaols and workhouses. . . ." See his *The English Utilitarians*, 3 vols. (London, 1900) vol. 1, p. 205.

57. Cited in S. and B. Webb, *op. cit.*, p. 108.

58. See Chapter Two, p. 32.

59. Cited in S. and B. Webb, *op. cit.*, p. 110.

60. Cited in *ibid.*, p. 111.

61. *Ibid.*

62. Cited in *ibid.*, p. 112.

63. *Ibid.*, p. 113.

64. See Chapter Two, p. 53.

65. D. Defoe, *op. cit.* (*supra*, ch. 2, n. 120) p. 23.

66. See Chapter Three, p. 68.

67. Bowring, viii, 371.

68. *Ibid.*

69. *Ibid.*, p. 398.

70. G. Himmelfarb, *op. cit.*, p. 97.

71. U.C. cliva, 224. Written in pencil at the top of this page was "not to be inserted but preserved."

72. Bowring, viii, 383.

73. *Ibid.*, 430.

74. *Ibid.*, 395.

75. U.C. cli, 258.

76. *Ibid.*, 254.

77. U.C. clivb, 345.

78. U.C. cliib, 458.

79. *Ibid.*, 517.

80. For an example of whipping as a punishment for beggars and others, see Chapter One, p. 21.

81. Bowring, viii, 393–94. As Gertrude Himmelfarb remarks, however, the "unexampled degree of protection" which the paupers were supposed to enjoy did not entail an exactly reciprocal relationship between pauper and official. Officials would not be punished for infractions; paupers would. Paupers would be listed by name in a "misbehaviour book"; but there would not necessarily be an official counterpart, only a "complaint book," and if there were a counterpart, the "name of the offender *need* not be entered." *Ibid.*, 393; G. Himmelfarb, *op. cit.*, p. 86n.

82. Bowring viii, 392ff.

83. *Ibid.*, 431.

84. *Ibid.*, 432.

85. *Ibid.*, 379 (emphasis in original).

86. See C. W. Everett, *The Education of Jeremy Bentham* (New York, 1931) pp. 171–75; and Bowring, x, 176.

87. U.C. clivb, 544.

88. *Ibid.*

89. For the discussion of idleness, see Chapter Seven, pp. 164ff.

90. Mss. Dumont, 63–85 (with the exception of 68, which is dated 3 June 1806 at Woodbridge).

91. *Ibid.*, 71 (emphasis added).

92. U.C. cli, 302.

93. U.C. cliva, 111; "politics of the day" was written in the ms. as an alternative for "the state of political warfare."

94. U.C. cxlix, 5.

95. U.C. cliiib, 323.

96. Bowring, viii, 416.

97. *Ibid.*, 414.

98. U.C. cli, 276–77.

99. *Ibid.*

100. "Their standard is that of a class of men who by forecast and self-command have fixed themselves on vantage ground, and secured themselves against that sort of degradation, that mixture of distress and degradation to which their neighbors for want of . . . those qualities remain exposed" (*ibid.*).

101. *Ibid.*

102. *Ibid.*

103. U.C. cxxxiii, 81.

104. Bowring, viii, 370n. Bentham also argued that the "pecuniary benefit" would be more extensively diffused "by bringing to light *small* hoards, hitherto barren, enabling them to bear an interest." He neglected to point out, however, that "small hoards" bring correspondingly small benefits.

105. "Abstract of Compressed View of a Tract Intituled Circulating Annuities" (Stark, vol. 2, pp. 203–350). Part of the work's subtitle reads, "The means for providing for futurity upon the securest terms placed for the first time within the reach of the inferior orders: and their attachment to the established government (the basis of national security and tranquility) strengthened by new ties."

106. *Ibid.*, p. 205 (emphasis in original).

107. *Ibid.*, p. 296.

108. *Ibid.*

109. *Ibid.*, p. 297. "Turning to Ireland, the demand for the remedy will be found the same in kind, but much more urgent in degree. The proportion of petty to great moneyholders much greater: the bias to turbulence and anarchy (not to speak of idleness and drunkenness) beyond comparison more prone."

110. *Ibid.*, pp. 297–98.

111. Bowring, viii, 420.

112. *Ibid.*

Chapter Six

1. Bowring, viii, 366–67.

2. *Ibid.*, 360ff., "Table of Cases Calling for Relief."

3. *Ibid.*

4. U.C. clivb, 349, 355.

5. *Ibid.*, 306.

6. U.C. cli, 222.

7. U.C. clivb, 283.

8. *Ibid.*, 339.

9. *Ibid.*, 391.

10. Bowring, viii, 368.

11. *Ibid.*, 382. "The value of the produce being thus not a nominal but a real value . . . will not be exposed to . . . degradation by competition, stagnation, or any other causes" (U.C. cli, 479).

12. U.C. clivb, 283. See also U.C. cli, 184 and 408; and see U.C. cli, 34.

13. Bowring, viii, 382–83.

14. U.C. clivb, 303. Bentham argued that contemporary poorhouses had attempted "self supply," but because of their size, the principle was "confined within limits too narrow . . . to save the establishment from dependence on external and precarious markets."

15. Bowring, viii, 362, "Tables of Cases Calling for Relief."

16. U.C. cli, 143.

17. *Ibid.*, 142; U.C. cliiib, 319.

18. U.C. cli, 145.

19. *Ibid.*, 146.

20. U.C. clivb, 528.

21. U.C. cli, 220–21.

22. For Bentham's arguments on "excess" wages, see Chapter Two, pp. 55–56.

23. U.C. cli, 220.

24. *Ibid.*, 153–54.

25. *Ibid.*, 154.

26. U.C. cliiib, 315 (emphasis added).

27. *Ibid.*, 316.

28. *Ibid.*, 317. "Even in the existing order of things," Bentham added, "I have instances before me, manuscript as well as print, of Parish goods not saleable for so much as the cost of the materials."

29. *Ibid.*, 318.

30. U.C. clivb, 311 (emphasis added).

31. U.C. cliiib, 300; and see 317.

32. *Ibid.*, 315.

33. Bowring, viii, 300.

34. U.C. cli, 480.

35. U.C. clivb, 300.

36. Bowring, viii, 374 (emphasis omitted).

37. *Ibid.*, 390. And see U.C. clivb, 290, where Bentham worried that in cases of "stigmatized, suspected, unavowed-employment" and "unchaste hands, once they had acquired a modicum of skill, "their continuance in the employment will become precarious." See also U.C. cli, 377.

38. U.C. cli, 201; and see Bowring, viii, 382.

39. U.C. cli, 202; and see 203 and 207, where Bentham argues that "unwholesome" work should be done only through choice, never compulsion, and, citing Smith, that such work is always higher paid. He thought that many should perform a small amount of necessary, unhealthy labor so that the unwholesomeness would be done away with just as "most deleterious affluvia is done away with by diffusion through the vast body of the atmosphere."

40. U.C. clivb, 307.

41. See this chapter, p. 130.

42. U.C. cli, 209.

43. *Ibid.*, 210. And see 216, where cutthroat competition with private enterprise is categorically forbidden. See also Bowring, viii, 317.

44. U.C. cli, 218.

45. *Ibid.*, 212, and U.C. clivb, 307. And see U.C. cxxxiii, 9.

46. U.C. cli, 200.

47. *Ibid.*, 186.

48. *Ibid.*, 189ff.

49. U.C. clivb, 310.

50. *Ibid.*, 285–88; and see Bowring, viii, 382.

51. U.C. clivb, 287.

52. *Ibid.*, 305 (emphasis added).

53. *Ibid.*, 365; and see Bowring, viii, 398–401.

54. Bowring, viii, 400. This was another instance of Bentham's attempting to co-opt religious organization for his own more secular purposes. See the discussion in Chap-

ter Seven, pp. 197ff.

55. *Ibid.*, 398–99.

56. *Ibid.*, 400.

57. *Ibid.*, 398.

58. See *In Defence of a Maximum*, Stark, vol. 2, pp. 257–58.

59. Bowring, viii, 400n.

60. U.C. clivb, 383. And see Bowring, viii, 390.

61. U.C. clivb, 367. And see Bowring, viii, 399, where Bentham omitted the distinction between prices which fell and those which were prevented from rising.

62. Bowring, viii, 399–400.

63. U.C. clivb, 386.

64. Bowring, viii, 430.

65. U.C. cliia, 65.

66. U.C. cli, 348.

67. Bowring, viii, 382, 368 and 433.

68. U.C. clivb, 292, 334 and 327.

69. U.C. cli, 474.

70. U.C. cliia, 263.

71. U.C. cli, 301.

72. Bowring, viii, 382.

73. U.C. cliia, 5 (emphasis added).

74. Bowring, viii, 377n.

75. U.C. cliib, 490 (emphasis added).

76. Bowring, viii, 384.

77. U.C. cliib, 474.

78. U.C. clivb, 329.

79. *Ibid.*, 329–30 (emphasis added); see also 331. And see U.C. cxxxiii, 8, where Bentham added that private charity lacked not only the authority but also the funds "to collect them for this purpose," that is, the purpose of putting them to work.

80. U.C. cli, 238 (emphasis added).

81. *Ibid.*, 242.

82. Bowring, viii, 392.

83. *Ibid.*, 389.

84. *Ibid.*, 382. For further discussion of the principles of management, see Chapter Seven, pp. 186ff.

85. *Ibid.*, 374.

86. *Ibid.*, 385; see also 380. And see U.C. cliiia, 198, where the "no-waste principle" is given as an alternative title.

87. U.C. cliiia, 199. "Note" was later appended to the heading.

88. *Ibid.*

89. *Ibid.*, 201. Bentham argued that farmers habitually chose the worst sites for dunghills so that their fertilizer value was diminished before it could be used.

90. Bowring, viii, 388n; and see 384 and 387.

91. U.C. cliv, 343.

92. Bowring, viii, 384. A similar principle was adopted with respect to clothing: "frugality" was its heart and soul. Materials were to be the cheapest, and the form of clothing was to be governed exclusively by "*necessity* and *use* . . . not fashion." One can imagine the effect of this clothing on morale, especially considering that Bentham intended in this way to resurrect the hideous old practice of badging the poor. See *ibid.*, 388–89.

93. *Ibid.*, 388. The independent poor, however, would receive no such period of

grace; rather they would be subject immediately to the strict regime, being seated separately from the others to save them from "the pains of regret and privation" and from "envy and discontent" (*ibid.*).

94. *Ibid.*, 384–85. And see U.C. clivb, 552.

95. Bowring, viii, 387.

96. *Ibid.*, 436.

97. U.C. cliii, 188.

98. Bowring, viii, 407–17.

99. *Ibid.*, 408.

100. U.C. cliia, 109.

101. Stark, vol. 1, p. 138.

102. *Ibid.*, pp. 109–10.

103. *Ibid.*, pp. 117 and 109.

104. Bowring, viii, 407–08 and 408n.

105. *Ibid.*, 409–10.

106. *Ibid.*, 410. Bentham's language in this passage is surely not a case of *double entendre*: it is most unlikely that he would risk a somewhat off-color pun in a serious work of persuasion such as this.

107. Bowring, viii, 410.

108. U.C. cliia, 118.

109. U.C. cliib, 384.

110. *Ibid.* Whether *de facto* "obligations" can in fact be morally obligatory is a question which is beyond the scope of this discussion.

111. See Chapter One, pp. 15–17.

112. Bowring, viii, 401–02. Bentham had originally planned to include the JPs in deciding who would go to a "House of Industry"—JPs would actually make the decision —but, obviously, he changed his mind by the time he published his article in the *Annals*. See U.C. cliva, 244.

113. Bowring, viii, 370.

114. For the list of "Unchaste Hands," see U.C. cli, 161, and "Table of Cases Calling for Relief," Bowring, viii, 355–56. The same "Table" describes "Suspected Hands" as those "acquitted or (after trial or examination) discharged without punishment, *through uncertainty of guilt, or technical defect in procedure or evidence.*" (Children of thieves or smugglers were likewise suspect.) The reference to "technical defect in procedure or evidence" serves to underline Bentham's contempt for the operation of the legal machinery of his day and gives notice of his intention to undo its mischief one way or another. Only a few years later he was hard at work on the reform of legal procedure and evidence.

115. U.C. cliva, 230.

116. U.C. cli, 163 (emphasis added).

117. *Ibid.*, 164.

118. *Ibid.*, 165.

119. *Ibid.*, 162.

120. See U.C. cliia, 35, for Bentham's account of his encounters in France and Italy with beggars playing on the sympathy of diners in restaurants. And see U.C. cliva, 183, where Bentham includes annoyance "in respect of the filth and other causes of disgust with which the persons of the beggars are apt to be encompassed" among the arguments for rounding them up.

121. Bowring, viii, 401.

122. U.C. cli, 4.

123. U.C. cliva, 189.

124. *Ibid.*, 187; Bowring, viii, 401.

125. *Ibid.*, 227; and see 228, where he says that "unavowed employment hands" would be "compelled to come in."

126. *Luke* 14:23. St. Augustine cites the same passage to justify coercing unbelievers and heretics into the Roman Church for the sake of their salvation. Bentham's secularized version of salvation masked but did not entirely obscure the religious or quasi-religious impulse behind it. See St. Augustine, Letters, XCIII, 5-10, reprinted in Henry Paolucci, ed., *The Political Writings of St. Augustine* (Chicago, 1962) p. 193.

127. Bowring, viii, 401; U.C. cliia, 64.

128. U.C. cliia, 65.

129. Bowring, viii, 402.

130. *Ibid.* U.C. cliia, 64. (For a second offense the charge "may be doubled or otherwise encreased—and so on *toties quoties*"). The children, wives, and cohabitating women of beggars, convicts, and suspected persons would all be taken directly to the workhouse.

131. U.C. cliva, 232.

132. *Ibid.*, 257-59.

133. *Ibid.*, 262.

134. *Ibid.*, 238.

135. U.C. cliib, 382.

136. Bowring, viii, 402.

137. U.C. cliib, 449.

138. U.C. cli, 372. For Bentham's arguments that current law inflicted unnecessary pain and provided little employment, see U.C. cliva, 192 and 202; and Bowring, viii, 402-03.

139. Bowring, viii, 435-36.

140. *Ibid.*, 436. And see D. G. Long, *Bentham on Liberty* (*supra*, ch. 1, n. 37) p. 188.

141. See Chapter One, pp. 16-17.

142. U.C. cliva, 252.

143. See, for example, *ibid.*, 193ff. and 252ff.

144. *Ibid.*, 245. And see 238 for Bentham's proposal for a census in order to control the poor. This, he said, would be alarming to the dishonest, but it would be "acceptable to all honest subjects."

145. Bowring, viii, 432n.

146. U.C. cxlix, 169.

147. U.C. cli, 360. Similarly, Bentham used visual imagery in arguing for a large-scale poor relief system: "Transparency, like beauty, is a faculty of a relative kind, the utility of which supposes the existence of an observing eye. To the eye of the public, an object may not be transparent if it be not of a certain magnitude" (*ibid.*).

148. U.C. cliiib, 278.

149. Bowring, viii, 428.

150. U.C. cli, 451.

151. U.C. cliib, 557.

152. Bowring, viii, 431-42.

153. *Ibid.*, 420.

154. U.C. cli, 351.

155. U.C. cliib, 552.

156. Bowring, viii, 432.

157. U.C. cli, 453.

158. Bowring, iv, 42n.

159. Bowring, viii, 400.

160. U.C. cxxxiii, 31.

161. *Ibid.*

162. Bowring, viii, 421.

163. *Ibid.*, 405. The idea of the Frankpledge, it will be noticed, closely resembles the notion of "the formation of the people into little combinations and fraternities" in the passage cited in Chapter Six, p. 156.

164. U.C. cliiib, 351.

165. The cells of Panopticon, writes Michel Foucault, "are like so many cages, so many small theatres, in which each actor is alone, perfectly individualized and constantly visible." See his *Discipline and Punishment* (New York, 1977) p. 200. For his treatment of the Panopticon idea, see pp. 195–228.

166. U.C. cliib, 303.

167. *Ibid.*, 286.

168. *Ibid.*, 283.

169. *Ibid.*, 284.

170. *Ibid.*, 289.

171. Even Bentham himself made some concession to admitting that poor-Panopticon was not so unlike Panopticon prison. "Though in respect of their main objects in view nothing could be more different, nothing more opposite than a Poor House and a Prison, yet among the purposes for which a Poor House is designed to answer . . . it can never answer without enclosing a good deal of the same company as are enclosed in Prisons" (U.C. cliib, 290).

172. *Ibid.*, 285.

173. *Ibid.*

174. U.C. cliva, 99; Bowring, viii, 378.

175. Part of the rationale for separating classes within the House was the "prevention of unsatisfiable desires"; "indigenous" and "quasi-indigenous" youth were to be separated from the "coming and going stock," who might "excite hankerings after emancipation, by flattering pictures of the world at large" (Bowring, viii, 373–74). As Gertrude Himmelfarb so acutely remarks, "This is surely the ultimate in revolutionary ideals—security against unrequited desire." (G. Himmelfarb, "Bentham's Utopia" [*supra*, Introduction, n. 2] p. 112.) For the full statement of the purposes of the "sequestration belt," see U.C. cliva, 99. One was "to prevent the introduction of spiritous liquors and other forbidden articles."

176. For the prevention of escape, see U.C. cliiia, 210 ; for the reference to watchtowers, see U.C. cliib, 281.

177. "[W]ith his own hand," writes Professor Trevor-Roper of Philip, "he would minutely regulate the disposition of hospital beds in the Escorial [his palace], or the sailors' berths in the Armada, just as he would carefully ration the . . . wine in his ships or dole out ultramarine paint to his artists, or specify, in exact detail, how his pictures were to be packed for carriage. . . ." The similarity to Bentham is remarkable. See H. R. Trevor-Roper, *Princes and Artists* (New York, 1976) p. 68.

178. U.C. cliib, 485–86 (emphasis added).

179. U.C. cli, 353.

180. U.C. cliiia, 205. And see, for example, Bowring, viii, 375–76, where additional details are given.

181. Bowring, viii, 375.

182. *Ibid.*, 389.

183. U.C. cliib, 352. Bentham evidently earmarked this material for early publication, since it was reproduced in a copyist's hand. See U.C. clivb, 602–04. For similar arguments briefly presented, see U.C. cli, 5.

184. *Ibid.*, 353.

185. *Ibid.* Bentham went out of his way to say that he did not intend to make a point of badging, that the distinctiveness of the clothing provided made that unnecessary: "What I mean to say is that should the same effect follow from that or any other operation, with or without that view, so much the better: and that the principle upon which the effect is grounded is a principle not to be censured, but adopted with applause."

Chapter Seven

1. See R. H. Tawney, *Religion and the Rise of Capitalism* (Mentor edition, New York, 1954) pp. 98–101 and p. 221. And see II Thessalonians 3:10. For Bentham's "no work—no eat" principle, see U.C. Cli, 5; and U.C. cliia, 263.

2. Tawney, *op. cit.*, pp. 217ff. And see Max Weber, *The Protestant Ethic and the Spirit of Capitalism* (Scribner edition, New York, 1958) pp. 177–78. Tawney's point is that Puritan attitudes reversed the recognition by the Elizabethan Poor Law that idleness is the result of economic circumstances beyond the control of the poor and taught that paupers' "idle, irregular and wicked courses" were the cause of their distress. We are not implying that no one in the eighteenth century argued the opposite case but only that belief in it was not general. It has already been pointed out that Bentham insinuated more than once that indigence was the fault of the paupers; and it has also been shown that he was well aware of (and in fact discussed) many causes of poverty unrelated to any fault of the poor. He argued what he chose as it suited his purpose.

3. U.C. cli, 153.

4. U.C. cliva, 76. In the same passage he adds that idleness is a danger to those who are opulent but possess uncultivated minds.

5. U.C. cliia, 245.

6. U.C. cli, 280.

7. U.C. cxlix, 54.

8. Tawney, *op. cit.*, p. 102.

9. U.C. cliib, 401. Bentham also referred to the "uneludable discipline of the inspection house plan" (U.C. cli, 134).

10. See Bowring, viii, 420.

11. Bentham argued the superiority of his own system over one of allowing paupers to live at home while not working since "in the half and half plan, association being promiscuous and inspection interrupted, if ninety-nine out of the hundred were pure, the one [morally infected] sheep would be sufficient to innoculate and keep up the contagion in the whole flock" (U.C. cliib, 401).

12. Bowring, viii, 375. For a similar discussion on discipline, see also U.C. cliiia, 208.

13. U.C. cliia, 232.

14. Bentham first discussed the "habit of obedience" in *A Fragment on Government* (1776). See ch. 1, paras. 10, 12, 14, and 32, and ch. 4, para. 35 (*CW*, 428, 429, 432–34, and 489).

15. U.C. cliia, 65.

16. U.C. cli, 4 (emphasis added).

17. U.C. cliib, 540 (emphasis added). Injustice to the productive was the second of the reasons listed. Such "injustice," however, as it should be clear by now, was by no means always given place when Bentham argued against outdoor relief.

18. U.C. cli, 4.

19. Bowring, viii, 377.

20. *Ibid.*, 396–97.

21. *Ibid.*, 384. Other such methods included pairing the lazy with the industrious when the reward could be divided according to effort; giving last choice to the maker of articles for self-supply; and, also for self-supplied articles giving each individual "what he has individually been concerned in producing; he will then be his own re-warder and his own punisher." For these and other examples such as the piece-rate system and sponsorship of competition, see *ibid.*, 383–84.

22. U.C. cliiia, 168–69.

23. *Ibid.*, 165 (emphasis added).

24. *Ibid.*, 166.

25. U.C. cliib, 545.

26. Weber, *op. cit.*, pp. 161, 167, and 171. For the definition of a calling, see p. 205.

27. Bowring, viii, 408.

28. Weber, *op. cit.*, pp. 158 and 261 n. 12; p. 262 n. 18.

29. Bowring, viii, 431. For the nature of the "physico-theological lectures," see *ibid.*, 427.

30. *Ibid.*, 396 and n.

31. *Ibid.*, 373. These were to be watched by "corruption-proof" inmates. See also U.C. cliib, 288.

32. *Ibid.*, 438.

33. *Ibid.*, 419.

34. *Ibid.*

35. *Ibid.*, 433.

36. U.C. cliia, 178. "Promiscuous intercourse" was a generic term as used here, but Bentham surely meant to include sexual "vices."

37. U.C. cliib, 551.

38. Bowring, viii, 430.

39. U.C. cliiib, 262. See also U.C. cli, 451, where the impossibility of "uncleanness in the scriptural sense" was given as an advantage of the inspection principle.

40. Bowring, viii, 437.

41. "In the proposed order of things, among *our* apprentices—there need be no such loss at all" (*ibid.*).

42. *Ibid.*

43. U.C. cli, 290–91.

44. Bowring, viii, 405.

45. U.C. cli, 247–49.

46. Bowring, viii, 404–05.

47. *Ibid.*, 423.

48. U.C. cli, 284.

49. Bowring, viii, 390.

50. U.C. cliiia, 107.

51. *Ibid.* For the view that "rational education" would substitute "garden culture to barrenness. . . ," see U.C cli, 284.

52. U.C. cxxxiii, 101.

53. U.C. cliib, 391.

54. *Ibid.*, 392. Bentham also feared that the *energy* lost through travel and play would be lost to labor. See *ibid.*, 395.

55. *Ibid.*, 393.

56. *Ibid.*, 392.

57. U.C. cxxxiii, 102.

58. Bowring, viii, 391.

59. U.C. cliiia, 93.

60. See Bowring, viii, 435. Although Bentham seems to have evaded it, the masters of Westminster School were known to make liberal use of the switch. This undoubtedly goes far to explain his comment that in schools the kind and quantity of punishment depend "not on the real demand for correction, but upon the habits and temper of the master and his subordinates" (*ibid.*). See also U.C. cli, 170; U.C. cliib, 294; and U.C. cliiib, 262–63.

61. U.C. cliiia, 85. And see U.C. cxxxiii, 102. Such slaps at the system of upper-class education (and at the upper classes themselves) were as far as Bentham went in the 1790's; it was nearly two decades later that he (however subtly) declared all-out war on the system through the publication of *Chrestomathia* (1816).

62. U.C. cxxxiii, 102.

63. U.C. clivb, 390.

64. Bowring, viii, 385.

65. U.C. cliv, 531 and 525.

66. *Ibid.*, 531.

67. Bowring, viii, 436 and 430. See also U.C. cliiia, 101.

68. *Ibid.*, 396 and n. This passage seems to have been modified directly from U.C. cxlix, 103, where it reads "[s]leep is not life, but temporary death: if without dreams, death followed by annihilation; if occupied by dreams, death followed by resurrection in another world." The continuation follows the Bowring text verbatim. See also U.C. cxxxiii, 32; and U.C. cliiia, 101.

69. U.C. cxxxiii, 103.

70. U.C. cli, 315. ". . . habit formed by a course of *practice* coeval with the *first dawn* of the thinking faculty, would, in infinitely the greater number of instances, banish every idea of *hardship*, and every sentiment of *reluctance*, from the situation of those, who found themselves, from an age anterior to that of *consent*, destined to this mode of life" (U.C. cliia, 217; and see also 250).

71. *Ibid.*, 335–36.

72. U.C. cliia, 250 (emphasis added).

73. *Ibid.*, 251.

74. U.C. cliiia, 104.

75. *Ibid.*, 104–05.

76. *Ibid.*, 105–06.

77. U.C. clivb, 530.

78. Hobbes, *Leviathan* (*supra*, ch. 5, n. 1), p. 63 (part I, ch. II).

79. U.C. clivb, 532.

80. U.C. cliiia, 111.

81. *Ibid.*, 113–15; U.C. cxlix, 111. In 1799 Bentham wrote a memorandum on Irish education saying that at public expense "men ought to be taught nothing but what is really *useful*. What is agreeable they will, in proportion as it is agreeable, teach themselves." Cited in G. Himmelfarb, "Bentham's Utopia" (*supra*, Introduction, n. 2) p. 105n.

82. U.C. cliiia, 113–15.

83. U.C. cxlix, 111.

84. Bentham's first published attacks on Blackstone were in the *Fragment on Government*; they continued until at least as late as 1829. See U.C. xxx, 124–164; and U.C. xxxi, 1–41.

85. U.C. cliiia, 119 (emphasis added).

86. *Ibid.*, 117.

87. *Ibid.*, 132.

88. *Ibid.*

89. *Ibid.*, p. 120.

90. *Ibid.*, p. 82.

91. U.C. cxlix, 110.

92. U.C cliiia, 14.

93. U.C. cxxxiii, 100.

94. U.C. cxlix, 54.

95. *Ibid.*, 64.

96. *Ibid.*, 105 and 107.

97. *Ibid.*, 65.

98. *Ibid.*, 59.

99. *Ibid.*, 63. An alternative for "transcendental" was "superior." The same idea is repeated at U.C. cxxxiii, 100, where Bentham found that "God Save the King" had its uses as "an anchor to the Constitution."

100. U.C. cxlix, 105–06.

101. The text of *Chrestomathia* . . . can be found in Bowring, viii, 1–191. Part of the subtitle reads, ". . . for the extension of the new system of instruction to the higher branches of learning, for the use of the Middling and Higher Ranks of life."

102. G. Himmelfarb, *op. cit.*, p. 87.

103. Bowring, viii, 392.

104. *Ibid.*, 374.

105. U.C. cli, 343.

106. U.C. cliiia, 154.

107. U.C. cli, 309. ". . . let it be a rule to render the management the same as to each point in every branch of the management—that is in every one of the Industry Houses" unless some special reason were to "outweigh the general advantages dependent on uniformity" (U.C. cliib, 363).

108. U.C. cli, 325.

109. U.C. cliva, 36.

110. U.C. cli, 309–10.

111. *Ibid.*, 322.

112. S. Pollard, *The Genesis of Modern Management* (*supra*, ch. 5, n. 10) pp. 2–6; 250–51.

113. U.C. cliib, 522–23.

114. U.C. cli, 322.

115. U.C. cliiia, 143.

116. *Ibid.*, 144. The five names were "1. Inspection-Architecture principle. 2. Panopticon principle. 3. Simultaneous—Inspection principle. 4. Principle of omnipresence. 5. Central-Inspection principle."

117. *Ibid.*, 160–64; and see Bowring, viii, 381–84. See also U.C. cli, 302ff.

118. *Ibid.*, 164.

119. *Ibid.*, 175; and 174–85 *passim*.

120. *Ibid.*, 187.

121. *Ibid.*, 169 and ff.; Bowring, viii, 383.

122. *Ibid.*, 170-71.

123. *Ibid.*, 161 and 166. And see Bowring, viii, 383. For the complete list of the "Principles of Management," see 380-86 *passim*.

124. U.C. cli, 473.

125. Bowring, viii, 380. After the initial years of the Company's existence, the position of manager would actually be auctioned off—"The price a man gives will be proof of the degree of his fitness, so far as depends upon inclination" (*ibid.*, 386).

126. U.C. cli, 358.

127. *Ibid.*, 361.

128. U.C. cliiib, 281.

129. U.C. clivb, 582.

130. Bowring, viii, 381.

131. U.C. clivb, 578.

132. U.C. cli, 337.

133. U.C. clivb, 582.

134. Bowring, viii, 380-81. See also U.C. cliiia, 45.

135. Bowring, viii, 391-92. For accounts of Bentham's ideas on accounting, see Louis Goldberg, "Jeremy Bentham, Critic of Accounting Method," *Accounting Research*, vol. 8 (1957) pp. 218-45; and L. J. Hume, "The Development of Industrial Accounting: the Benthams' Contribution," *Journal of Accounting Research*, vol. 8, no. 1, (Spring 1970) pp. 21-33. For an account of Bentham's ideas on management, see L. J. Hume, "Jeremy Bentham on Industrial Management," *Yorkshire Bulletin of Economic and Social Research*, vol. 22, no. 1, (May 1970) pp. 3-15.

136. U.C. clivb, 406.

137. Bowring, viii, 414.

138. *Ibid.*, 392.

139. U.C. cliib, 361; and see U.C. cli, 354.

140. U.C. cliib, 360n.

141. Bowring, viii, 392-93. For Protestantism and moral bookkeeping, see Weber, *op. cit.*, pp. 124 and 238 n. 100.

142. Bowring, viii, 393.

143. There were, for instance, ten varieties of "subsidiary" books—cash sales, bill, and receipt and letter books to name a few.

144. Bowring, viii, 392.

145. U.C. cliia, 170 (emphasis added).

146. Bowring, viii, 393-94 (emphasis omitted). See also U.C. cliib, 311-12.

147. U.C. cliva, 34 (emphasis in original). A scribbled note at the bottom of the ms. is not without historical interest. Referring to *les affaires panoptique et française*, Bentham wrote, "Mr Pitt, who knows not what dispatch is, unless it be in going to war with or without a cause . . ."—and the passage breaks off.

148. U.C. cli, 448.

149. Bowring, viii, 392.

150. L. J. Hume, "Jeremy Bentham on Industrial Management," p. 4.

151. *Ibid.*, p. 14.

152. Bowring, viii, 423-25. For a brief account of Bentham and social engineering, see H. L. Beales, "Jeremy Bentham, Social Engineer," *The Listener* (August 3, 1932) pp. 148-50.

153. Bowring, viii, 425.

154. *Ibid.*, 425-27.
155. U.C. cliiib, 300.
156. *Ibid.*, 337 (emphasis added).
157. Bowring, viii, 425 and 429.
158. *Ibid.*, 425 and 437.
159. *Ibid.*, 425.
160. *Ibid.*, 395.
161. *Ibid.*, 427.
162. See Chapter Four, p. 85.
163. Bowring, viii, 386-87.
164. *Ibid.*, 400.
165. U.C. clivb, 380.
166. U.C. cliia, 175.
167. Bowring, viii, 414.
168. U.C. cliva, 138-39.
169. Bowring, viii, 414.
170. *Ibid.*, 420-21.
171. *Ibid.*, 427. Visitors, Bentham speculated, would come to the Sunday Lectures for scientific education, the rich, perhaps, paying a small fee. The only concession to less than strictly utilitarian activities on Sunday seems to have been his willingness for paupers to visit their friends in the parishes; but even here the visit was not purely social, for it would be an apt occasion, he suggested, for the indigent to do his banking at the local church (*ibid.*, 417).
172. *Ibid.*, 431.
173. U.C. cli, 452.

Conclusion

1. *An Introduction to the Principles* . . . mentions sympathy, but not as a sanction. Only later, in *Deontology*, was sympathy elevated in status to a sanction. See the edition in *CW*, ed. Amnon Goldworth (Oxford University Press, 1982).
2. Bowring, iv, 39.
3. U.C. cliiia, 215-16.
4. See Chapter Two, n. 8, p. 225.
5. See Chapter Six, p. 129.
6. See Chapter Seven, p. 178.
7. Emigration to North America from the United Kingdom as a whole averaged roughly 25,000 a year between 1815 and 1830. Even the exceptionally high rate of 1829-30 amounted to approximately 77,000, of which 34,000 were Irish and 7,500 Scots. The population of England, Wales, and Scotland rose from roughly 11 million in 1801 to some 16.5 million in 1831 and to some 21 million in 1851. The rate of emigration was thus quite low. See J. H. Chapman, *An Economic History of Great Britain* (Cambridge, England, 1930) pp. 63-64; and 53-54. For conditions of life among ordinary laborers, see Peter Mathias, *The First Industrial Nation: An Economic History of Britain* (London, 1967) pp. 207ff.
8. Warren Roberts, "Bentham's Poor Law Proposals," a paper delivered at the Bentham Conference, University College London, July 1979. A version of the paper is published in *The Bentham Newsletter*, no. 3 (December 1979) pp. 28-45. See pp. 34-35.

9. Bowring, viii, 443.

10. See W. Roberts, *op. cit.*, p. 35.

11. B.M. Add. Ms. 33550, f. 372; and see f. 369, dated 29 August 1831.

12. *Ibid.*, f. 378.

13. Bowring, xi, 103.

14. B.M. Add. Ms. 33550, f. 369. The subject of his *History*, Bentham wrote, is the "history of the wrath of one man and its baneful effects—a counterpart to the Iliad—among the innumerable baneful effects are instances of individual depravity springing from matchless constitution and corruption."

Index

of refuse in NCC, 144; and diet, 145;
instilled by desire, 148; and pauper
children, 177. *See also* Saving

Future-regarding behavior: a foundation
of civilization, 50; to be engrained in
poor, 57, 109; poor unattentive to,
111; prediction of future markets,
138; prudent savings encouraged,
147; need to postpone gratification,
148; and pauper education, 179; education as, 181; need to inculcate concern for, 204

George III, King of England, 35, 123,
216f.
Gilbert, Thomas, M.P., 32, 116
Gilbert's Act, 32
Globe Theatre, compared to Panopticon,
106
Gratification: increased among taxpayers with lower taxes, 54; need for
poor to postpone, 109, 148; of taxpayers maximized under NCC, 120;
education and, 179–180; reward the
means of future, 204. *See also* Future-regarding behavior
Gratitude: as social bond, 76, 78f., 81;
Bentham on, 84. *See also* 'Cohesion
of society'
Greatest Happiness Principle, 99, 121,
206, 238–239n., 240–241n. *See also*
Happiness; Utilitarianism

Habeas corpus, denied beggars under
NCC, 152
Habit: of industry, 49, 71, 165; of
obedience, 166, 251n.; of sloth, 152;
of frugality, 177; of sobriety, 177;
of privation, 179; children to retain
good, 185–186
Hammond, J. L. and B., 23, 38, 42
Happiness, 10, 179; its relation to population and means of subsistence, 100–
101; of poor and sexual pleasure,
171ff.; and satisfaction of basic appetites, 180; relation to wealth, 180;
as end of society, 201; sacrifices of
one's, for others, 201. *See also*
Greatest Happiness Principle
Hardy, Thomas, 34

Hay, William, 23
Health: of paupers in NCC to be ensured,
136–137; preserved by labour, 142;
not to be undermined by diet, 145f.
History, Bentham's views on study of,
181–182. *See also* Education
Himmelfarb, Gertrude, 104, 111, 186
Hinduism, 127
Hobbes, Thomas, 103, 134, 180, 241n.
Hogarth, William, 145
Home relief. *See* Outdoor relief
Homosexuality, 97f., 171, 173, 239n.,
240n.
Howard, John, 157
Howlett, John, 24, 40
Humanity: exclusively private charity as
tax on the humane, 19, 81–82, 214;
claims of, as influence on Bentham,
48; considerations of, to temper na-
tional justice, 112; possible interfer-
ence of feelings of, with adoption of
NCC, 113; as permission to work,
166; Bentham's disregard of, 209

Identification, personal: use of tattoos
for, 28, 158, 205; need for means of
in penal law, 205; civil liberty threat-
ened by universal, 158f. *See also* Employment Gazette
Idleness: Bentham's attempt to abolish,
3; only necessity forces man out of,
54–55; an evil, 87; as treason in NCC,
122; and unemployment, 131; and
drunkenness, 132f., 134; out-allowances an inducement to, 142; as pre-
lude to evil, 164ff.; and "less eligibility," 215
Impressment, Bentham's early defense
of, 18
Independent poor: assisted by Bentham's
plan, 11; eat worse diet than workhouse inmates, 145; compared to
NCC inmates, 170
Indigence: definition of, 4; necessity of
national policy for relief of, 13;
natural alliance of with vice, 48;
contrasted with poverty, 86. *See also*
Poverty
Individualism: Bentham's connection of
with labor, 86, 167; limits of in Ben-